RESOLVING CONFLICT

RESOLVING CONFLICT

HOW TO MAKE, DISTURB, AND KEEP PEACE

LOU PRIOLO

P.O. BOX 817 • PHILLIPSBURG • NEW JERSEY 08865-0817

Italics within Scripture quotations indicate emphasis added.

Printed in the United States of America

Library of Congress Cataloging-in-Publication Data

Names: Priolo, Lou, author.
Title: Resolving conflict : how to make, disturb, and keep peace / Lou Priolo.
Description: Phillipsburg : P&R Publishing, 2016.
Identifiers: LCCN 2016016392| ISBN 9781596389090 (pbk.) | ISBN 9781596389106 (epub) | ISBN 9781596389113 (mobi)
Subjects: LCSH: Conflict management--Religious aspects--Christianity.
Classification: LCC BV4597.53.C58 P75 2016 | DDC 248.4--dc23
LC record available at https://lccn.loc.gov/2016016392

To Fern Gregory

Thanks oodles for teaching me how to make my ideas fit for human consumption!

CONTENTS

ACKNOWLEDGMENTS

SEVERAL INDIVIDUALS have helped me with this project in various ways over the five years it has taken me to write this book. Andy and Beth Beano, David and Leesa Street, and Johnny and Dianne Phillips have each provided me with a "writer's getaway" that has enabled me to focus my attention on this project without the distractions that typically occur when I write at home. Mrs. Fern Gregory has been my crackerjack proofreader for years and has done another masterful job at clarifying my message, largely by correcting my atrocious spelling and grammar and checking that my Scripture references are accurate. My wife, Kim, encourages me to write and helps with entering Fern's corrections (and makes a few of her own emendations to the manuscript).

I also want to acknowledge two of my mentors who have taught me much and, though they are cited in this volume at various places, have influenced much more of this book than even I can fully recognize. They are Wayne Mack (who has taught me more about how to make biblical counseling practical and effective than anyone else has) and Jay Adams (who has invested himself in my life in a variety of ways). The Institute in Basic Life Principles years ago gave me the tools to develop the working definitions that I have included in part one of this book.

I thank Christ Jesus, my Lord, who has strengthened me and entrusted to me the ministry of helping His people through writing.

PREFACE

THOSE WHO HAVE READ some of my other books will notice some familiar material in this volume. Because most of the previous books also have to do, in one way or another, with improving our relationships with others (spouses, former spouses, children, manipulators, and so on), some overlap of material was necessary. I trust that revisiting those concepts will serve as a helpful review to you if you have read my other works.

It is my prayer that *Resolving Conflict* will be used by Christians in a broad variety of contexts. As a marriage counselor, I hope that the book will be a blessing to many couples who want to learn how to resolve conflicts quickly, effectively, and with a minimum amount of sin. As a family counselor, I believe that the concepts in this volume, if practiced regularly, will help many parents and children learn to do likewise. As a pastor/elder, I know that church members who understand and practice the biblical principles and directives contained in the following pages will be able to prevent and resolve church-splitting schisms that dishonor God, wreck friendships, and sometimes spiritually cripple those who have been involved in them. (I recently taught this book as a Sunday school class in my local church. The response was overwhelmingly positive.)

As a counselor to missionaries, I know that Christian workers who are willing to conduct their relationships according to the Bible will be more effective in ministry and will prevent many of the interpersonal relationship problems (or so-called "personality conflicts") that account for the majority of missionaries returning from the field years before they imagined. (The same is true of conflicts between staff members of local churches.) As a college and seminary professor, I have written this book in the hope that it will be used as a textbook for biblical conflict-resolution courses. As a father, I imagine that such a course could be used even in Christian high schools (and home education programs).

What is different about this book?

Ken Sande has written a wonderful book on conflict resolution entitled *The Peacemaker.*[1] If you have not yet read it, you should. It is a classic! Ken unfolds the entire Matthew 18:15–20 process better than I could ever dream of doing. There is no way I can improve upon what Ken has written. What I have tried to do in this volume is to zoom in and take a very practical look at the first step of the process—resolving conflicts "between he and thee alone." Solomon said,

> Do not go out hastily to argue your case;
> Otherwise, what will you do in the end,
> When your neighbor humiliates you?
> *Argue your case with your neighbor,*
> And do not reveal the secret of another,
> Or he who hears it will reproach you,
> And the evil report about you will not pass away. (Prov. 25:8–10)

This is a much more informal, more "down and dirty," less forensic approach to solving conflicts than *The Peacemaker* is. It deals in great detail with approaching conflict with the proper motives and attitudes. Other fine biblically based books address this topic in one way or another. My book is written through the eyes and experience of a biblical counselor. As such, it offers useful material not found anywhere else, although I make no claim that it is infallible.

1. Ken Sande, *The Peacemaker: A Biblical Guide to Resolving Personal Conflict*, 3rd ed. (Grand Rapids: Baker, 2004).

INTRODUCTION

WHAT COMES TO MIND when you hear the word *conflict*? Do you see conflict as something that is always wrong, or perhaps as something to be avoided at all cost? Or do you see conflict as something that can be good—and even *necessary*—something that God Himself requires you to participate in and even to initiate[1] at times? Do you see conflict as something that, if avoided (or eschewed), may displease God?

I recently had an opportunity to minister in Sao Paulo, Brazil. During my presentation, I used the word *conflict* to express the idea of two people being able to passionately disagree with each other without either one of them necessarily resorting to sin. My translator faithfully translated the word *conflict* into Portuguese. At the break, an English-speaking Brazilian brother came up to me and said that he had "a doubt" ("a question," as it turns out) about how a conflict could occur without sin. After I explained what I meant, he went on to explain that in the Portuguese language (or at least in Brazilian Portuguese), the word *conflict* necessarily connotes the employment of sinful forms of communication (sort of like our word *quarrel*). The Portuguese word for "argument," however, does not necessarily involve sin. From a biblical perspective, to have a conflict with someone (or even to start one) is not *necessarily* a sin.

Where, may I ask, does the Bible say that conflicts, arguments, debates, disputes, and disagreements are necessarily wrong and are, therefore, always to be avoided? Sure, generally speaking, Christians are

1. I'm currently reviewing an interesting book about "being a gentleman" in which the author suggests that a gentleman should never start an argument. Although I certainly appreciate that sentiment, I do not fully agree, because sometimes Christians must initiate conflict.

exhorted to be cool-spirited, calm, cheek-turning, quarrel abandoning peacemakers who make every effort to make and keep peace (in fact, that phrase is central enough that it once formed the working title of this book!). And, of course, on the other side of the same coin, we are exhorted to avoid being contentious, to keep away from strife, to not quarrel or fight or battle, and to avoid a dozen other things that are usually thought of as conflict.

Yet *conflict* is a general term under which many biblical forms of good and proper communication may rightly be placed. For example, the process of restoring a sinning brother in Matthew 18:15–18 is essentially a command to initiate a course of action that (even as the text suggests) might result in conflict. Scripture speaks of additional conflicts (or confrontations) that Christians sometimes must initiate. Christians must at times "convict" (Jude 15), "rebuke" (2 Tim. 4:2), "admonish" (Rom. 15:14), "resist" (or "oppose," Gal. 2:11) and "solemnly charge" (2 Tim. 2:14) people. There are even times when they may have to "contend earnestly" with people for the sake of the faith (Jude 3). These words all imply some form of confrontation if not conflict. So to throw out all conflict as wrong is to, as the saying goes, "throw out the baby with the bathwater." Indeed, sometimes, in order to obey God, followers of Jesus Christ are called upon to disturb the peace. Disrupting the status quo is something that Jesus and His followers were accustomed to doing. Those who proclaim the gospel (who put on the shoes of "the preparation of the gospel of peace," Eph. 6:15) publicly and privately ought to expect that, despite every attempt to make and keep it, the peace is often disturbed—sometimes even to their own physical detriment. The truth is divisive!

When I use the word *conflict* throughout this volume, I do not necessarily mean something that is wrong or unhealthy. Indeed, as we shall see, sometimes conflicts are biblically necessary and therefore good. There is a difference between having a conflict and having a fight, between arguing and quarreling, between having a contestation and being contentious. One is not necessarily sinful; the other is.

This should become more apparent as the book develops, but I trust for now that this will help you to properly interpret the term *conflict* as it occurs quite frequently in this book.

Part One

PREREQUISITES FOR CONFLICT RESOLUTION

WOULD IT SURPRISE YOU to learn that there is a passage of Scripture that, when violated, produces virtually every kind of interpersonal conflict? When couples whom I counsel have serious difficulties resolving their differences, before I even start exploring their backgrounds I know that at least one of them is out of sync with this passage of Scripture. But the amazing thing about it is that there is absolutely nothing anywhere near the text about marriage. Can you guess what that passage is?

It's Ephesians 4:1–3. Four character traits listed in this passage are essential to conflict resolution. See if you can pick them out.

> Therefore, I, the prisoner of the Lord, implore you to walk in a manner worthy of the calling with which you have been called, with all humility and gentleness, with patience, showing tolerance [forbearance] for one another in love, being diligent to preserve the unity of the Spirit in the bond of peace.

The very last line of this passage is sort of a summary statement of the entire sentence. It is an imperative—a command that we are to obey. The Holy Spirit, through the pen of the apostle Paul, is giving us a very important directive: "*make every effort*," He says, "to keep the unity of the Spirit through the bond of peace" (v. 3 NIV).[1] What precedes this summary statement are the four prerequisites: humility, gentleness, patience, and loving forbearance.

You may have noticed that this book is divided into two sections: "Prerequisites for Conflict Resolution" and "Biblical Principles of Conflict Resolution." In this section, we will take an in-depth look at the four prerequisites in verse two of Ephesians 4. In the next, we will unpack some of the most important components of resolving conflicts biblically.

But before we go any further, please allow me to give you a word of warning. There may be a moment or two as you read the prerequisite materials in this section of the book when its contents will seem to have little to do with conflict resolution. (Some of the working definitions of these prerequisite character traits will go way beyond the scope of resolving conflicts or even communication.) You might even be tempted to read ahead in order to get to the nuts and bolts of what you purchased this book for—to learn the mechanics of biblical conflict resolution. Let me assure you that plenty of very helpful, practical material of that nature follows in the second half (and in the appendices) of this book. But learning all of those wonderful, biblically based principles of conflict resolution will do you little good if you don't meet the prerequisites. (In fact, my prayer for you is that the first part of this book will have a greater impact on you than the latter half.) Believing that you can skip prerequisites is as shortsighted as a building contractor believing he can erect a skyscraper without first driving the pilings upon which its foundation will be laid deep into the bedrock. Such a building may stand for a moment, but it simply will not endure the test of time—it will not be able to stand up to the tempestuous forces of nature and will soon crumble.

Let me explain why the prerequisites are essential. Communication proceeds from the heart. The Bible speaks often of the connection

1. Paul reminds the Ephesians in chapter 2 (vv. 11–17) that Christ's death on the cross established "peace" both between God and man and between Jew and Gentile (believer and believer). The unity of (or the unity that comes from) the Spirit is the result of both groups having been brought together in Christ.

between the heart and the mouth (and lips and tongue—see Job 33:3; Pss. 12:2; 17:10; 19:14; Prov. 15:2, 28; 16:23; 26:23–24). Matthew 15:8 looks at the hypocrisy shown when the heart and the lips say different things. Many verses in Scripture compare the way that the thoughts of the heart proceed through the mouth in terms of flowing water. Proverbs 15:2 says, "The *tongue* of the wise makes knowledge acceptable, but the *mouth* of fools *spouts* folly." Or see Proverbs 15:28: "The *heart* of the righteous ponders how to answer, but the *mouth* of the wicked pours out evil things." Proverbs 10:11 tells us, "The mouth of the righteous is a *fountain* of life, but the mouth of the wicked conceals violence."

Imagine a fountain or a waterfall. Whatever is at the source will come out. If the basin is salt water, don't expect fresh to come from the fountain. If the water at the top has arsenic in it, what comes down the waterfall won't be good to drink. Likewise, Luke tells us, what is in the heart will be expressed in the words: "The good man brings out of the good treasure of his heart forth what is good; and the evil man brings out of the evil treasure forth what is evil; for his mouth speaks from that which fills his heart" (Luke 6:45).

You simply can't expect to speak that which is good (or to resolve conflicts well) when evil attitudes are ruling your heart. Jesus asked the question, "How can you, being evil, speak what is good?" (Matt. 12:34). The only way we can have our hearts truly cleansed is through the sanctifying work of the Holy Spirit.

So please work hard to meet the preconditions of effective conflict resolution discussed in chapters one through four. Just as you will have to work hard to practice the skills you will learn in part two of this manual, so you will need to practice developing these prerequisites—even *after* you have finished reading the book. It is as Paul told Timothy: "Discipline yourself for the purpose of godliness; for bodily discipline is only of little profit, but godliness is profitable for all things, since it holds promise for the present life and also for the life to come" (1 Tim. 4:7–8).

But really now, who can say, "I have met the prerequisites"? Which of us have become so totally proficient in each of these virtues that we can now claim to have arrived?

None of us is able to do that. But we can all commit ourselves to learning how to walk in these qualities so that day by day we become increasingly more prepared to resolve conflicts God's way—and thereby to glorify Him.

1

PREREQUISITE ONE: HUMILITY

THE FIRST PREREQUISITE for being a biblical peacemaker is humility.

> I . . . implore you to walk in a manner worthy of the calling with which you have been called, *with all humility*. (Eph. 4:1–2)

What is it that most often prevents conflicts from being resolved? What is the opposite of humility? Pride is the *one* sin, *above all others*, that hinders our ability to resolve conflicts with others. "Pride only breeds quarrels" (Prov. 13:10 NIV). It comes in many show-stopping forms. See if you can recognize any of them in your life.

- ☐ Unwillingness to admit when I am wrong
- ☐ Resorting to defensiveness, blame shifting, justification, or anger when I'm lawfully reproved by another
- ☐ Becoming impatient or upset when contradicted in speech—especially when publicly contradicted
- ☐ Oversensitivity to correction
- ☐ Being unwilling when wronged to forgive an offender who has not demonstrated extreme submission or repentance
- ☐ Difficulty in being pleased by others

Conflicts often occur when one person sins against another.[1] Such conflicts cannot be resolved effectively without confession[2] (and repentance) on the part of the sinning party. And that takes humility. But pride often gets in the way.

WHAT IS PRIDE?

Acquired Immune Deficiency Syndrome is a disease that renders the body's immune system *unable to resist* invasion by several microorganisms that cause serious infections. According to my encyclopedia,

> The AIDS virus causes so much damage to the immune system that the body becomes susceptible to a variety of opportunistic infections—infections that are less harmful to people with normal immune systems but take advantage of the breakdown in an AIDS sufferer's immune system to produce devastating and eventually lethal diseases.[3]

The sin of pride is the AIDS of the soul. Almost like a cataract, the HIV/AIDS virus blinds the eyes of its victim's immune system, preventing it from seeing those bodily enemies that threaten his life.

Pride blinds us not only to itself, but to every other sin tucked away in the recesses of our hearts and lives. It causes us to hate correction and reproof. It hides our sin from us, it justifies our sin, it excuses our sin, and it keeps us from repenting of our sin. It deceives us into thinking that we are spiritually well when, in fact, we have a deadly cancer and are in desperate need of the Great Physician's balm.[4] (Of course, when

1. As we will explore later in this book, sin is not the only cause of conflict. Sometimes conflicts can occur when (non-sinful) differences in people's views, personas, values, lifestyles, or approaches to problems cause them to disagree.

2. The first person to whom we must always confess our sins is God, who promises that "if we confess our sins, He is faithful and righteous to forgive us our sins and to cleanse us from all unrighteousness" (1 John 1:9; cf. Pss. 32:5; 51). This is necessary if we want to be in proper relationship with God and man (see Acts 24:16). We need God's grace—that is, His supernatural enabling power and desire (see Phil. 2:13)—to properly repent of those sins that mess up all of our interactions.

3. *Encarta* (Redmond, WA: Microsoft Press, 1993), CD-ROM, s. v. "Acquired Immune Deficiency Syndrome."

4. When people die as a result of contracting AIDS, they do not die of AIDS. They die from other diseases commonly referred to as AIDS-related complications, such as pneumonia or tuberculosis.

it comes time for us to confess our sin, we expect those whom we have offended to overlook our "little mistakes.")

Look at what Richard Baxter, the prolific Puritan writer, had to say about the pathology of this horrible plague of the soul:

> Pride is a deep rooted and a self-preserving sin; and therefore is harder to be killed and rooted up than other sins. It hinders the discovery of itself. . . . It will not allow the sinner to see his pride when he is reproved; neither will it allow him to confess it if he see it; nor . . . to loathe himself and forsake it. . . . Even when he recognizes all of the evidences of pride in others, he will not see it in himself. When he feels himself despising reproof, and knows that this is a sign of pride in others, yet he will not know it in himself. If you would go about to cure him of this or any other fault, you shall feel that you are handling a wasp or an adder; yet when he is spitting the venom of pride against the reprover, he does not perceive that he is proud; this venom is a part of his nature and therefore is not felt as harmful or poisonous.[5]

The proud person doesn't understand the dynamics of Proverbs 15:33 and 18:12 that "before honor is humility."

Notice the terms that Solomon uses to describe the persons whose pride will not allow them to accept reproof or instruction.

> The fear of the Lord is the beginning of knowledge;
> *Fools* despise wisdom and instruction. (Prov. 1:7)

> Do not reprove a *scoffer*, or he will hate you,
> Reprove a wise man, and he will love you. (Prov. 9:8; cf. Prov. 15:2)

> Whoever loves discipline loves knowledge,
> But he who hates reproof is *stupid*. (Prov. 12:1)

5. Richard Baxter, *Baxter's Practical Works*, vol. 1, *A Christian Directory* (Ligonier, PA: Soli Deo Gloria Publications, 1990), 207.

He is on the path of life who heeds instruction,
But he who forsakes reproof *goes astray*. (Prov. 10:17)

Humility, on the other hand, causes people to realize that because of the effects of sin on the human mind, we don't know everything. Each of us is quite capable of misperceiving, misjudging, misunderstanding, and miscommunicating. More than this, God didn't give any of us the entire loaf of bread (all wisdom). The humble person recognizes and appreciates the fact that God has blessed *others* with gifts, abilities, and information from which we may learn. A humble person realizes that he is a great sinner capable not only of doing wrong, but also of being blinded to the sin about which he is being confronted. The humble person can be grateful for the gift of counsel—for both the correction and the corrector.

If you're not quite sure of the connection between pride and lack of forgiveness, let's look at two brief conversations, first between two proud people and then between two humble people:

Jim: You are so messed up. Who do you think you are talking to me that way? I'm not a child! I deserve to be treated with respect.

Bob: So you don't think the way you're acting right now is childish? Look, I'm having a bad day. You're just going to have to get over it (and while you're at it, you need to get over yourself) and forgive me.

Jim: I'm not quite ready to extend my forgiveness to the likes of you. You haven't offended just any ol' person, you've offended *me!* And I don't go around granting people my forgiveness simply on the basis of their word without them somehow otherwise *propitiating* my anger.

Whoops, rerun. Let's try that again.

Jim: Hey Bob, you know I have a lot of respect for you and the way you conduct yourself in general. But the way you spoke to me yesterday left me a bit puzzled and frankly disturbed. I might be wrong, but what I heard you say was ______________. It seemed you were angry at me or something. It came across as rather condescending and even a bit vindictive. But it was bugging me, and so I thought I should check and see if I heard it right.

Bob: Thank you for caring enough to say something. You know, I haven't quite got that off my conscience. God didn't let me sleep well last night, and I'd already decided to talk to you in order to try to make it right. I'm sorry. I probably did have a condescending attitude toward you. I wasn't actually angry at you. Two hours before we spoke one of my subordinates at work embarrassed me very badly in front of my boss, who proceeded to falsely accuse me in front of lots of people. At any rate, will you forgive me for having such a proud and dismissive attitude and for setting a bad example for you and for any others who might have been watching? Is there anything else I need to ask your forgiveness for?

Jim: I forgive you, brother. Thank you for hearing me and, more importantly, for listening to what the Lord was convicting you of.

A humble believer recognizes the enormity of his own debt of sin that Christ has forgiven and considers any offenses that he must forgive as minutia in comparison (see Matt. 18:21–35). He willingly grants forgiveness to those who sincerely ask for it. In the absence of hard evidence to the contrary, he takes the repentant brother at his word.

> Be on your guard! If your brother sins, rebuke him; and if he repents, forgive him. And if he sins against you seven times a day, and returns to you seven times, *saying*, "I repent," forgive him. (Luke 17:3–4)

Humble people have realistic expectations of themselves and are willing to give others grace. Because they understand the importance of respect and honor, they grant them to others. If someone's action can be taken two different ways, they choose to see it through the eyes of love and grace. Baxter again says it well.

> As godly, humble men rightly amplify their sins in light of the greatness and excellency of God whom they offend; so the proud man foolishly amplifies every little wrong that is done to him, and every word that is said against him, and every supposed omission or neglect of him, because of the high estimation he has of himself.[6]

In what ways may our desire to be too highly esteemed by others affect our ability to resolve conflicts successfully? Here are just a few possibilities. (As you view this list, remember that we may still manifest pride in conflict even if the person with whom we are speaking is not one by whom we want to be esteemed. Of course, we might think ourselves better than that person and therefore consider his opinion irrelevant, which is still pride.)

- ☐ It may tempt us to respond defensively (to shift the blame to someone or something else, to justify our sin, or to become angry) when reproved.
- ☐ It may tempt us to exaggerate (lie about) our virtues and minimize our flaws.
- ☐ It may produce in us a censorious, critical, condemning, accusing, judgmental attitude toward others (especially toward those in positions of authority). Others—especially those who know us best—may be repulsed by our pride and consequently try to humble us by putting us in our place.
- ☐ It may tempt us to include in our discussion superfluous tidbits of information about our own accomplishments that have little or nothing to do with the issue at hand. In addition to distracting from the resolution (wasting time), our pride may again tempt others to a sinful response.
- ☐ It may tempt us to outwardly agree with others even though we don't inwardly agree.

6. Baxter, *Baxter's Practical Works*, 203.

- ☐ It may also tempt us to say "yes" when we should say "no."
- ☐ It may tempt us to show partiality in a conflict—to favor one person's opinion (the one whose esteem we are longing for) over another's.
- ☐ It may tempt us to be indecisive. We may be so concerned about how a decision will be seen by the one whose esteem we are seeking that we spend inordinate amounts of time trying to look at the decision from every vantage point.
- ☐ It may make us prone to command rather than to obey, prone to teach rather than to be taught, prone to speak rather than to listen.
- ☐ It may tempt us to become impatient or upset when we are contradicted—especially when others are witnessing the conflict.
- ☐ It may render us inordinately curious about things that we do not have a biblical need to know, thus causing us to be reproved for being meddlesome.

WHAT IS THE DIFFERENCE BETWEEN PRIDE AND HUMILITY?

Next I'd like to give you four working definitions of the sin of pride[7] and four definitions of its antithesis, humility.

To really get the most out of the definitions in this chapter (and the following three chapters) I'd like to suggest that you internalize (memorize) them so that you may suck as much of the flavor out of them as you can. And let me remind you again that the character traits we will be looking at will go outside the bounds of conflict resolution. These are matters of the heart—of sin and righteousness—and as such should not be viewed primarily as a means to some temporal end. Even our desire to be conflict resolvers (peacemakers) should have a higher motive than merely getting along with others.

7. These definitions were originally published in my book *Pleasing People: How Not to Be an "Approval Junkie"* (Phillipsburg, NJ: P&R Publishing, 2007), 109–13.

1. Pride is the delusion that our achievements are primarily the results of our own doing.

A delusion is an erroneous belief or opinion. The dictionary defines it as a false belief that is strongly held in spite of invalidating evidence, *especially as a symptom of mental illness.* (By this definition, our mental hospitals are filled with people who are crazy . . . *about themselves!*)

Whatever we have has been given to us by God and should be used as a means of bringing honor to Him. "For who regards you as superior? And what do you have that you did not receive? But if you did receive it, why do you boast as if you had not received it?" (1 Cor. 4:7). God has given us the blessings and achievements in our lives. Those blessings are bestowed on us to promote the glory and reputation of the One who is truly responsible for them and for the good of others. Yet pride tempts us to take credit and to focus on ourselves.

To use any of our gifts to promote ourselves is to use them for purposes other than those for which they were given. Not that it is wrong to take pleasure in these things, or even to enjoy a certain sense of satisfaction as they are used for God's purposes. But to consume them in the pursuit one's lusts is to pervert the ends to which they were given and to rob the Giver of the glory that is due Him.

On the other hand, humility is the realization that God (and, to a certain extent through His grace, others) is responsible for our achievements. "Every good thing given and every perfect gift is from above, coming down from the Father" (James 1:17).

"What does this have to do with conflict resolution?" you may be wondering.

Let me ask you a few questions about the last conflict you had. For whom (for whose glory) were you fighting? To what extent were you *consciously trying* to use your communication skills, your logic, the Scriptures, and so on for the purpose of showing love to your neighbor (or enemy) and bringing glory to God? Would a bit more humility (regarding what God has given you) have done anything to improve your ability to solve that dispute?

Sometimes when we are in a conflict, we can lose sight of the fact that defending our reputation is not the most important thing. Glorifying God, telling the truth, edifying others, and finding a biblical resolution to the matter as quickly as possible with a minimum amount of sin should all trump our desire to defend our reputation—or to bolster it by showing off our verbal prowess (see 2 Cor. 12:19).

An ungrateful attitude—especially toward a person in position of authority—can be especially provocative in a conflict.

2. Pride is esteeming ourselves above and beyond the condition and proportion that God has appointed for us.

By "condition" I mean our state of being, from the state of our health to our IQ, our social standing, or anything that might cause others to esteem us more highly. In other words, our condition would be the situation or circumstances (and the honor associated with them) into which the Lord has chosen to place us. By "proportion" I mean the relative magnitude, quantity, or degree of those conditions (or circumstances) that God has chosen for us.

Humility allows us to be content with our status in life, whether we have authority, honor, influence, and wealth, or whether we have a position that is lowly by human standards. Humble people are thankful for what they have been given and for God's wise distribution of blessings to all people for His purposes, and they understand that all the parts of the body work together anyway, whether our own part is that of an eye or of a thumb. Perhaps the saddest thing about being proud is that we will never be satisfied, no matter how much approval we are able to generate. What Solomon says about material wealth—"He who loves money will not be satisfied with money, nor he who loves abundance with its income" (Eccl. 5:10)—is applicable to any idolatrous desire. Temporal things do not satisfy; they only tempt us to further discontentment.

Over-esteeming ourselves in the midst of a conflict will usually produce a condescending "know-it-all" attitude that disposes others to resist agreeing with our point of view—not because we are necessarily wrong but because we appear wise in our own eyes (and therefore in need of a little embarrassing opposition).

In the book of Esther, Haman esteemed himself *above* and *beyond* the condition and proportion that God had appointed for him. He is a prime example of the fool who Paul spoke of in Galatians 6:3: "For if anyone thinks he is something when he is nothing, he deceives himself." His pride deceived him into thinking that he was the man most worthy of honor in the king's court, though God thought otherwise. God chose to exalt a young orphaned Jewish girl named Esther and her wise uncle Mordecai, and to let Haman's pride be the snare that entrapped him.

On the other hand, *humility is esteeming ourselves soberly according to the condition and proportion God has appointed for us.* Do you have a sober assessment of yourself? "For through the grace given to me I say to everyone among you not to think more highly of himself than he ought to think; but to think so as to have sound judgment, as God has allotted to each a measure of faith" (Rom. 12:3).

To have a sober understanding of the wisdom, gifts, and abilities that God has given you is not necessarily pride. To have no understanding of one's "giftedness" is to have no cause to glorify God for His goodness to you in that area. In fact, to be ignorant of such things is to not become good stewards of them. What's more, it is not necessarily proud to derive a certain measure of delight and pleasure in such God-given things as wisdom, gifts, and abilities. "With the fruit of a man's mouth his stomach will be satisfied; he will be satisfied with the product of his lips" (Prov. 18:20).

So then, humility *is* aware of its own blessings, but it is also very mindful that God has blessed others as well. "Do nothing from selfishness or *empty conceit,* but with humility of mind let each of you *regard one another as more important* than yourselves" (Phil. 2:3). Regarding others as more important than ourselves helps to minimize and resolve conflicts. (It disposes people to want to affirm and agree with us where they can, rather than to resist us.) To regard others is to regard their opinions. It is not that we are always going to agree with them or even believe that they are right, but that we are going to treat them as though (all things being equal) their opinions are just as valuable to the conversation as our own (or even more so).

3. Pride is the desire to be esteemed by others above and beyond the condition and proportion that God has appointed for us.

It's bad enough to esteem ourselves above and beyond the condition and proportion appointed to us by God. It's *worse* to want others to do so.

Do you remember the account of that married couple in the book of Acts who were snuffed out by God within hours of each other because of something they said? A cursory reading of the text might lead you to believe that Ananias and Sapphira were judged just for their deception. But if you really look, you will see that it was their *pride* that motivated them to lie!

> But a man named Ananias, with his wife Sapphira, sold a piece of property, and kept back some of the price for himself, with his wife's full knowledge, and bringing *a portion* of it, he laid it at the apostles' feet. But Peter said, "Ananias, why has Satan filled your heart to lie to the Holy Spirit and to keep back *some* of the price of the land? While it remained unsold, did it not remain your own? And *after it was sold, was it not under your control*? Why is it that you have conceived this deed in your heart? You have not lied to men, but to God." And as he heard these words, Ananias fell down and breathed his last; and great fear came over all who heard of it. (Acts 5:1–5)

How and why did Ananias and Sapphira lie? They lied by leading the church to believe that they gave the *entire portion* of the proceeds from the sale of their property to the Lord. They were free to give only a portion of the sale to the church. It was *under their control*. They lied because they wanted the church to esteem them above and beyond the proportion of what they had given. Another man in the New Testament had an inordinate desire for others to esteem him above and beyond what he had been given. He had a rather serious conflict-resolution issue. The Bible says of him that he "loved to be first" among his peers. His name was Diotrephes.

> I wrote something to the church; but Diotrephes, who loves to be first among them, does not accept what we say. For this reason, if I come,

> I will call attention to his deeds which he does, unjustly accusing us with wicked words; and not satisfied with this, he himself does not receive the brethren, either, and he forbids those who desire to do so and puts *them* out of the church. (3 John 9–10)

Haman, Ananias, and Diotrephes all tried to exalt themselves and were rebuked for their pride. A scary principle that runs through the Bible about humility says that *either we humble ourselves or God will humble us!* King Nebuchadnezzar and Pharaoh both learned that the hard way. (Pharaoh never learned it at all.)

On the other hand, *humility is the desire for others not to esteem us above and beyond the condition and proportion that God has appointed for us.*

> For though I might desire to boast, I will not be a fool; for I will speak the truth. But I refrain, lest anyone should think of me above what he sees me to be or hears from me. (2 Cor. 12:6 NKJV)

> Have this attitude in yourselves which was also in Christ Jesus, who, although He existed in the form of God, *did not regard equality with God a thing to be grasped,* but emptied Himself, *taking the form of a bond-servant,* and being made in the likeness of men. And being found in appearance as a man, He humbled Himself by becoming obedient to the point of death, even death on a cross. For this reason also, God highly exalted Him, and bestowed on Him the name which is above every name. (Phil. 2:5–9)

In what ways can humility help us to love others even as we face conflict with them?

- ☐ It will enable us to listen when reproved.
- ☐ It will help us to resist the temptation to exaggerate (lie about) our virtues and minimize our flaws.
- ☐ It will produce in us a gentle, compassionate, respectful, and teachable attitude toward others (especially toward those in positions of authority).

- ☐ It will enable us to focus on the other person and on the problem at hand more than on how we are coming across in the conversation.
- ☐ It will help us to listen to what others are saying and to look for ways to agree with and encourage them.
- ☐ It will enable us to show impartiality in a conflict—to avoid favoring one person's opinion (the one whose esteem we are longing for) over another's.
- ☐ It may help us to be objective by obliging us to look at the decision from every vantage point without trying to see which angle will serve our own desires best.
- ☐ It should make us prone to listen and more willing to understand our opponent's perspective.
- ☐ It will encourage us to be patient even when we are contradicted or shown to be wrong—even if others are witnessing the conflict.
- ☐ It will prevent us from being inordinately curious about things which we do not have a biblical need to know and thus will keep us from being reproved for being meddlesome.

4. Pride is the desire to exalt ourselves above and beyond the condition and proportion that God has appointed for us.

This is the pinnacle of pride: to exalt *ourselves* to a higher position than we know we deserve.[8] It's bad enough to esteem oneself above and beyond the condition and proportion appointed by God. It's *worse* to want others to do so. It's *worse yet* to *exalt oneself* above that position. It's what the Devil did that got him thrown out of heaven. It's what Eve and Adam did to get them thrown out of the garden. As we've seen, it's what Ananias and Sapphira did to get thrown out of the church!

On the other hand, *humility is contentment with the condition and proportion God that has appointed for us.*

Are you content with your condition in life? Are you content with your house, your social status, your clothing, your looks, your earning

8. Of course, a truly humble individual knows that the thing he deserves most is to spend eternity in hell. The point here is not that we should think of ourselves as "deserving" but rather that we should not exalt ourselves (boast) beyond what God has seen fit to give us.

power, your other stuff? Richard Baxter said, "Humility is a willingness and desire that others should not think of us, or speak of us, or use [i.e., treat] us as greater or wiser or better than we are: that they should give us no more honor, praise or love than is our due."[9]

> O LORD, my heart is not proud, nor my eyes haughty;
> Nor do I involve myself in great matters,
> Or in things too difficult for me. (Ps. 131:1)

> Let your conduct be without covetousness; be content with such things as you have. For He Himself has said, "I will never leave you nor forsake you." (Heb. 13:5 NKJV)

The apostle Paul learned how to regulate his level of desire to the condition and proportion into which God chose to place him from day to day.

> I am not saying this because I am in need, for I have learned to be content whatever the circumstances. I know what it is to be in need, and I know what it is to have plenty. I have learned the secret of being content in any and every situation, whether well fed or hungry, whether living in plenty or in want. (Phil. 4:11–12 NIV)

The same is often true of us. Be it our health, finances, jobs, friendships, or reputations, we can find ourselves to have paucity or plenty. But contentment is the "secret" in any and every situation.

If we were content with food and clothing, we would save ourselves from many unnecessary conflicts.

> What is the source of *quarrels and conflicts* among you? Is not the source your pleasures that wage war in your members? You lust and do not have; so you commit murder. You are envious and cannot obtain; so you *fight and quarrel.* You do not have because you do not ask. You ask

9. Baxter, *Baxter's Practical Works*, 193.

> and do not receive, because you ask with wrong motives, so that you may spend it on your pleasures. You adulteresses, do you not know that friendship with the world is hostility toward God? Therefore whoever wishes to be a friend of the world makes himself an enemy of God. Or do you think that the Scripture speaks to no purpose: "He jealously desires the Spirit which He has made to dwell in us"? But He gives a greater grace. Therefore it says, "God is opposed to the proud, but gives grace to the humble." (James 4:1–6)

We will unpack this passage in chapter 2, but for now suffice it to say that the opposite of contentment is covetousness (idolatry), and James makes a definite correlation between sinful conflicts and our covetous desires.

Of the four godly attitudes we will look at in this section, humility has the broadest scope. It is something we must all strive to develop (to clothe ourselves with—see 1 Peter 5:5) every day of our lives on this earth. The more you understand and can recognize the many facets of pride in your heart and life, the easier it will be for you to repent of them by God's grace. As with the Spirit's help you learn to clothe yourself with humility day by day, you will find that your ability to resolve conflicts will dramatically improve.

2

PREREQUISITE TWO: GENTLENESS

> Walk in a manner worthy of the calling with which you have been called, with . . . gentleness. (Eph. 4:1–2)

THERE IS NO EXACT English translation for the Greek word for gentleness (or meekness). It is related to the character trait that we looked at in the first chapter—humility—because you cannot truly be meek without being humble.

A NECESSARY RESPONSIBILITY

From time to time, all Christians find themselves in a position where they will have to implement Galatians 6:1. "Brethren, even if anyone is caught in any trespass, you who are spiritual, restore such a one in a spirit of gentleness; *each one* looking to yourself, so that you too will not be tempted." Granted, obeying this passage correctly might result in a conflict. But not following it properly (to the letter) will all but ensure one.

When someone we know who professes Christ has fallen into a pattern of sin from which he is not able to extricate himself, we are told to restore him—in a spirit of gentleness.

It is sometimes easier to illustrate something by its antithesis. So try to imagine how effective it would be to restore someone like this:

"What a boneheaded move that was! How could you do something so unbiblical? I never would have done such a thing! I'm really disappointed in you! You had better listen to me carefully because I really don't want to have to rescue you again." This is *not* the way to restore someone with meekness.

Gentleness does not present itself as "holier than thou" but rather communicates an awareness of its own shortcomings. "The things I'm telling you today, I had to tell myself just last week" is the attitude it conveys, or "I'm just one beggar showing another beggar where to find the bread." I occasionally explain to my counselees, "Today, I'm giving you advice. Next week, you may be on this side of the desk giving me counsel because I'm every bit as much a sinner as you are (and maybe more of one)."

The second element in gentleness has to do with controlling one's temper (restraining one's anger). Anger is given lots of print in the Bible. It is mentioned, in one form or another, over 500 times in the Bible (far more than fear, which appears in various forms over 350 times).

Biblical counselors have to deal with the sin of anger more than almost any other sin. Apart from the sin of selfishness, sinful anger is probably the most prevalent sin in all of life.

In this chapter, we will look at seven perspectives or working definitions of gentleness—seven slices of the pie, if you please. These descriptions relate to the second element of meekness (controlling one's temper).

1. Gentleness is the ability to distinguish between righteous anger and sinful anger.

There is righteous anger (holy passion, if you please) and there is sinful anger. They actually both appear in the same chapter of the Bible where the primary text for this book is found.

> Be angry [an *imperative* in the original Greek], and yet do not sin; do not let the sun go down on your anger. (Eph. 4:26)

> Let all bitterness and wrath and anger and clamor and slander be put away from you, along with all malice. (Eph. 4:31)

Now, before we proceed any further, let me be clear about one thing: most of the references to anger in Scripture are of the unholy variety. Although it is possible for us to be angry and *not* sin, sinful anger is much more common. I daresay the majority of the anger that most of us experience is sinful. Nevertheless, the mature Christian can distinguish one from another, especially in his own heart. "But solid food is for the mature, who because of practice have their senses trained to discern good and evil" (Heb. 5:14; cf. 4:12).

When our anger is due to concern that a holy God has been offended by another's behavior (or by our own—see 2 Cor. 7:11), then that anger is lawful. In other words, if we are angry because God's revealed will (as found in the Bible) is violated (that is, if we are angry as a result of someone's sin), our anger is not rooted in our own sin.

On the other hand, if our anger is the result of our not having our personal desires met, then that anger is probably sinful. That is, if we are angry merely because someone prevented us from having what we really wanted, our anger is unlawful.

Of course, it is possible (even probable, in those situations in which another person's sin against God is also an offense against us) to have *both* righteous anger and sinful anger residing in our hearts at the same time.[1] We are often presented with scenarios in which others do something quite unbiblical but the offense, in addition to being a sin against God, is also against us.[2]

In such cases, communication is usually required (see Matt. 18:15; Luke 17:3). Conflict between the offended and the offender is a real possibility. But sinful anger on the part of the offender as he communicates his concerns will complicate resolving the matter. It is essential that the offended party deal with his sinful anger (i.e., that he get his heart in such a state that he is sure he has much more of the proper anger than he does the sinful anger, if any anger at all) before he proceeds with the

1. Just as it is possible to hold only righteous anger at a sin against another, it is possible to have only righteous anger when the sin is against ourselves. But it is also easy to use a justification like "I have good reason to be angry" (Jonah 4:9) and to descend into bitterness.

2. For example, a teenager lies to her parents about the use of her cellular telephone. Or a wife is blatantly disrespectful to her husband in front of their mutual friends.

process. Indeed, as we have seen, one of the conditions required to restore a sinning brother is to go "with all humility and gentleness" (Gal. 6:1).

I am indebted to David Powlison, who provided the idea for the following diagram. It is one of the best tools I know of to help people determine whether or not their anger is sinful.

Unholy Anger	**Holy Anger**
When I don't get what I want	When God doesn't get what He wants†
I am the lord of my life	Christ is the Lord of my life
My will is violated	God's will is violated
Motive: my heart's idolatrous desire	Motive: God's glory
I am god	God is God

2. Gentleness is refusing to allow any desire to become so deep-rooted that it produces anger (either in an attempt to obtain it or as a result of not being able to obtain it).

A very helpful passage of Scripture that speaks of conflict and its relation to idolatrous desires is found in the fourth chapter of the book of James.[3] The Christians to whom the Lord's brother was writing were having such conflicts with one another that James used the words *wars* and *fighting* to describe the outward manifestation of their anger. The question that he asks in verse 1 cuts right through such outward symptoms and focuses on the internal causes or motives of the anger. "What is the *source* of quarrels ["wars" NKJV] and conflicts ["fights" NKJV] among you?" He then answers his own question to reveal to his readers exactly what is at the heart of their angry disputes (i.e., what is in *their* hearts that produced their angry disputes). "Is not the source [of these quarrels and conflicts] the pleasures that wage war in your members?" "Yes" is the understood reply.

† I'm speaking here, of course, not of the decretive will of God but rather of the revealed will of God. The point here is that the anger that we experience because someone has violated God's will (as revealed in the Bible) is (at least in part) righteous anger.

3. Much of the material in this section has been adapted from my book *The Heart of Anger* (Sandy Springs, OK: Grace & Truth Books, 2015), 105–7.

We have angry conflicts with one another because our pleasures (desires that are not necessarily sinful *in and of themselves*) have become so intense that they are waging war within our members. When our desires (as good as they may be) become so strong that they wage a military campaign in our hearts, otherwise lawful desires become sinful, idolatrous desires—not because they are sinful desires (per se) but because they are desired *inordinately*. Our hearts covet them so intensely that we are willing to sin (to go to war and fight) either in order to obtain our desires or because we are not able to obtain them.

God wants us to desire Him with the same kind of desire with which He desires us. "Or do you think that the Scripture speaks to no purpose: 'He jealously desires the Spirit which He has made to dwell in us?'" (v. 5).The Spirit of God earnestly desires that we not displace our love for Him with a love for anything that the world has to offer.

The best evidence that a Christian desires (loves) something more than he desires (loves) God is his willingness to sin against God *in order to acquire that desire* or *because he cannot acquire it*. "If you love Me, you will keep My commandments," Jesus said (John 14:15). The surest evidence that our desires are inordinate is when we become angry because we cannot get what we want.

Sinful anger is sort of like our built-in smoke detector. It lets us know that we are *coveting* something to the point of idolatry. Twice in the New Testament, idolatry is connected to covetousness.

> Therefore put to death your members which are on the earth: fornication, uncleanness, passion, evil desire, and *covetousness, which is idolatry*. (Col. 3:5 NKJV)

> For this you know with certainty, that no immoral or impure person or *covetous man, who is an idolater*, has an inheritance in the kingdom of Christ and God. (Eph. 5:5)

When we find ourselves getting angry in the midst of conflict, it is wise to ask ourselves a couple of questions: "What is it that I want that my opponent is not giving me?" and "Is what I want something that God also wants?" If the answer to the latter is "no" or "not necessarily," it may be wise to reevaluate your argument in light of Scripture (or even to postpone the discussion until you can thoroughly do so).

3. Gentleness is knowing how to harness righteous anger so that it may be used to destroy only those things that God would approve being destroyed.[4]

When we are faced with a problem, there is often great potential for us to become angry. People often resort to one of two extreme expressions of sinful anger. On one end of the spectrum is *internalization*. Some of us "clam up" when we get angry. We withdraw, cry, pout, sulk, walk away, retreat to another room, go for a walk or drive (without first committing to resolve the conflict later), and give those whom we believe caused the problem a "cold shoulder."

At the other end of the spectrum is *ventilation*. The fool gives *full vent* to his anger (see Prov. 29:11). Some of us "blow up" when we get angry. We resort to raising our voices, calling others inappropriate names, using profanity, throwing, hitting, kicking things, using biting sarcasm, and various other forms of vengeance. Some individuals mix and match these responses. They blow up first and then clam up, or else clam up until the internal pressure builds to overflowing, at which time they blow up.[5]

How do you respond when you get angry?

- ☐ Blow up
- ☐ Clam up
- ☐ Blow up, then clam up
- ☐ Clam up, then blow up
- ☐ All of the above
- ☐ Neither

4. Much of the material in this section (and in section 5 later) has been adapted from chapter 2 of my book *Keeping Your Cool: A Teen's Survival Guide* (Phillipsburg, NJ: P&R Publishing, 2014).

5. We are indebted to Jay E. Adams for this paradigm. See *What Do You Do When Anger Gets the Upper Hand?* (Phillipsburg, NJ: P&R Publishing, 1975).

In what *specific* ways have you preferred to express your anger?

Blow up responses

- ☐ Yelling/screaming
- ☐ Throwing/kicking/hitting
- ☐ Talking back (quarreling)
- ☐ Using biting sarcasm
- ☐ Name-calling
- ☐ Using profanity
- ☐ Contemptuous speech
- ☐ Saying hurtful things that you later regret
- ☐ List the other forms of hateful or vindictive actions you prefer: ______________
____
____
____

Clam up responses

- ☐ Sulking
- ☐ Pouting
- ☐ Crying
- ☐ Giving the silent treatment
- ☐ Giving the cold shoulder
- ☐ Withdrawing/retreating
- ☐ Refusing to talk
- ☐ Going for a walk or drive
- ☐ List the other forms of hateful or vindictive actions you prefer: ______________
____
____
____
____

When my wife and I are having a conflict, we each try to express our differing opinions to each other in the hope that one of us will persuade the other of his or her point of view. So we banter back and forth for five, ten, or twenty minutes until I persuade her, or she persuades me, or we meet somewhere in the middle (or we both conclude that it is perfectly fine to agree to disagree). Back and forth we go, trying with each exchange of words to reach an agreement with each other with a minimal amount of sin (unbiblical communication). But the moment one of us becomes sinfully angry, the conflict comes to a halt. The communication circuit is broken, and no further progress is made. Typically, an angry person exits the conflict prematurely or his opponent exits the conflict in fear. The conflict is aborted midstream without biblical resolution. I will illustrate this dynamic further in part 2.

The expression of sinful anger is probably the greatest obstacle to resolving conflicts quickly. How is it with you? Think about your last conflict with someone. Did it go south rather quickly after someone got angry? Chances are that someone's anger stopped the matter from being resolved swiftly.

Anger, properly focused, can give us energy to attack and destroy something that needs to be destroyed. But too often we direct it toward the wrong target and offend others in the process. Or we push it inside and destroy ourselves (and anyone and anything around us) with its detonation. Godly communication can help us to avoid either of these dangerous outcomes. When you blow up, you are *mis*communicating. When you clam up, you are *not* communicating.[6]

4. Gentleness involves knowing how to think during times of provocation.

Conflicts can evoke a wide spectrum of emotions within each of us—from excitement to dread, from a sense of accomplishment to feelings of exasperation. When we are in intense conflict, adrenaline and other chemicals pour into our blood, causing our hearts to beat faster, our respiration to increase, our blood pressure to rise, and our perspiration to flow. Our thoughts race at upward of a thousand words per minute. And this all happens even if we are not being provoked by our opponent. But when we are in a conflict in which we are being irritated and goaded by another, we seem to respond without thinking at all.

This is a problem for Christians, who are not to be easily provoked (see 1 Cor. 13:5) and are supposed to control and captivate their thoughts (see 2 Cor. 10:4–5) and respond with gentleness.

"But in the heat of the battle, it's hard to control our thoughts!"

Being in the heat of battle makes it harder, perhaps[7]—but it is not impossible for the Christian. And there is good news: God has a remedy for this dilemma.

6. You often are communicating something when you clam up in the midst of a conflict—an attitude of pride, fear, selfishness, and/or rudeness.

7. All those biological factors mentioned above are God-given and therefore have a good purpose. Perhaps they were given to us to help our brains (and mouths) to function better in the heat of the battle.

PRAYERFUL PONDERING

One of the best ways to put on gentleness is to pray and think (to talk to God and talk to yourself) before you open your mouth. In fact, it may sometimes be wise to simply ask to postpone the discussion until a later date.†

> The heart of the righteous ponders how to answer. (Prov. 15:28)

> Respect what is right in the sight of all men. (Rom. 12:17)

Few translations bring out the exact meaning of the verb that begins this imperative. It's actually a participle that literally means to think of beforehand. God is saying (in the contexts of personal battles against evil) that you must plan your next response before the next battle. Of course, because you don't know what the exact nature of the next battle will be, planning ahead may involve considering several scenarios (based upon the history of your opponent's fighting style and *where* you're likely to be tripped up). We are to anticipate beforehand how to respond to conflict so that, when we find ourselves in the heat of the battle, we will not retaliate in kind but rather respond to evil (or provocations) with good. Soldiers are prepared for battle in basic training drills in this way so that in the heat of combat they will automatically respond properly.

Who is the one person with whom you find yourself in conflict the most? Do you know exactly how you are going to respond to him the next time he sins against you? Have you prepared your arsenal? Have you cleaned and loaded your weapons? Have you practiced fighting with them? If not, you'll likely pick up the first

† I have known people to do this quite effectively by acknowledging their own weakness before (or as a basis for) appealing for a rain check on the conflict: "I'm really upset (or angry or struggling with ________) right now. Would it be all right if I prayed and thought through a more righteous response to your argument (or question or position or request), and returned to this conversation within 48 hours?"

weapon at hand (a familiar but sinful one) when the bullets start to fly and will thus be overcome by his evil rather than overcoming his evil with good as Romans 12:21 commands.

Another mental weapon that gentle people have at their disposal is the ability to interrogate themselves about their provocations. That "humble" element of the Greek word for "gentleness" is willing to consider its own contribution to (culpability in) the conflict.

- ☐ Has the other person really *sinned* against me?
- ☐ Is there an idolatrous desire in my life after which I am lusting?
- ☐ Do I have all the facts, or am I jumping to a hasty conclusion?
- ☐ Is my heart magnifying a tolerable trial to the level of an intolerable one?

Gentleness is also mindful of how to fight in God-honoring ways.

- ☐ What Scripture passages should guide my thoughts and words in this matter?
- ☐ How can I respond in a way that will attack the problem and glorify God?

5. Gentleness is knowing how to command not only your thoughts, but also your tongue, countenance, and body language during times of provocation.

Communication involves more than just words (see Prov. 16:24). It also involves our tone of voice (see Prov. 16:21) and our nonverbal communication (see Acts 12:17). If we are going to learn how to communicate (and resolve conflicts) properly, we must learn how to do so in all three areas.

Of the three slices of the communication pie, the Bible places the greatest emphasis on words. If there is ever a time when a believer ought to premeditate what he is going to say, it is in those circumstances when he is most likely to become angry. When we are angry (or experiencing other intense emotions), we are at the greatest risk of sinning with our words. Being gentle means choosing our words carefully, especially when a problem exists that makes us angry.

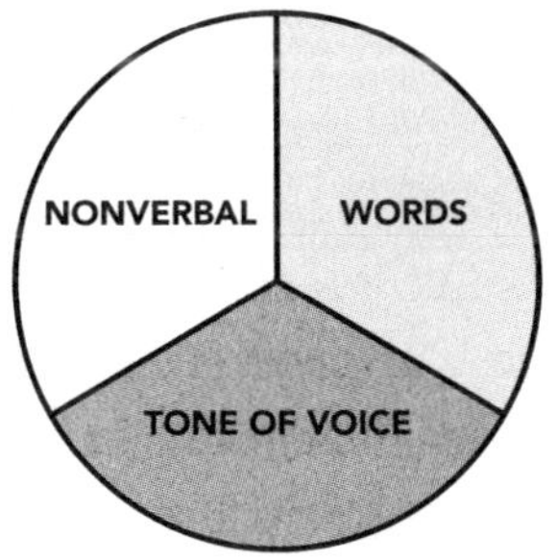

The Bible also addresses the importance of using the proper tone of voice. "A gentle answer turns away wrath, but a harsh word stirs up anger" (Prov. 15:1). "Sweetness of speech increases persuasiveness" (Prov. 16:21; cf. Prov. 16:24; 18:23; Col. 4:6). It is not enough for us to choose the right words. We must say the right words in a tone that is appropriate.

Teenagers, for example, probably provoke their parents to anger more quickly by being disrespectful than by any other behavior. Yet it is more often the tone of the teen's voice, rather than the words, that communicates disrespect. In fact, some communication professionals believe that in the English language, the message is communicated up to seven times more by the tone of one's voice than by one's words.

Imagine that a manager asks his assistant if she has read the report that he left on her desk this morning. Her "of course" could mean "Of course [sigh, eye roll], I read it, you incompetent moron. Don't I read every time-wasting report you give me?" or "Of course [smile, polite nod of the head], I read it eagerly and am about to finish it up. Is there anything else I can for you today?"

Or how about a teenager who responds to his mother's question, about wanting to earn some extra money this weekend by helping with a household project, with "Sure." Depending on the teen's inflection and body language (use your imagination), that "sure" may be interpreted in several different ways.

1. "Sure, I've got nothing better to do with my Saturday than helping you with your worthless project."
2. "Sure, I could use the money—but how long will it take, and how much money will I make?"
3. "Sure, I could use the cash, and I'd be happy to help. When can I get started?"

Think about the many bad attitudes that our voice inflection is capable of communicating. There is disrespect, anger, hatred, bitterness, contempt, vengeance, fear, anxiety, pride, condescension, harshness, superiority, self-righteousness, sarcasm, criticism, callousness, impatience, and indifference, to name a few. On the other hand, with the tone of our voice, we can also communicate such righteous attitudes as love, acceptance, compassion, forgiveness, patience, submissiveness, forbearance, humility, and gentleness.

The Bible has much to say about nonverbal forms of communication. Nonverbal communication encompasses such things as your facial expressions, eye contact, gestures, posture, and touch. Some believe that our body language carries even more of the total communication message than our words and tone of voice put together.[8]

Perhaps the best place to begin is with your face. "Why are you angry?" the Lord asked Cain (Gen. 4:6), "and why has your countenance fallen?" Anger is one of several sins that the Bible specifically indicates can show up on your face.[9] What is in your heart also bleeds through your countenance (see Neh. 2:2; Prov. 15:13; Eccl. 7:3). In the Bible, the word *heart* represents the "inner man," and it is invariably held over against the "outer man" (the mouth, tongue, lips, eyes, countenance, hands, feet,

8.This is probably not as it should be. Although the Bible addresses all three forms of communication, the sheer preponderance of references argues that our *words* should be given the most significant attention.

9. For further information on the specific sins that can mar our countenances, please see Lou Priolo, "How to Improve Your Looks from the Inside Out 1–2," MP3 Audio, http://www.noutheticmedia.com/mp3-library/how-to-improve-your-looks-from-the-inside-out-1-2-mp3/.

and so on). Isaiah put it this way: "The expression of their faces bears witness against them, and they display their sin like Sodom" (Isa. 3:9).

David refers to God as "the help of my countenance" (Pss. 42:11; 43:5). He realized that only God could remove from one's heart the sins that mar the countenance. Solomon also understood the connection between man's heart (the reservoir of wisdom; see Prov. 2:10; 14:33) and his face. "A man's wisdom illumines him and causes his stern face to beam" (Eccl. 8:1).

Another important element of nonverbal communication is eye contact. In some cultures of the world, it is considered rude to look a person in the eyes. In our culture, it is generally considered rude *not* to look at people while talking to them. The Bible says in 1 Corinthians 13:5 that love is not rude (ESV). When God counsels us, He is said to do so with His eye upon us (Ps. 32:8). Job said to one of his counselors, "Now please look at me, and see if I lie to your face" (Job 6:28). One of the clues that may indicate a potential lie is the dilation of the speaker's eyes. Look at those with whom you are having a conflict. As much as possible, make it a habit to practice "Stop, Look, and Listen" when they are addressing you. *Stop* whatever else you may be doing when they begin talking to you, *look* directly at their eyes, and *listen* intently to what they are saying to you.

A final element of nonverbal communication that we should consider addressing is touch. Jesus showed His compassion for quite a few people as He touched them in the process of healing their infirmities, including touching a leper who was ceremonially unclean/untouchable (Matt. 8:3). In the context of marriage and the family, affectionate touch can communicate feelings such as love, compassion, comfort, and sympathy. How affectionate are you with those with whom you argue?

6. Gentleness is remaining quiet when angry in order to ponder an appropriate response.

The Bible has much to say about the importance of thinking before we speak.

> The heart of the righteous ponders how to answer,
> But the mouth of the wicked pours out evil things. (Prov. 15:28)

> When there are many words, transgression is unavoidable,
> But he who restrains his lips is wise. (Prov. 10:19)
>
> He who is slow to anger has great understanding,
> But he who is quick-tempered exalts folly. (Prov. 14:29)
>
> A hot-tempered man stirs up strife,
> But the slow to anger calms a dispute. (Prov. 15:18)
>
> The heart of the wise instructs his mouth,
> And adds persuasiveness to his lips. (Prov. 16:23)
>
> The beginning of strife is like letting out water,
> So abandon the quarrel before it breaks out. (Prov. 17:14)
>
> A man's discretion makes him slow to anger,
> And it is his glory to overlook a transgression. (Prov. 19:11)
>
> Let every man be swift to hear, slow to speak, slow to wrath.
> (James 1:19 NKJV)

A gentle person slows down when he becomes angry in order to be certain that his brain is engaged before he opens his mouth. He realizes that until he gains composure, it will hurt his argument (and accelerate the conflict) should he open his mouth.

> He who restrains his words has knowledge,
> And he who has a cool spirit is a man of understanding.
> Even a fool, when he keeps silent, is considered wise;
> When he closes his lips, he is considered prudent. (Prov. 17:27–28)

In certain circumstances, it may be helpful to politely and humbly confess your anger to the person with whom you are in conflict. Perhaps something along these lines would be fitting: "I have purposed with God's help to resolve this conflict biblically, but I confess I am struggling right now. Will you please help me to express my concerns without getting angry by listening carefully to my perspective?" Or possibly something like this: "I really want to have a good attitude about this, but I am not succeeding right now because I think that you are not understanding my point of view. Will you please pray for me that I will be able to talk to you about this without getting sinfully angry?"

Several years ago, one of my children did something inappropriate that not only deserved discipline, but also provoked me to anger.

"Go to your room and prepare for a spanking," I said rather gruffly.

"Dad, aren't you a little too angry to spank me right now?" my daughter responded.

"I am angry!" I said. "Go to your room and pray for me!" I have long since forgotten what she did to deserve to be chastised that day, but the lesson she taught me that day I will probably never forget.

7. Gentleness is forgiving your offender quickly, thus not allowing yourself to meditate on and muse over the provocation.

Juliet is happy as she prepares her husband's favorite meal. She doesn't make it very often because it is time consuming (not to mention a bit expensive). Romeo has been asking for weeks to have this anniversary make-up meal. She decided on cooking it tonight because the children were all away at Christian camp. Romeo should be home in just ten more minutes, and the first course (stuffed fried zucchini flowers) is ready to be lowered into the fry machine. The ingredients for the second course (four cheese and mushroom risotto) are on the stovetop awaiting Romeo's arrival (it should take him twenty minutes to change and unwind once he walks through the door). The vegetables for tonight (Sicilian stuffed artichokes) are sitting in the pressure cooker waiting to be pressurized. The rosemary coated and garlic infused leg of lamb is roasting in the oven with about fifty minutes left to go. The Caesar salad (and homemade dressing) are in the fridge along with the $35 bottle of Chianti that Uncle Dominic brought back with him from Verona and the chocolate chip cannoli (made with sheep mill ricotta which had to be special ordered from some place in upstate New York).

The phone rings, and Juliet picks it up. Romeo's name shows up on the screen. Her heart begins to race. "Hey, honey," she says with a smile.

"Hi," he says, obviously distracted by something. "Just wanted to tell you that I am going to be a little late for supper tonight. The board is in town tomorrow and the boss asked me to go over the budget with him before he presents it to them in the morning."

"Did you forget what tonight is?"

"It's Thursday, right?"

"It's the night I told you at least three times this week that I was going to cook you our make-up anniversary meal." She should have expected him to do this—he *always* does this, now that she thinks about it.

"Oh no, I forgot all about it! I'm so sorry! Can it wait? I should be home in ninety minutes."

"You are sorry! You are the sorriest husband I have ever met! Goodbye!"

WHAT IS BITTERNESS?

Bitterness is the result of not forgiving others. To be bitter at someone is to have not truly forgiven that person. In other words, bitterness is the result of responding improperly (unbiblically) to an offense.

The Scripture speaks of bitterness as a root. "See to it that no one comes short of the grace of God; that no root of bitterness springing up causes trouble, and by it many be defiled" (Heb. 12:15). When someone hurts you,[10] it is as if that person dropped a seed of bitterness onto the soil of your heart. At that point, you can choose to respond in two ways. You can either reach down to pluck up the seed by forgiving your offender, or you can begin to cultivate the seed by reviewing the hurt over and over again in your mind. Bitterness is the result of dwelling

10. The hurt can be real or imagined; it makes no difference. The result is the same. If you do not deal with it biblically, you will become bitter. If I hurt you as a result of my sin and you choose not to overlook it or cover it in love (see Prov. 17:9; 1 Peter 4:8), you must follow Luke 17:3 and pursue me with the intent of granting me forgiveness, and I must repent. If you get your feelings hurt as a result of something I did that was not a sin, you must repent of your unbiblical thinking that caused you to be "offended" at something that was not a sin.

too much on a hurt. Again, it is indicative of the fact that one has not truly forgiven an offender (see Matt. 18:34–35).

Let's follow the cultivation of Juliet's seed of hurt into a root of bitterness:

Juliet's Internal Thoughts	Cultivation of Juliet's Bitterness
"I can't believe he's done it again! He is the most self-centered, inconsiderate man I've ever met."	Juliet presses the seed an inch or two into the soil of her heart.
"He never keeps his promises! He loves that job and his stupid boss than he loves me!"	Juliet covers the seed with more soil.
"He's such a coward! Why couldn't he stand up to his boss and tell him that he couldn't stay after hours tonight (or at least that he would come in early tomorrow)?"	Juliet aerates the soil.
"How would he like it if he planned a weekend getaway with me and I found something more important to do? He wouldn't like that one bit."	Juliet waters the seed.
"He reminds me all the time not to waste money. As soon as he comes home I have a good mind to tell him exactly how much money it cost to prepare this meal that *he wasted!*"	Juliet fertilizes her hurt, and it starts to sprout.
"It's not just the money. I wasted three hours of my life trying to please my sorry excuse for a husband. And it isn't the first time he's done this."	Juliet weeds her little sprout, and its roots grow deeper.

"He can't get away with this! I'm going to purposely overcook the meal so that he'll really regret being so inconsiderate and will learn to be more thoughtful in the future."	Juliet puts the finishing touches on the greenhouse that houses her stinkweed and begins charging people admission to see it.

Juliet was obviously displeased that Romeo had forgotten their important date, but her response was out of proportion to the insult. When we exert inordinate amounts of emotional energy over trivial disappointments, it's a good indication that we may be bitter.

The fact is, when Juliet heard her husband explain why he would be late, mentally she wrote a list called "Specific Ways Romeo Has Offended Me Through the Years." "Coming home late" was entry number 892 on the list. This list of past similar offenses provoked her to respond to more than just the current issue. Meditating and musing over past offenses is the surest way to cultivate bitterness.

BIBLE BASICS ABOUT FORGIVENESS

Most of the principles that follow have been extrapolated from Luke 17:3–10. Other passages have been cited where applicable.

> Be on your guard! If your brother sins, rebuke him; and if he repents, forgive him. And if he sins against you seven times a day, and returns to you seven times, saying, "I repent," forgive him. (vv. 3–4)

1. Forgiveness is to be granted only if a sin has been committed against you.

Jesus said, "If your brother sins." He didn't say, "If he doesn't give you what you want," "If he lets you down," "If he hurts your feelings," or "If he profoundly disappoints you." Your brother may do any and all of these things in the process of sinning, but he is not in need of your forgiveness unless he sins against you.

If what your brother has done to upset you is not a sin, it may be appropriate for you to talk with him about the matter at some point, but not before your thinking about the "offense" has changed. In other words, it is not your offender who must repent, but you may have to repent of any unbiblical thinking that took offense at something that God did not.[11]

2. Sometimes the offended party must initiate forgiveness.

If you cannot overlook the transgression (Prov. 19:11) or cover it in love (1 Peter 4:8), you are obligated as a Christian to go to a brother who has sinned against you and to "rebuke him." Sometimes it is necessary to go to our sinning brother and tell him about his sin with the intention of being able to grant him forgiveness.

"But *he* sinned against me!" you protest. "Why does his sin obligate me to go to him? Didn't Jesus say somewhere that he is supposed to come to me before he brings his gift to the altar?"

He did. In Matthew 5:23–24, Jesus tells us to seek forgiveness from those whom we have offended. In that passage the *offending* party is told to go. But Luke 17 says that the *offended* party should go. Since you, as the offended party, are the one who has knowledge of the wrong, you are to go. The one who knows about the offense is the one who goes. Perhaps your offender doesn't know about his sin, or maybe he doesn't want to seek reconciliation. Or, as it happens rather frequently, it could be that there is a misperception on someone's part that requires a discussion to clear up the issue. It might even be discovered that no real sin was actually committed.

3. Forgiveness is costly.

When you forgive someone, it costs you something that is tremendously expensive. It costs you the *price* of the *offense* that you forgive![12]

But more importantly, what it costs you is *minutia* compared to what

11. Of course, we might be grieved, and God along with us, at results of living in a fallen world that are not actually sin. If a driver has a heart attack behind the wheel and his car slams into your vehicle and cripples you, the driver has not sinned—but the process of accepting what God has sovereignly allowed into your life might still resemble forgiveness. All sin is evil, but not all "evil" is the result of someone's sin.

12. One of my graduate school professors used to speak of forgiveness as being analogous to giving an expensive gift. Basically, what we do when we forgive someone is to pick up his offense, place it in a colorful box, tie a pretty ribbon around the box, place a lovely bow on top, and then hand it back to the person whom we are forgiving.

it cost the Lord Jesus to forgive you of your sins. That is why unforgiveness is such an odious crime in the eyes of Him who is the judge of the whole earth. In the parable of the unforgiving servant, Jesus referred to the protagonist—the one who, after being forgiven an incalculable debt, refused to forgive a much smaller debt— as "wicked."

> "You *wicked* slave, I forgave you all that debt because you pleaded with me. Should you not also have had mercy on your fellow slave, in the same way that I had mercy on you?" And his lord, moved with anger, handed him over to the torturers until he should repay all that was owed him. (Matt. 18:32–34)

In light of how much we have been forgiven by God, for us not to forgive those who offend us is *wickedness*. It doesn't matter how much the offense that we are struggling to forgive hurt us; by comparison to our offenses against God and the hurt we put His Son through, the offense that hurt us is minutia!

When Jesus Christ died on the cross for your sins and mine, He said, "It is finished." Our incalculable debt was paid in full. What ingratitude it is for Christians not to forgive their offenders! Dare we slap Him in the face by refusing to forgive those petty little offenses in light of all He's done for us?

4. Forgiveness is fundamentally a promise.

In his insightful book *From Forgiven to Forgiving*, Jay Adams explains,

> When God forgives, He goes on record. He says so. He declares, "I will not remember your sins" (Isa. 43:25; see also Jer. 31:34). Isn't that wonderful? When He forgives, God lets us know that He will no longer hold our sins against us. If forgiveness were merely an emotional experience, we would not know that we were forgiven. But praise God, we do, because forgiveness is a process at the end of which God declares that the matter of sin has been dealt with once for all.
>
> Now what is that declaration? What does God do when He goes

> on record saying that our sins are forgiven? God makes a promise. Forgiveness is not a feeling; forgiveness is a *promise!*[13]

When you forgive, you are promising to no longer hold your offender's trespasses against him.[14] You are also promising to impute your forgiveness to him (much as Christ imputed His righteousness to you when you became a Christian). The dictionary defines the verb *impute* as follows: (1) "to charge with the fault or responsibility for"; (2) "to attribute or credit."[15] When you promise not to impute your offender's trespasses against him, you are promising to no longer charge him for what he has done. This means that you are not going to allow yourself to dwell on the offense. You will refuse to cultivate those seeds of hurt, but rather will immediately pluck them out of the soil of your heart. You will relinquish all "rights"[16] to get even.

When you promise to impute your forgiveness, you credit your offender's account with your forgiveness, much as Christ credited your heavenly account with His righteousness. You make every effort to think well of him, to pray for him, and to speak well of him, if possible. This promise, to some extent, can be made in the form of a personal commitment in your heart even if your offender does not acknowledge his sins to you. This is what is sometimes referred to as "forgiving someone in your heart" (see Mark 11:25).

If he does acknowledge his sins and asks for your forgiveness, you will make this promise to him as you verbally grant him forgiveness. In such cases, you will be making him two additional promises. The "not remembering his sins" concept is an implicit promise to never bring up the offense to him again. If you have forgiven him, there is no need to discuss it again. Similar sins that he may commit in the future may

13. Jay E. Adams, *From Forgiven to Forgiving: Learning to Forgive One Another God's Way* (Amityville, NY: Calvary Press, 1994), 11–12.

14. This is not to say that the person we forgive is absolved of all consequences or that any trust that has affected the relationship will be instantly restored.

15. *American Heritage Dictionary of the English Language*, 3rd ed. (Boston: Houghton Mifflin, 1992), s. v. "impute."

16. As a Christian, you really don't have such a right anyway, as personal vengeance is something you are not allowed to take (see Rom. 12:17–21).

require new confrontations. In addition, when you verbally grant someone forgiveness, you are promising not to gossip about the offense.[17]

5. Forgiveness is not the same as trust.

If someone sins against you, it is incumbent upon you as a Christian to forgive that person as you have been forgiven by God in Christ (see Matt. 18:21–35). However, it is incumbent upon that person to earn back the trust that he lost as a result of his sin. Forgiveness should be immediate. Trust may take time (see Matt. 25:14–30; Luke 16:10–12). But to withhold trust after it has been earned is unloving. The Bible says, "Love . . . believes all things" (1 Cor. 13:7). This means that if we love someone, in the absence of hard evidence to the contrary, we will put the best possible interpretation on what he does. In this case, that means believing that the fruit of repentance that he has brought forth is genuine. And, whether or not you are able to quickly trust your offender, you must trust God to work through the person in your life and to protect you from whatever consequences you suspect might happen.[18]

6. Forgiveness focuses not on secondary causes but on the sovereignty of God.

Joseph had to *learn* to trust in God's sovereignty. We sometimes think that, when Joseph was sold into slavery by his brothers (the secondary causes of his trial), he somehow said to them, "Don't worry, guys; you mean this for evil, but someday you'll see that God means it for good." But, in reality, he was a proud young man who was happily telling his whole family about dreams in which he came out as their superior, was going off to find his brothers and their sheep while wearing the

17. If other individuals have a biblical need to know about the offense, you can lovingly urge the offender to confess to all necessary parties so that you will not be obligated to disclose anything to anyone. If he refuses to "turn himself in," you may rightly question his repentance. And if the other person has a biblical need to know about the offense, you may lawfully be able to inform such a person without being uncharitable or unforgiving. Of course, there are circumstances when it will be impossible (or even unwise) to extend this courtesy to an offender, such as if you are no longer in contact with the person anymore, or where the law requires you to report criminal or suspicious activity.

18. Of course, having faith in God does not mean that one cannot use all necessary biblical means to protect oneself—especially in cases when harm is at risk.

coat that reminded them "I'm Dad's favorite," and in general was used to seeing himself as the center of his world. Only after years of unjust imprisonment was he in a position for God to use him and for him to recognize that God had been using circumstances in his life all along.

In the final analysis, God could have prevented the offenses that tempt us to bitterness—but He didn't. Forgiveness focuses not on the offender's sin but on how God (in His wisdom and goodness) may be using the offense for His glory. We should assume that God is concerned more about our response to the offense than about the offense itself.[19]

7. Forgiveness involves an act of the will—not of the emotions.

If your offender repents, you must forgive him—quickly.[20] Jesus phrased this concept in such a way as to make it clear that (in the absence of evidence to the contrary) you have to take your offender at his word and grant him forgiveness. Look again at Luke 17:4: "And if he sins against you seven times a day, and returns to you seven times, saying, 'I repent,' forgive him." Even if it is the seventh time in one day that he has asked you to do so, you are to forgive him.[21] Jesus does not give you very much time to get your feelings in line *before* you forgive. You are to do it as an act of your will in obedience to God. Your feelings will follow. If you wait until your feelings change before you forgive, you may never obey the Lord's command.

You may not always feel like forgiving the person, and after you have forgiven him, the offense may come back into your mind. Don't let that seed of hurt develop into a root of bitterness by dwelling on it.

19. Sometimes an offense is God's way of revealing to us a need in our offender's life so that we might pray for him (or even minister to him).

20. If your offender does not repent, to prevent bitterness you will have to apply Mark 11:25. Jesus said, "Whenever you stand praying, forgive, if you have anything against anyone." You must, in other words, somehow forgive your offender "in your heart." I have prayed something like this on occasion: "Lord you know what my offender did and how much it hurt. You also know that what I really feel like doing is to give him a taste of his own medicine. But I know that to retaliate in kind is wrong. So, in obedience to You, as an act of my will, I impute my forgiveness to his account just as You imputed Your forgiveness to mine."

21. This is not to say that *for his sake* you cannot call into question (and urge him to examine) the sincerity of his repentance before you grant him forgiveness. Indeed, when there is *hard evidence* to refute his claim of repentance, it would be unloving not to call him into question (by asking him to explain the incongruity between his claim and the evidence).

Pray for him and put your mind into a Philippians 4:8 thought pattern ("Whatever things are true, whatever things are noble, whatever things are just, whatever things are pure, whatever things are lovely, whatever things are of good report, if there is any virtue and if there is anything praiseworthy—meditate on these things" NKJV).

Thomas Watson asked and answered this same question of how we know when we have forgiven another. "When do we forgive others? When we strive against all thoughts of revenge,—if it be in our power to do our enemies mischief, we will not,—we wish well to them, grieve at their calamities, we pray for them, we seek reconciliation with them, we shew ourselves ready on all occasions to relieve them,—this is gospel-forgiving."[22]

Rather than reviewing hurtful mental images from the past or laying vindictive plans for the future (seeing the face of your offender on a dartboard or on a baseball that you are about to pulverize with your "Louisville Slugger"), picture his face with the words "I've forgiven you" boldly imprinted across the image. Put your imagination to work on Philippians 4:8 (or other relevant passages of Scripture). You may be surprised at how much better you will feel, as well as how quickly you will forget once you truly forgive. Forgetting is the result of forgiving, not the means of it. It is the final step of the process, not the first one.

Before you go on to the next chapter, let me point out something quite interesting about these first two prerequisites of humility and gentleness. During His earthly ministry, the Lord Jesus said much about His Lordship. He referred to himself as "the bread of life" (John 6:35, 48; cf. 41, 51), "the light of the world" (John 8:12), "the door" (John 10:9), "the good shepherd" (John 10:11, 14), "the resurrection" and "the life" (John 11:25), "the way," "the truth," and "the life" (John 14:6), and "the vine" (John 15:1, 5). In Revelation, the glorified Christ referred to himself as "the Alpha and the Omega," "the first and the last," and "the beginning and the end." But as far as I can determine, the only thing He ever said about His character has to do with our first two prerequisites.

22. Thomas Watson, *Body of Divinity: In a Series of Lectures on the Shorter Catechism* (New York: Robert Carter & Brothers, 1855), 551.

He said, "Take My yoke upon you and learn from me, for I am *gentle* and *humble* in heart" (Matt. 11:29). The words *gentle* and *humble* in the original are cognates of the words in Ephesians 4:2. Ponder that between now and whenever you begin chapter 3.

3

PREREQUISITE THREE: PATIENCE

> Walk in a manner worthy of the calling with which you have been called . . . with patience. (Eph. 4:1–2)

WHEN WAS THE LAST TIME you had an IQ test? Not an Intelligence Quotient test, but rather an Impatience Quotient test. With the help of Dr. Wayne Mack and Puritan pastor Richard Baxter, I've put together a little inventory that should provide you with some idea of how impatient you really are.[1]

Using the rating scale below, record next to each statement the number that best describes the frequency with which the specific symptom of impatience occurs.

Rating Scale	Points
Never (Hardly Ever)	5
Seldom	4
Sometimes	3
Frequently	2
Always (Almost Always)	1

1. This IQ test is not a scientifically normed instrument. Because the questions were developed from biblical constructs, persons taking the test are being compared more closely to the character of Jesus Christ than to the character of those in our secular society.

1. When another motorist cuts me off as I am driving my automobile, I become so annoyed that I say or think something critical, unkind, or nasty to or about that motorist. ________

2. When I fail to perform according to my expectations, I put myself down in thought or word. ________

3. When I want to leave for an appointment on time and others hinder me from doing so by their procrastination, I become restless and scold those who are slowing me down. ________

4. When I am trying to be serious and others seem to be more interested in kidding around or goofing off, I become miffed and withdraw myself from their company. ________

5. When someone for whom I have been waiting for twenty or thirty minutes shows up late and does not apologize, I take it personally and assume that he does not think that I'm important. ________

6. When I make a conscientious effort to do my best and am still criticized for my efforts, I wonder what the use is in trying, or I think about quitting and giving up. ________

7. When someone hurts or offends me, I write that person off, having little or no desire for reconciliation. ________

8. When someone has a dismissive attitude toward me or teases me, I respond as though he had done something much more serious (like punching me in the nose or stabbing me in the arm). ________

9. When I suggest something to someone and my suggestion is either ignored or ridiculed, I automatically cease from making suggestions to that person in the future. ________

10. When people don't treat me with the respect and honor that I believe I deserve, my willingness to communicate with them and minister to them is diminished. ________

11. When people expect more of me than I am realistically capable of doing, I become exasperated, aggravated, or resentful. ________

12. When others are ungrateful for the things that I have done for them, I vindictively cease doing those things for which they have been ungrateful. ________

13. When I am working against a deadline and realize that I might not be able to meet it, I become irritable and grouchy toward those who are around me, or I blame them for my inability to meet the deadline. ________

14. When I am tired or sick, I become irritable, grumpy, and short-tempered. ________

15. When someone tries to convince me that something is wrong, which I know is not wrong according to the Bible, I struggle with feelings of contempt for that person. ________

16. When someone with whom I am acquainted does not change as quickly as I think he should, I automatically assume that this individual is not really trying to change. ________

17. When I dearly want something, I am tempted to employ sinful means in order to obtain my desire (rather than waiting for the Lord to provide). ________

18. When others don't meet my expectations, I withdraw from them, pout, or sulk rather than express to them what my expectations are. ________

19. When facing trials and tribulations, I am more concerned that God shorten my suffering than that He strengthen my character. ________

20. When God does not execute His judgment on the unrepentant as quickly as I think He should, it really troubles me and I question His justice. ________

Total Score ________

RATING SCALE

After calculating your score by adding together your total number of points, use the scale below to determine how patient or impatient you are.

94–100%	Excellent! You have no problem with impatience. (You may have a problem with dishonesty!)
84–93%	Very good! You are probably a patient person!
74–83%	You could use more patience.
64–73%	You are probably an impatient person.
63% or below	You should probably plan on reading this chapter regularly until you bring your score up to at least a 74.

IT DOESN'T WORK FOR ME

Have you ever felt as though, no matter how hard you tried, you just couldn't do what God requires? My counselees express this sentiment quite often. "I tried it God's way, and it didn't work!"

For instance, "I've told myself a thousand times, 'I'm not going to get sinfully angry at my husband the next time he shifts the blame from himself to someone or something else.' But halfway into his blame-shifting exercise, I lose it!"

"What exactly have you tried to do in your attempts to do it God's way?"

"I've prayed before and during our conflict; I've tried carefully not to interrupt him in the middle of his tirade; I've praised him often; I've appealed to him; I've tried to see and commend any valid points he makes; I've even bitten my tongue, smiled, and tried to walk away. But by that point he could tell that I was furious with him. And that's on a good day!"

"I see. What else did you do?"

"You're kidding, right?"

"No. It's just that you said you did it God's way, and I was wondering if you really did everything that the Bible says you could have done."

"Like what?"

"Well, have you been actively working on developing that gentle and quiet spirit that Peter says wives ought to have in relation to their husbands? Have you considered whether you are bitter at him and whether your bitterness is somehow affecting your communication toward him (if not somehow provoking him)? Have you asked the Lord to show you if there is some idolatrous desire in your heart for a humble, reasonable husband? Have you been studying what the Bible says about blame shifting and taking responsibility so that you can convict your believing husband with God's Word? Have you considered whether or not you ought to enlist the help of another Christian to help him to see the pattern of sin that you believe you see in him?"[2]

"No, I guess I really haven't done it God's way as well as I thought I have."

But sometimes those who I counsel claim to have done everything that the Bible says they ought to do in a given situation. And, when I inquire, they have indeed basically been sincerely trying to apply the relevant biblical directives and principles to their circumstances. At this point I ask, "About how long have you been doing this (trying to be a loving husband or respectful wife or biblical parent)?"

"Oh, I would say for about six weeks."

"That's not long enough to solve a stubborn problem like yours. The Scripture says, 'You have need of endurance so that *after* you have

2. Many Christians fail to understand that solving problems God's way usually involves not only putting off sinful behaviors but also putting on biblical alternatives. Consequently, where they fail to "do things God's way" is in trying to simply stop doing what is wrong (getting angry, for example) without making it their goal to become proficient in the corresponding biblical antithesis (kindness, tenderheartedness, forgiveness, and gentleness.) Indeed, often the best way to put off a character flaw is by putting on its corresponding character trait.

done the will of God'—not while you're doing it for a week and a half, but after you've done it day in and day out for a longer period of time—'you may receive the promise'"(Heb. 10:36 NKJV).

Endurance is something we don't hear much about today, except perhaps in the area of athletics. But the Bible has a lot to say about it (and about its little cousin, patience).

Is there a difference between endurance and patience?

Although they are used interchangeably in some New Testament English translations, the primary Greek word for *endurance* is a military term that has to do with bearing up under suffering, while the principal word for *patience* carries with it the idea of being steadfast and longsuffering. Another interesting distinction that some make between the two is that *endurance* is used for being patient in circumstances, whereas *patience* refers to being patient with people.[3] I will say a bit more about this in a moment.

WHAT IS PATIENCE?

We will look at six definitions of this third peacemaking prerequisite. Once again, the scope of some of these characterizations may go beyond any obvious connections to conflict resolution.

1. Patience is the ability to accept a difficult situation from the Lord without accusing Him of wrongdoing or giving Him a deadline to remove it.[4]

Did you notice that almost all the criteria for our IQ inventory had to do with trials? Life is filled with difficult situations of all shapes and sizes. Some are gigantic; others are tiny. Many of us think that we are patient when we handle the larger trials well. But what about those minitrials—how do you handle them?

3. Richard C. Trench, *Synonyms of the New Testament* (Grand Rapids: Eerdmans, 1983), 198; cited in John MacArthur, *Colossians & Philemon*, The MacArthur New Testament Commentary (Chicago: Moody, 1992), 34.

4. This definition of *patience* has been adapted from the Institute in Basic Life Principles "Character Bookshelf Series" game entitled Character Clues (Oak Brook, IL: Institute in Basic Youth Conflicts, 1974).

What is a minitrial?

How about having to sit at the same red light for a second go-around because the elderly gentleman in the car in front of you wasn't paying attention to the traffic and lollygagged around until the light changed back to red—or how about being late for church because one of your family members overslept, or took too long to dress, or had to run back into the house because she forgot something inconsequential?

I daresay that the things that most often tempt us to impatience are life's little trials!

Did you ever stop to consider that in the Bible the word *patience* is often found in conjunction with some kind of trial?

James commends Job to us as an example of patience during trials. (Notice how many times the words *patience* and *endurance* occur.)

> Therefore, be *patient*, brethren, until the coming of the Lord. The farmer waits for the precious produce of the soil, being *patient* about it, until it gets the early and late rains. You too be *patient*; strengthen your hearts, for the coming of the Lord is near. Do not complain, brethren, against one another,[5] so that you yourselves may not be judged; behold, the Judge is standing right at the door. As an example, brethren, of *suffering* and *patience*, take the prophets who spoke in the name of the Lord. We count those blessed who *endured*. You have heard of the *endurance* of Job and have seen the outcome of the Lord's dealings, that the Lord is full of compassion and is merciful. (James 5:7–11)

Do you remember how Job—that man who was perfect and upright, who feared God and eschewed evil—responded when he was first tried?

> Then Job arose and tore his robe and shaved his head, and he fell to the ground and worshiped. He said,

5. Here is the short version of the IQ Test: do you grumble and complain when going through minitrials?

> "Naked I came from my mother's womb,
> And naked I shall return there.
> The LORD gave and the LORD has taken away.
> Blessed be the name of the LORD."
>
> Through all this Job did not sin nor did he blame God. (Job 1:20–22)

What exactly was "the outcome of the Lord's dealings" with Job? How was he "full of compassion" and "merciful"? We often think of Job as having lived a life of misery. But, according to the biblical account, he lived a very blessed life before his trial and a very blessed life after it. His severe trial was just a small blip in the midst of an incredibly long and happy life.

In 1 Corinthians 2:9, we find a very familiar but often misinterpreted passage of Scripture: "But as it is written, Eye hath not seen, nor ear heard, neither have entered into the heart of man, the things which God hath prepared for them that *love* him" (KJV). The misinterpretation has to do with thinking that this passage refers to what awaits us in heaven. But this verse has to do with the here and now. In its context, Paul is quoting Isaiah to make the point that only those who love God and have the Spirit of God to teach them (vv. 10–11) can truly understand spiritual truth. It cannot be understood through mere intellectual pursuit or empirical study (through the eyes or ears).

But the thing I want you to notice about this passage is that the Holy Spirit through Paul's pen changed the wording from the original. Check out Isaiah 64:4 in comparison to the New Testament's rendering above, and notice especially the very last phrase: "For from days of old they have not heard or perceived by ear, nor has the eye seen a God besides You, who acts in behalf of the one who *waits* for Him." Do you see what happened? The word *wait* has been changed to the word *love*. Isaiah, looking forward to the Messiah, used the word *wait* in anticipation of His coming. Paul used the word *love* because the Messiah had already come, and also to make the point that only those who love Him will be given supernatural spiritual (i.e., from the Holy Spirit) discernment.

But don't miss the analogy: to *love* God is to *wait for* Him (to be patient). The very first item on the list about love is that it "is patient" (1 Cor. 13:4). One of the best tests of our love for God (and neighbor) is our level of patience.

"Now what does all this have to do with conflict resolution?" you may be wondering. We often have conflicts with trying individuals—those who regularly cause us some amount of misery. It is with these troubling individuals that we must exercise great patience. If not, our impatience will serve to retard or aggravate the resolution of the conflict.

The Greek word used in Ephesians 4:2 for patience is *makrothumía.* As I mentioned a moment ago, some argue that when the word *makrothumía* is used, it is largely to indicate patience in respect to persons, while the word for endurance *(hupomoné)* connotes patience in (or putting up with) things or circumstances.[6] The words sometimes appear together (see 2 Cor. 6:4, 6; 2 Tim. 3:10). Do you find yourself tempted to impatience more often with people or with circumstances?[7]

In the counseling office, when trying to help someone identify impatience *with people,* I look for a couple of attitudes. The first is an unwillingness to work any longer on the relationship. Relationships take effort. But impatient people are too quick to throw in the towel on friendships and even family relationships that are difficult.

"But how long do I need to wait before I throw in the towel?"

6. Spiros Zodhiates, *The Complete Word Study Dictionary: New Testament* (Chattanooga: AMG Publishers, 2000), Logos Bible Software e-book, Strong's number G3115. Barclay says, "*Makrothumia* . . . is the characteristic Greek word for *patience with others.* John Chrysostom defined it as the spirit which has the power to take revenge but never does so. J. B. Lightfoot, the New Testament scholar, defined it as the spirit which refuses to retaliate. To take an imperfect analogy—it is often possible to see a puppy and a large dog together. The puppy yaps at the big dog, worries it, bites it, and all the time the big dog, which could put the puppy in its place with one snap of his teeth, bears the puppy's impertinence with a forbearing dignity. *Makrothumia* is the spirit which bears insult and injury without bitterness and without complaint. It is the spirit which can suffer unpleasant people with graciousness and fools without irritation" (William Barclay, *The Letters to the Galatians and Ephesians,* The New Daily Study Bible, 3rd ed. [Louisville, KY: Westminster John Knox Press, 2002], 159–60).

7. Impatience with your circumstances is being impatient with the One who controls those circumstances. Loving God involves being patient with (waiting for) Him (see 1 Cor. 13:4).

"How long must I put up with her crying (or nagging, or disrespect, or lying, or laziness)?"

"How long must I put up with his drinking (or temper, or silence, or foolishness)?"

I am often asked "how long" type questions when counseling people who are going through difficult relationships. Patient people are committed to handling relationships and the "difficult" people in them biblically. They are willing to go the second and even the third mile with them.[8] They are willing to persevere through not just one or two conflicts but, if the Lord wills, many years of them. This is so because some relationships are very difficult to terminate without sinning. And in the midst of each conflict they have with difficult people, patient people understand that, if the conflict can be resolved at all, it is apt to take longer than it would with people who are not so difficult.

The second attitude that lets me know that I'm dealing with an impatient person is one that unduly pressures or even demands that a loved one change according to one's own (subjective) schedule. I sometimes tell them, "If the Lord were to show you all your remaining sin in one moment and told you that you had until the end of next week to 'get things together,' how would you like it?" The Holy Spirit has His own sanctification agenda for each of us. And that agenda is almost certainly different for our loved ones than we might like to think. Superimposing our agenda for another person's sanctification over that of the Holy Spirit's is not only a manifestation of impatience, it's the epitome of spiritual arrogance.

When we are in conflict with another believer, it is easy for us to become angry and impatient with the immaturity of our opponent. We sometimes wish that we could argue with someone more mature. But a

8. Of course, there may be times when there really is little else that can be done to move forward (if you have truly made every effort "as much as depends on you" to make peace; see Rom. 12:18 NKJV; Eph. 4:3). It may be wise (after receiving biblical counsel) to back off of the relationship biblically—making it clear to the other person that the relationship is changing not because the counselee is throwing in the towel, but because the other person isn't willing to play by God's rules. In fact, sometimes it is an error to stay in a relationship—in cases such as a friendship with a person who is a sexual temptation for you or your spouse, for example, or a friendship with a person who entices you to sin in an area where you are weak. Sometimes fleeing is the godliest response (Gen. 39:6–12).

patient person accepts the fact that his opponent is where he is spiritually and does what he can to spur his opponent to greater maturity—without allowing himself to be provoked into temporarily obscuring his own maturity by sinful responses.

2. Patience is the ability, while experiencing physical or mental distress, to keep one's emotions (grief, fear, and anger) from developing into sinful thoughts, words, attitudes, or actions (especially toward God and others).

It is easier for us to sin when we are physically ill. Job again serves as an example. He handled the initial part of his trial (up until he was physically afflicted) amazingly well. Then his thoughts and words about God began to change. The Bible says much about trials and suffering. It's a fact of life. Perhaps the most obvious characteristic about individuals who don't suffer well is that they complain about their circumstances, often putting the worst possible interpretation on them. God calls His people to suffer and gives them the grace to suffer well. He tells us not to be surprised by it. "Beloved, do not be surprised at the fiery ordeal among you, which comes upon you for your testing, as though some strange thing were happening to you" (1 Peter 4:12).

Trials come in all shapes and sizes. They come for many reasons: to test our faith, to sanctify us, to discipline us, to teach us to better depend upon God, to show His strength in our weakness, and to teach us patience.

> Consider it all joy, my brethren, when you encounter various trials, knowing that the testing of your faith produces endurance. And let endurance have its perfect result, so that you may be perfect and complete, lacking in nothing. (James 1:2–4)

> And not only this, but we also exult in our tribulations, knowing that tribulation brings about perseverance. (Rom. 5:3)

If you have been a Christian for any time, you have no doubt read Hebrews 11, which speaks of the faithfulness of God's saints through the ages. Their faith in God is what stood by them through various trials. What you may have failed to notice, however, is that in the first few verses of the following chapter (Heb. 12), the words *endure* and *endurance* occur again and again.

> Therefore, since we have so great a cloud of witnesses surrounding us, let us also lay aside every encumbrance and the sin which so easily entangles us, and let us run with *endurance* the race that is set before us, fixing our eyes on Jesus, the author and perfecter of faith, who for the joy set before Him *endured* the cross, despising the shame, and has sat down at the right hand of the throne of God. For consider Him who has *endured* such hostility by sinners against Himself, so that you will not grow weary and lose heart. . . . It is for discipline that you endure; God deals with you as with sons; for what son is there whom *his* father does not discipline? (1–3, 7)

We are to endure our trials (especially those that involve God's discipline) with our eye on Jesus (who, by the way, never complained). It's easy, when we take our eyes off of Jesus, to allow the trials and tribulations of life to tempt us to sin. But rather than murmuring and complaining, accusing God of things that are inconsistent with His character, or negatively infecting others with our discouragement, the Lord tells us to rejoice!

But how do we do that? It's largely a matter of perspective. I currently live in Alabama, where we have a tradition every November called the Iron Bowl. The University of Alabama and Auburn University football teams play each other in the most anticipated game of the year. Now the interesting thing is that, in Alabama churches, there are almost always fans that cheer for each side.[9] So here you have members of the same church seeing the exact same football game, perhaps even sitting in the same set of box seats, but when the game is over some are elated and some are depressed. This is so because one member values Auburn above Alabama and the other values Alabama above Auburn.

9. I've actually met married couples in which one partner roots for one team and one for the other (although that usually changes in time).

So it is with our trials. If we value God's purposes in our trials more than man's purposes, we will be able to endure the trial with grace. If we value man's purposes more than God's, we will be tempted to all manner of sin.

> And He began to teach them that the Son of Man must suffer many things and be rejected by the elders and the chief priests and the scribes, and be killed, and after three days rise again. And He was stating the matter plainly. And Peter took Him aside and began to rebuke Him. But turning around and seeing His disciples, He rebuked Peter and said, "Get behind Me, Satan; for you are not setting your mind on God's interests, but man's." (Mark 8:31–33)

It requires setting our minds on the things of God to keep from sinning in the midst of suffering. And it requires the ability to do that for the duration of the trial. It requires endurance!

God does not owe us an explanation for why He does what He does. He is God, and He can do what He pleases. And whatever He does will always be good.

> But indeed, O man, who are you to reply against God? Will the thing formed say to him who formed it, "Why have you made me like this?" Does not the potter have power over the clay, from the same lump to make one vessel for honor and another for dishonor? (Rom. 9:20–21 NKJV)

Even if you knew the answer to that perplexing "why" question, it might not help you as much as you think. You may not like God's answer or agree with His reasoning. In time, God may see fit to show you why He allowed the difficult circumstance that He has brought into your life. Or He may not. When you get to heaven, you'll certainly understand. But in the midst of trials, perhaps the question you should be asking is not a "why" question but rather a "what" (or a "how") question: "What does God want me to do about (how does he want me to respond to) the problem He has brought into my life?"

I mentioned earlier that to love God is to wait on Him. But to love Him is also to believe the best about Him. Love "believes all things" (1 Cor. 13:7).

Do you love God so much that you are accustomed to putting the best possible interpretation on His dealings with you? "Love believes all things" means that we are to believe the best about others. In other words, if there are ten possible interpretations or explanations of why someone took a particular course of action, nine of them being evil and only one of them being good, the person who loves will, in the absence of evidence to the contrary, *choose* to reject the bad in favor of the good. Now, if you are commanded to view other sinners with this kind of optimism, how much more should you interpret God's dealings with you in the best possible light? How much more should you forsake the harsh interpretations of His providence in your life and believe that He does what He does for your good?

How do you like it when others put the worst spin on your actions? What do you suppose you do to the Spirit of God when you do so to Him?

"God is surely going to pour out His judgment against me."

"God intends to make my life miserable."

"He is going to fill my life with trials and misery."

"He has brought me here to slay me!"

If there is any *good* interpretation that you can make about the Lord's dealings with you, you ought to make it!

But this is a book about solving conflicts with people. So let's talk for a moment about how impatience can manifest itself in sinful words, attitudes, or actions toward others.

Several communication issues are associated with impatience (an unwillingness to *wait*).

- ☐ Interrupting others while they are speaking (not waiting until others have finished expressing their thoughts before I express mine)
- ☐ Jumping to hasty and unfounded conclusions (not waiting until I have collected all the information necessary to come to a biblical conclusion)

- ☐ Judging motives (not waiting until I have asked others what their real motives are before I accuse them of having improper ones)
- ☐ Demanding immediate answers to difficult questions (not waiting until those I question have had sufficient time to consider their response)
- ☐ Pressuring people to finish what they are saying quickly (not waiting until others have finished expressing their thoughts before I express mine)
- ☐ Finishing others' sentences[10] (not waiting until others have finished expressing their thoughts before I express mine)
- ☐ Taking vengeance verbally (not waiting for God to execute His justice in His time)
- ☐ Prematurely terminating a discussion in order to do something more pleasurable (not waiting to do what I want until after I do what God wants me to do)
- ☐ Prematurely terminating conflicts due to an unwillingness to tolerate the sinful attitudes of my opponent

When our opponents are not playing by the rules we can be tempted to pull the plug on the conversation quickly. Thoughts like this may run through our minds and short-circuit the entire process.

"He's only interested in expressing his own opinion."
"He is a fool. I'm not going to waste any more of my words on him."
"There's no hope; she'll never admit that she's wrong."
"God's going to have to show him. I'm tired of trying."
"It's hopeless. She's not going to listen to reason."
"A man persuaded against his will is of the same opinion still. I'm outta here!"
"I'm not going to put up with her disrespect (or other bad attitude). This conversation is over!"

10. There may be circumstances when someone is struggling to find the right word that suggesting a possible "fit" will be appreciated. But if this is done too often, it might be perceived as impatience.

But there are more patient (loving) ways to think during such times of provocation by an opponent. Why not make a list of the ones that counteract the impatient thoughts you tend to have when you are being antagonized by an adversary? Here are a few to get you started.

> "I'm going to give this conflict at least two more rounds (exchanges)."
> "There's got to be a way to help him see things differently."
> "God has been patient with my sin. I'm going to be patient with him!"
> "Just because his attitude stinks doesn't mean that his reasoning is wrong."
> "God calls me to use 'great patience' when I am in conflict."
> "Lord, help me to know how much longer to stay in this fight and how and when to terminate it politely."

3. Patience is the ability to endure tribulation without resorting to any sinful means of deliverance.[11]

At the time of 1 Samuel 24, David was being pursued by Saul. Saul, looking for a place to relieve himself, came into the very cave where David was hiding. Though David's people urged him to take advantage of what seemed a divine opportunity, he chose instead to cut off only a piece of Saul's cloak in order to show the king that he had indeed had opportunity to kill him but chose not to (vv. 1–6).

Similarly, the apostle Paul and Silas were preaching the gospel when they were thrown into prison and put in stocks in the dungeon (Acts 16:22–24). God sent an earthquake that set the prisoners free. But, rather than seeing this as a wonderful opportunity to escape and put as much distance behind them as possible, they stayed near, ready to be used by God in an unexpected way.

> But about midnight Paul and Silas were praying and singing hymns of praise to God, and the prisoners were listening to them; and suddenly there came a great earthquake, so that the foundations of the prison house were shaken; and immediately all the doors were opened and everyone's chains were unfastened. When the jailer awoke and saw the

11. The next three definitions for patience are technically subsets of the previous one.

> prison doors opened, he drew his sword and was about to kill himself, supposing that the prisoners had escaped. But Paul cried out with a loud voice, saying, "Do not harm yourself, for we are all here!" And he called for lights and rushed in, and trembling with fear he fell down before Paul and Silas, and after he brought them out, he said, "Sirs, what must I do to be saved?"
>
> They said, "Believe in the Lord Jesus, and you will be saved, you and your household." And they spoke the word of the Lord to him together with all who were in his house. And he took them that very hour of the night and washed their wounds, and immediately he was baptized, he and all his household. And he brought them into his house and set food before them, and rejoiced greatly, having believed in God with his whole household. (Acts 16:25–34)

As it turns out, Paul and Silas were released after all, without becoming jailbirds. But God's agenda for their lives (following His will) was more important to them than their own agendas or their comfort. Imagine how many lives would have been negatively impacted if they had taken the easy way out. Consider how many people were positively impacted (even down through the centuries) because they refused to use sinful means to extricate themselves from the prison into which the Lord had sent them.

Impatient people are often on the prowl for something—anything—that will bring them relief (e.g., divorce, suicide, rebellion, gossip, manipulation, running away, or even neglecting personal responsibilities).

Sometimes those I counsel can feel trapped by their trials—sort of like they are in stocks in the dungeon themselves. And, with every day that goes by, the shackles seem to become more unbearable. Occasionally it even appears that the stocks are tightening on their limbs and that they will soon be crushed by the ever-tightening walls of the prison dungeon.

The Bible has some very important things to say to them (and to us) about that sense of being trapped and imprisoned. First Corinthians 10:13 says, "No temptation has overtaken you but such as is common to man; and God is faithful, who will not allow you to be tempted beyond what you are able, but with the temptation will provide the way of escape also, that you may be able to endure it."

According to this passage, you are not the only one who has ever undergone trials. Your own trials are not unique, though the exact details of them might be rare. But others of God's children are undergoing some of the same trials right now, and others throughout history have too.

God promises that He will not allow the temptation to become so difficult that you will not be *able* to deal with it biblically (in a way that is not sinful and that will bring glory to God). In other words, He will not let the jailer lock you up and throw away the key!

This promise does not tell us how God will release us from the trial, only that He will do it. Scripture is full of examples of how He has done so with His children. (Sometimes the release is even through death, as for many of His people in Hebrews 11.)[12] But we can trust that He is faithful, even when we cannot see the next step (see Heb. 13:5). We can trust that He will give us strength to endure it.

Recently I found myself in a conflict with an individual who, because of his history of not proactively addressing a problem with those under his care, was causing unnecessary grief to someone I loved very much. The fact that my loved one and I had been in that trial for what I thought was "way too long" (notice the impatience in that phrase) became a great temptation for me to sin in at least two ways.[13] First, my impatient spirit tempted me to speak with so much passion that sinful forms of communication might have easily flowed out of my mouth. Second, I was tempted to prematurely fix the problem by not going through the proper channels to try to get the issue resolved. Which "sinful ways of deliverance" from conflict have you attempted (or been tempted) to employ?

12. Even those Christians who are suffering with incurable or terminal illnesses have hope that someday God will let them out of the boxes of their fleshly tents (their physical bodies) and will deliver them into the freedom (see Rom. 8:18–22) of their heavenly home ("a building from God, a house not made with hands, eternal in the heavens"—2 Cor. 5:1).

13. When you are in a trial, don't be surprised if other Christians encourage you to take matters into your own hands, as David's men did to him.

- ☐ Personally attacking your opponent (or his argument) so that he will get angry and walk away (or you will be able to walk away and blame him for prematurely ending the conflict)
- ☐ Lying your way out of the conflict (saying "yes" when you mean "no") just to "get it over with"
- ☐ Falsely accusing your opponent (or exaggerating his culpability)
- ☐ Intimidating (bullying) your opponent into agreeing with you
- ☐ Manipulating your opponent into agreeing with you through guilt
- ☐ Becoming excessively emotional so that your opponent will back off
- ☐ Purposely misusing Scripture
- ☐ Unjustly pulling rank (abusing your position of authority over your opponent)
- ☐ Saying "whatever" and walking away
- ☐ Becoming physical (pushing, shoving, hitting, slapping, pinching, and so on)
- ☐ Other: ______________________________
- ☐ Other: ______________________________
- ☐ Other: ______________________________

4. Patience is the ability to endure suffering while continuing to acknowledge and be thankful for God's sovereignty, justice, wisdom, love, and goodness.

Let's look again to the example of Job. Throughout the account, Job never questioned God's sovereignty over his circumstances. He didn't focus on secondary causes—like the Sabeans or the Chaldeans or the fire from heaven or the wind that destroyed the house in which his children were banqueting. Rather, he attributed everything to the decretive will of God. He apparently knew that God had sovereignly instigated the trial.

Have you ever gone through a trial in which there seemed to be almost nothing for which you could praise God—nothing *in the circumstance* for which you could be thankful? Yet we are instructed to give thanks in every situation.

> In *everything* give thanks. (1 Thess. 5:18)

> I will bless the Lord *at all times.* (Ps. 34:1)

During such times, as difficult as it may be, we can praise God for who He is. *Patience* is required for us to see what God is up to and how He is going to work our trials together for our good. When we are facing trials, one of the most profitable things we can do is to spend some extra time studying God's perfections.

> I would have despaired unless I had believed that I would see *the goodness of the* Lord
> In the land of the living. (Ps. 27:13)

> He who comes to God must believe that He is and that *He is a rewarder* of those who seek Him. (Heb. 11:6)

Do you lose sight of God's perfections when you are in conflict? If so, you will be more likely to lose your cool rather than patiently enduring the conflict. If you really believed these things and acted on them (or acted out of an abiding assurance of them even though you might not be able to see them operating at the moment), wouldn't you be much less likely to resort to unbiblical means of communication in your attempts to resolve matters? Wouldn't you have a certain calmness (if not winsomeness) that would make your arguments even more persuasive? Wouldn't it strengthen your resolve to contend without being contentious? Wouldn't it be easier for you to trust God for the outcome even if the other person is unwilling to play by God's rules? Wouldn't it enable you to hang in there a bit longer with your opponent (or at least to not throw in the towel prematurely)? In the space provided below, record how an awareness of God's perfections could have helped you during your last conflict (or how it might help you in the next one).

God's sovereignty ______________________________
God's justice ______________________________

God's wisdom ______________________
God's love ______________________
God's goodness ______________________

5. Patience is the ability to keep a biblical perspective about one's troubles by not magnifying a tolerable trial so that it appears to one's mind as an intolerable one.

Patience is a mind-set. It's a matter of how the mind interprets life—of how one views reality. Consider the characteristic of the first contemplation listed in Philippians 4:8. "Finally, brethren, whatever is *true*, whatever is honorable, whatever is right, whatever is pure, whatever is lovely, whatever is of good repute, if there is any excellence and if anything worthy of praise, let your mind dwell on these things." To think about things that are *true* is, in part, to think about that which conforms to reality (as held over against that which is a fantasy). Our minds can magnify the misery of our trials way beyond reality. There are even some interesting biblical examples of those who magnified tolerable trials so that they appeared to their own minds as intolerable ones. Although we may see our need to depend on God's grace more in the larger trials than in smaller ones, for the Christian all trials are tolerable because of the grace that is promised to us throughout any trial we may experience (see 1 Cor. 10:13). It may be more accurate to say that we don't so much magnify the trial as we minimize our view of God in proportion to it (make Him not as large as it is).

Cain: "And Cain said to the LORD, 'My punishment is too great to bear!'" (Gen. 4:13).

Rachel: "Now when Rachel saw that she bore Jacob no children, she became jealous of her sister; and she said to Jacob, 'Give me children, or else I die'" (Gen. 30:1).

Moses: "So Moses said to the LORD, 'Why have You been so hard on Your servant? And why have I not found favor in Your sight, that You have laid the burden of all this people on me?'" (Num. 11:11).

The Israelites: "Then they said to Moses, 'Is it because there were no graves in Egypt that you have taken us away to die in the wilderness? . . .

Would that we had died by the LORD's hand in the land of Egypt, when we sat by the pots of meat, when we ate bread to the full; for you have brought us out into this wilderness to kill this whole assembly with hunger'" (Ex. 14:11; 16:3).

Elijah: "He said, 'I have been very zealous for the LORD, the God of hosts; for the sons of Israel have forsaken Your covenant, torn down Your altars and killed Your prophets with the sword. And *I alone am left*; and they seek my life, to take it away'" (1 Kings 19:10).

Jonah: "When the sun came up God appointed a scorching east wind, and the sun beat down on Jonah's head so that he became faint and *begged with all his soul to die*, saying, 'Death is better to me than life.' Then God said to Jonah, 'Do you have good reason to be angry about the plant?' And he said, 'I have good reason to be angry, even to death'" (Jonah 4:8–9).

Like the Israelites whose impatience in the wilderness tempted them to sarcastically complain to Moses (and against God), impatience tempts us to similar verbal and attitudinal sins by exaggerating the scope and intensity of our trials. Such exaggerations can magnify the importance of the issues of our conflicts way beyond that which conforms to reality—especially to God's reality. Patient people train their minds not to perceive a pinprick as though they had been mortally wounded. Consequently, they do not see every potential conflict as something to be eschewed at all costs. Neither do they use nuclear (sinful) tactics in conflict when conventional (biblical) ones will do just fine.

6. Patience is the ability to rejoice in the assurance that one's present distress will produce godly character, which is of great value not only in this life, but also in the next.

I have previously used Jay Adams's "man in a box" illustration. I often conclude it with words to this effect: "God is preparing you, while you are in the box, for what He has prepared for you once He lets you out of the box." Focusing on God's purposes for sending trials will give hope, and hope, as we shall see in a moment, is inseparably linked to patience.

Do you know what God's purposes are for trials in the life of the believer?

Trials are often God's catalysts for our sanctification. We grow, mature, are completed and perfected, become more Christlike, develop proven character, or whatever other biblical synonym you care to use for progressive sanctification, through trials. I daresay that most of us wouldn't grow much at all apart from them! It is trials that impel the vast majority of counselees into my office for counseling.

> Consider it all joy, my brethren, when you encounter various trials, knowing that the testing of your faith produces endurance. And let endurance have its perfect result, so that you may be perfect and complete, lacking in nothing. (James 1:2–4)

Our sanctification is of tremendous value, not only in this life, but also in the next.

> Bodily discipline is only of little profit, but godliness is profitable for all things, since it holds promise for the present life and also for the life to come. (1 Tim. 4:8)

> Therefore we do not lose heart, but though our outer man is decaying, yet our inner man is being renewed day by day. For momentary, light affliction is producing for us an eternal weight of glory far beyond all comparison, while we look not at the things which are seen, but at the things which are not seen; for the things which are seen are temporal, but the things which are not seen are eternal. (2 Cor. 4:16–18)

Learning to live in light of (in hope of) eternity is an essential element of developing patience.

Another purpose for enduring trials is ministry to others. When my counselees respond properly to trials (when they suffer well), they are comforted and assisted by the Holy Spirit in the trial and become better equipped to minister to others.

> Blessed be the God and Father of our Lord Jesus Christ, the Father of mercies and God of all comfort, who comforts us in all our affliction so that we will be able to comfort those who are in any affliction with the comfort with which we ourselves are comforted by God. (2 Cor. 1:3–4)

I'll never forget sitting across the desk from a hurting counselee and trying to minister to him when all of a sudden out of my mouth came the most spot-on, insightful counsel I had given in years. As I sat there amazed at what I was saying—knowing that through my words the Spirit of God was pouring oil into the wounds of my hurting friend—my eyes began to water as I said in my heart, "Thank You, Lord. Now I understand better than ever why I had to go through that horrible trial several years ago."

It's now time to connect the dots for you between *hope* and *patience*. Notice the progression in the following passage from trials to patience to character to hope.

> And not only this, but we also exult in our tribulations, knowing that *tribulation* brings about *perseverance*; and perseverance, proven character; and proven character, *hope*; and hope does not disappoint, because the love of God has been poured out within our hearts through the Holy Spirit who was given to us. (Rom. 5:3–5)

It is hope that enables us to persevere. Without hope, we are tempted to prematurely throw in the towel.

As an avid angler, I enjoy fishing even when I don't catch any fish. Why? Because I know that if I am using the right equipment and I tough it out, sooner or later I'm going to be rewarded. The hope of catching "the big one" enables me to sit there patiently (and pray) hour after hour until the Lord sends His fish to me (or doesn't).

Our hope of seeing the goodness of the Lord—presumably in the land of the living (but, if not, certainly in heaven)—is what enables us to patiently endure whatever God sends our way.

> For in this hope we were saved. Now hope that is seen is not hope. For who hopes for what he sees? But if we hope for what we do not see, we wait for it *with patience*. (Rom. 8:24–25 ESV)

In the final analysis, most of the conflicts that we have with people are of little eternal significance. But the character (godliness) that we are often willing to sacrifice in our attempts to win an argument costs us eternal (and sometimes temporal) rewards. God can use even the distress of conflict to build godly character in our lives.

Several years ago I had a serious conflict with an individual who tried to do me much harm. One of the best pieces of advice I received as I was trying to determine my response to this individual was simply this: "In ten years, no one will remember the details of what ________ has done to you. What they will remember is how you responded to him—for better or for worse."

We live in a world of fast food, microwave ovens, instant information, and high-speed air travel. We are accustomed to obtaining whatever our hearts desire at the moment through the use of credit cards. The desire for instant gratification can be a real enemy to the development of patience. But there is no such thing as instant spirituality. Learning to delay (for biblical reasons) the acquisition of some of the things that we want is a good exercise in putting off impatience. So patience really is a virtue—and a very worthy goal to be pursued by everyone who names the name of Christ.

4

PREREQUISITE FOUR: LOVING FORBEARANCE

> Walk in a manner worthy of the calling with which you have been called . . . showing tolerance for one another in love. (Eph. 4:1–2)

IT'S TIME FOR ANOTHER TEST. Wait—I didn't warn you about today's pop quiz, did I? Must have slipped my mind. Well, bear with me, please. Using the rating scale below, record next to each statement the number that best describes the frequency with which the specific symptom of impatience occurs in your life.

THE TEST FOR TOLERANCE

Rating Scale	Points
Never (Hardly Ever)	5
Seldom	4
Sometimes	3
Frequently	2
Always (Almost Always)	1

1. When others do not do things exactly as I would do them or in a way that I think is best, I criticize them verbally or mentally. ______

2. When people hold differing opinions from mine about things that are not clearly delineated in Scripture, I judge them to be wrong, immature, or unspiritual. ________

3. When talking to someone who holds a differing opinion from mine, I immediately try to persuade that person that he is wrong, rather than demonstrating respect for him by trying to understand more completely his point of view. ________

4. When other Christians disagree with me on minor doctrinal issues, I have difficulty fellowshipping with them. ________

5. When I am discussing political issues with someone who holds radically different views from my own, I become sinfully angry or end up saying something that I later regret. ________

6. When my spouse (or some other person with whom I am close) desires to do something differently than I do, I try to change his or her mind without first considering his desires (or point of view). ________

7. When those who are close to me persist in using annoying mannerisms and irritating idiosyncrasies, I have difficulty tolerating them. ________

8. When people of other races want to be my friend, I hesitate to befriend them or I determine to limit the scope of the friendship. ________

9. When people of greater or lesser socio–economic levels want to be my friend, I hesitate to befriend them or I determine to limit the scope of the friendship. ________

10. When I encounter individuals who zealously hold to religions other than Christianity, I angrily write them off as foolish rather than praying for their salvation. ________

11. When I see other parents allowing their children to do things that I would not allow my children to do, even though no clear sin is involved, I judge them to be poor parents. ________

12. When someone does something that my conscience would not allow me to do, I judge that person to be sinning before I evaluate whether or not the Bible classifies his behavior as wrong. ________

13. When a weaker brother has a scruple about something that I do which I am convinced the Bible does not prohibit, I struggle with feelings of contempt for that brother. ________

14. When other people sin, I reprove them for their sin before I consider whether or not the transgression should be overlooked. ________

15. When others do not follow my counsel to the letter, I assume that they really do not want to change, or I judge their motives in some other way. ________

16. When others who are struggling need my assistance with sin problems that I find especially repugnant, I struggle with not wanting to minister to them. ________

17. When others continue in sin, I become angry if I do not see them suffer the consequences of their sin as quickly as I think they should. ________

18. When I realize that a small sacrifice on my part would provide a great benefit to someone else, I struggle with sacrificing my desires for his happiness. ______

19. When I have a conflict with another church member, my first inclination is to withdraw or to write the other person off rather than to reconcile with him. ______

20. When I hear a message in church that does not directly pertain to what I want or think I need, I allow my mind to wander or wish that the speaker would be more practical, rather than trying to understand and apply the meaning of the text. ______

Total Score ______

RATING SCALE[1]

94–100%	You are a forbearing person.
86–93%	You could use some improvement.
75–85%	You probably need considerable improvement.
Below 74%	You urgently need improvement.

The word *tolerance* stirs up mixed feelings in the hearts of many contemporary evangelical Christians. This is so because we have been accused of being *intolerant* of certain practices and lifestyles that the Scriptures teach are wrong. And, up to a point, we are right to be intolerant of sin. But showing tolerance is biblical—especially about those things that other people do that are *not* sinful.

We all have nonsinful idiosyncrasies, quirks, and foibles that can be irritating to others. These are often a cause of serious conflict. But should they be? Not if we practice loving forbearance.

1. As with the IQ test in chapter three, this is not a scientifically normed instrument. The questions were developed from biblical constructs; consequently, persons taking the test are being compared more closely to the character of Jesus Christ than to the character of those in our culture.

WHAT IS FORBEARANCE?

The word *forbearance* literally means "to put up with" or "to tolerate." When used in conjunction with people, it means "to have patience with in regard to the errors or weaknesses of anyone."[2] But the word *forbearance* does not appear alone in this text. It is qualified by the word *love*: "forbearing one another in love." Loving forbearance is what this fourth prerequisite is all about.

Love is by nature forbearing, for it "covers a multitude of sins" (1 Peter 4:8, cf. Prov. 10:12). Like a Timex watch, forbearing love "takes a licking and keeps on ticking." It takes a shoving but keeps on loving.

Once again, I will offer several working definitions of this precondition for conflict resolution.[3]

1. Forbearance is the ability to recognize and appreciate the fact that God has made each person different.

Paul asked the Corinthians, "Who makes you differ from another?" (1 Cor. 4:7 NKJV). "God did" is the expected reply. The Lord has given to each of us different abilities, skills, gifts, ministries, backgrounds, tastes, skin colors, genders, and even body shapes. Forbearance recognizes and accepts this fact as a good thing. Perhaps nothing drives the reality of our differentness home to us better than marriage.

Oliver grew up on a farm in the country more than twenty-five miles from the thriving metropolis where his wife, Lisa, was raised. His father raised pigs and chickens and came to town only twice a month for the purpose of getting supplies. Lisa's father was a big-city lawyer who entertained people in his home regularly. Oliver's family was accustomed to going to bed at 9:00 p.m. Lisa's (because they entertained so much) would routinely retire for the evening at 11:00 p.m. He did chores on the farm (and at home) for many hours each day. She had a maid and was required to do little more than make her bed and keep her clothes off the bedroom floor.

2. Spiros Zodhiates, *The Complete Word Study Dictionary: New Testament* (Chattanooga: AMG Publishers, 2000), Logos Bible Software e-book, Strong's number G430

3. I am grateful to Dr. Wayne Mack, whose materials have been helpful in developing several of these "definitions."

Oliver's family had to make do with little. They bought their clothes at Wal-Mart, drove old American vehicles (pickups), never took vacations, and reupholstered their furniture every eight to ten years. Lisa's family bought their clothing at Brooks Brothers, Neiman Marcus, and expensive specialty shops; drove Mercedes Benz and BMWs; and vacationed frequently at their beach and lake houses. Oliver loved sports. He was on the varsity football, baseball, and basketball teams at the local public high school. Lisa went to prestigious private schools (including several in Europe), had no interest in sports, and loved the arts. He loved to fish and go to movies and rodeos. She loved to dance and go to the theater and the symphony. He liked country and gospel music. She liked classical music and opera. She spoke three languages; he spoke Southern! Suffice it to say that they came from two very different backgrounds (and you may be wondering how they were ever attracted to each other in the first place).

Lisa and Oliver were bound to have many conflicts in their marriage, not because one of them was necessarily a bigger sinner than the other (after all, is it a sin to shop at one store rather than another or to prefer the symphony to a tractor pull?), but rather because they were so different. Different is good! But now that they were married, what time would they retire for the evening? Where would they purchase their clothing? What kind of car would they buy? Where would they go on a date? Where would they travel on vacation? Where would they live? What kind of house would they buy? How would they furnish and decorate it? How much domestic help would they have? Attempts to resolve these normal marital issues would be more difficult for Oliver and Lisa than for couples whose differences were not so pronounced. But forbearing love can make it easier.

2. Forbearance is the ability to distinguish sin issues from nonsin issues.

Although we must sometimes show forbearance when people sin[4] (Luke 9:41), we will more often have to put up with the nonsinful things

4. In conflict, some individuals are prone to resort to unbiblical forms of communication that will require forbearance even though it may subsequently become necessary to convict (reprove) them.

that others are accustomed to doing. If we cannot distinguish between the two, we will find ourselves slow to tolerate anything because everything will become an offense to us. This will increase the number of potential conflicts we have with others and will unnecessarily extend the time it takes to resolve our legitimate differences. More importantly, what right do we have to get offended at something that doesn't offend God?

As we saw in chapter 2, the ability to distinguish right from wrong is one mark of a mature Christian (cf. Heb. 5:14). There are real problems associated with confusing the two. Isaiah 5:20 declares, "Woe to those who call evil good, and good evil." Not the least of these problems is legalism. The legalism that has the greatest impact on one's ability to resolve conflicts is the kind that elevates manmade rules (one's subjective personal standards) to the same level of authority as God-given commands. It has to do with sinfully judging others to be sinning when they are not. In James 4:11–12, we are given this warning:

> Do not speak against one another, brethren. He who speaks against a brother or judges his brother, speaks against the law and judges the law; but if you judge the law, you are not a doer of the law but a judge of it. There is only one Lawgiver and Judge, the One who is able to save and to destroy; but who are you who judge your neighbor?

When James says not to speak against your brother, he means speaking against him in the sense of judging him to be doing something wrong when he really isn't. There is a serious implication when you make such an uncharitable judgment about another. Do you know what it is? It's as if you are saying, "*So what* if the Bible does not condemn it? Everybody knows that it's a sin to do it."

When you judge things to be sinful that are not *clearly* delineated as such (at least in principle) in the Scriptures, you wrongly judge not only your brother who did the misjudged deed, but also the Bible for not condemning the deed, and the *Author* of the Bible, who apparently forgot to include it in Holy Writ. Think of how grave a matter it is to make such a presumptuous accusation against God!

Everyone who knows my wife knows that she loves her cup of coffee in the morning and in the afternoon. She doesn't abuse it; she just has two cups a day. Those cups must not be in Styrofoam, must have real cream, and must be made in a European way immediately before she consumes them piping hot. (Yes, most people are intimidated to make her a cup of coffee.) Many years ago, she was tremulously approached by a friend who had mustered up the courage to confront her about the sin of ruining her health by drinking coffee. Now, Kim appreciated the fact that her friend cared enough to plan this confrontation, but she was deeply saddened that her friend had obviously been influenced, and even coached in her confrontation, by other more censorious and proud friends, who drank only decaffeinated coffee. Obviously it is not a sin for Kim to have two cups of coffee a day, but this situation illustrated to us how a judgmental, proud, censorious attitude can cause us, as well as those we influence, to sin in the way that James chapter 4 describes. When we convict another, we must be certain that the issue we are confronting him about is really a sin.

Sometimes sin must be tolerated—at least for a period of time—but things that are not sinful ought always to be tolerated by the Christian. This is not to say that we cannot try to do something to reduce or eliminate the irritation from our life. But, after all is said and done, if the other person is unwilling or unable to change his annoying habit, we must lovingly forbear with him. This brings us to the next definition.

3. Forbearance is a willingness to allow others the freedom to develop and express their own unique lifestyles within the framework of Scripture without passing judgment on them or holding them in contempt.

What do I mean when I speak of *unique lifestyles*? We each have our own style or way of living life—a "bundle of behaviors," if you please, that sets us apart and distinguishes us from those around us. Some lifestyles are inherently unbiblical, such as the lifestyle of sexual immorality or hedonism. Others are acceptable within the context of Scripture. A forbearing individual does not make moral judgments of individuals whose lifestyles are not clearly delineated as sinful in the Scriptures.

We have tremendous freedom as Christians to live our lives with great diversity. There is a wide array of behaviors, customs, and activities in which we are free to participate. As with Oliver and Lisa, some live modest lifestyles, and some live more affluent lifestyles. Is it necessarily a sin to do either? Some people, like me, like to drive Volvos; others prefer Hondas; still others prefer American-made automobiles. Does it offend the Lord to drive any of these? Some people dress more formally, others more casually. Does the Bible forbid either? Some people prefer the English Standard Version of the Bible to the New American Standard version. Is it unbiblical to read either of these translations? Some Christians listen to traditional Christian music; others prefer more contemporary music. The list could go on to include matters of cuisine, entertainment, and use of idiomatic expressions. The point is, if the Bible doesn't condemn the lifestyle of another, we shouldn't either.

Another passage that speaks to this issue is Romans 14. As you read the first six verses below, notice that there are two types of Christians identified and two sins to avoid (one for each type of person).

> Now accept the one who is *weak in faith*, but not for the purpose of passing judgment on his opinions. One man *has faith* that he may eat all things, but he who is weak eats vegetables only. The one who eats is not to *regard with contempt* the one who does not eat, and the one who does not eat is not to *judge* the one who eats, for God has accepted him. Who are you to judge the servant of another? To his own master he stands or falls; and he will stand, for the Lord is able to make him stand. One person regards one day above another, another regards every day alike. Each person must be fully convinced in his own mind. He who observes the day, observes it for the Lord, and he who eats, does so for the Lord, for he gives thanks to God; and he who eats not, for the Lord he does not eat, and gives thanks to God.

Did you spot them? First, there is the Christian who is "weak in faith" (we sometimes refer to this person as the "weaker brother"). This is the person whose *conscience* is weak (see 1 Cor. 8:8–12). That is, his conscience has not yet been programmed biblically, and as a result he has scruples about things that a more mature Christian, whose conscience has been rightly developed (who, to put it in biblical language, "because of practice" has his "senses trained to discern good and evil"—Heb. 5:14), does not.

On the other hand, there is the person who "has faith." Paul later goes on to refer to this type of person (and this is what we all should aspire to) as the one who is able to stand strong (15:1).

Now, as to those special instructions for each: the weaker brother is not to *judge* the stronger, and the stronger is not to *regard with contempt* the brother who doesn't eat. In other words, the person with the scruple ought not to say (or even think), "How can he do such a thing? Doesn't he care about what the Lord thinks?" And the stronger brother (who is to avoid holding his brother in contempt) ought not to reason like this about his weaker brother: "Why doesn't he grow up? I hate that I have to limit my freedom in Christ when I'm around him lest I offend his unbiblical scruples!"

Stronger Brother	**vs.**	**Weaker Brother**
No unbiblical scruples	vs.	Unbiblical scruples
Biblically trained conscience	vs.	Unbiblically trained conscience
Sin: Holds weaker bro. in *contempt*	vs.	Sin: *Judges* stronger bro.

Here is the bottom line for both: Don't you dare presume to judge (don't slam down the gavel in your heart, or with your mouth, and pronounce judgment on) another's *actions* (e.g., the stronger brother) or *opinions* (e.g., the weaker brother) without the authorization of Scripture!

I have learned that this is particularly important in child-raising. When our oldest daughter was an infant and a toddler, we were constantly bombarded with dogmatic declarations about what we were doing wrong and what we were not doing that we should have been doing. Some friends thought we were too lenient with our daughter and told us frequently, "You need to spank her for that." On the other hand, some friends were convinced that we were too strict and were ruining and damaging our daughter by our firmness with her. They were actually quite hostile to us about it, to the point of breaking off the friendship. There are not many directives in Scripture pertaining to raising children. The Bible simply doesn't address things like breastfeeding, sleeping schedules, potty training, and so on, and parents are given much freedom to raise their children according to their convictions as long as they are following biblical principles.

Putting this all together, to be forbearing is to put up with (not to judge uncharitably or hold in contempt) the lawful lifestyles of other believers, remembering that God has accepted them.

Now as you can imagine, this weaker brother / stronger brother matter has been the source of many conflicts down through the centuries. It continues to this very day. But it doesn't have to be this way if we understand and apply what we have just learned. Imagine how much smoother your conflicts would go if you truly allowed other believers to express views that don't violate Scripture without judging them or holding them in contempt. Imagine how much smoother they would go if others were more forbearing with you.

4. Forbearance is the ability in close relationships to distinguish swing issues from fire issues (Luke 10:38–42).

When our oldest daughter was a toddler, my in-laws bought her a toddler swing. In case you don't know what that is, a toddler swing is a special dangling device (usually shaped like a bucket) with a safety harness. It is typically made of durable, colorful plastic, with nylon rope that may be attached to existing swing sets or tree limbs. Sophia loved this present and asked to use it often.

Try to envision an allegorical scenario in which my family and I are on our way to visit some friends in the country. It's a beautiful fall day. As we are driving up to their house, little Sophia spies a swing set. She asks if she can swing. I say to her, "Maybe later, honey." As the morning progresses, she asks me several more times if I will take her out to the swing set. After holding off as long as I can, I say, "Okay, honey, let's go take a look at that swing set." When we get up close, I realize (for the first time) that there is no toddler seat.

"Sophia, I'm sorry, but this is not the right kind of swing. You'll have to wait until we get home, and then I will swing you on your swing!"

"But Daddy, I want to swing now."

"I know you do, honey, but this swing is not really safe. If you get on it you may fall off and get hurt."

"But Daddy, you said we would swing. Can't I please swing? Please, Daddy!"

At this point, I say to myself, "I did sort of promise her she could swing. She has patiently waited for several hours without complaining. Besides, if I hold her while she swings, she probably won't fall off, and even if she did slip off I would probably be able to catch her before she hits the ground."

"All right, Munchkin, Daddy will hold you on the swing and you should be safe."

A swing issue is a matter (not involving sin)[5] in which I can easily go both ways. The person with whom I am in conflict may prefer to go in one direction while I prefer to go in another; but, because I am a forbearing person, I will "swing with it." If it means that much to you, I am willing to yield my personal desires to yours in order to prefer you in honor and pursue peace with you.

> Be devoted to one another in brotherly love; give *preference* to one another in honor. (Rom. 12:10)

> So then we *pursue the things which make for peace* and the building up of one another. (Rom. 14:19; see also Heb. 12:14)

A fire issue is an issue that, although not necessarily a sin, would be very difficult for me to agree to do. Perhaps it's a matter of personal preference, or taste, or enjoyment, but for whatever reason I find the matter objectionable (see 1 Cor. 16:12). It may be something that I might not refuse to do if I absolutely had to, but that I would really rather not do.

Here is another sort of silly scenario that may illustrate the point. Suppose we have just returned home from our visit to our friends in the country. I change clothes and commence to do some yardwork. After raking the autumn leaves into a large pile, I begin to burn them.[6]

5. Christians may not "swing" on matters that are clearly delineated in Scripture as sin.

6. For any firemen who are reading this, we will assume I have also gotten permission from the local fire department to do so!

After a few moments, Sophia comes out and says to me, "Daddy, can I please play in the fire?"

"What?"

"The fire looks pretty. May I jump in?"

"Sweetheart, the fire is very hot. You will get burned."

"But Daddy, the fire looks pretty. It's all different colors and makes funny noises. Can't I please jump in the leaves? Please, Daddy?"

"Absolutely not!"

Obviously a "fire" issue might not rise to *this* level of "no" in your heart, but it is something that you or another person feels very strongly about, and from which you cannot be lightly swayed. Sometimes firmness on the issue might come from genuinely righteous resolve (I will not attend movies that glorify adultery), sometimes it comes from selfishness (I will never let her have the last word), and sometimes it is morally neutral (I do not eat raw onion). Most commonly it is an extremely strong preference for which there is little to no biblical reason to be dogmatic.

Ideally, people in conflict ought to be "tripping over each other" to show forbearance to one another in order to put the other person's needs (or wishes) above their own.

5. Forbearance is the ability to put up with the idiosyncratic swing issues that you wish were different in another person and to sacrifice your own desires for his benefit.

The Bible has much to say about yielding one's personal desire for the good of others. Here are a few examples.

> We who are strong ought to bear the weaknesses of those without strength and not just to please ourselves. (Rom. 15:1)

> Give no offense either to Jews or to Greeks or to the church of God; just as I also please all men in all things, not seeking my own profit but the profit of the many, so that they may be saved. (1 Cor. 10:32–33)

> Do nothing from selfishness or empty conceit, but with humility of mind regard one another as more important than yourselves; do not

> merely look out for your own personal interests, but also for the interests of others. Have this attitude in yourselves which was also in Christ Jesus, who, although He existed in the form of God, did not regard equality with God a thing to be grasped, but emptied Himself, taking the form of a bond-servant, and being made in the likeness of men. Being found in appearance as a man, He humbled Himself by becoming obedient to the point of death, even death on a cross. (Phil. 2:3–8)

Part of the uniqueness of God's design (see Ps. 139:13–16)—and part of the consequence of the fall—is that we each have our own set of peculiarities, quirks, and foibles. These "oddities" sometimes prove to be irksome to our fellow sinners whose peculiarities don't exactly mesh with ours. What is more, the Bible teaches that there are certain people who are (at least temporarily) more peculiar ("weaker") than others and that these members of the body require special care.

> And the eye cannot say to the hand, "I have no need of you"; or again the head to the feet, "I have no need of you." On the contrary, it is much truer that the members of the body which *seem to be weaker* are necessary. . . . And if one member suffers, all the members suffer with it; if one member is honored, all the members rejoice with it. (1 Cor. 12:21–22, 26)

> We urge you, brethren, admonish the unruly, *encourage the fainthearted, help the weak*, be patient with everyone. (1 Thess. 5:14)

Remember that part of a person's idiosyncratic differences have to do with his internal thought processes—the preferences, opinions, beliefs, and desires that are peculiar to him. This is a big part of what I mean when I speak of putting up with "idiosyncratic swing *issues.*" As we reveal our hearts to others in conflict, the things that we value become apparent. Others may not value these things quite as highly as we do, if they value them at all.[7] But a forbearing individual always keeps in mind

7. I value (sometimes to the point of idolatry) gourmet cuisine and fly-fishing. My wife is

that the things he values most are not necessarily valued as highly by the person with whom he is in conflict. He understands that, for many things in life, there is more than one way to skin a cat (or ice a cake) biblically. And, armed with this understanding and with a desire to obey the second greatest commandment (to love his neighbor as himself), he is willing to yield to (to forbear with) the different desires of the other.

Who is it that you find yourself in conflict with the most? Is it your spouse, a family member, a friend, or a coworker? What is it about that person that irritates you? With what little quirk of personality or character do you find it difficult to forbear? In the space provided below, write down the initials of the persons to whom you have struggled to show forbearance, as well as the idiosyncrasies that you find the most difficult to tolerate. Make these a matter for prayer, find someone to help hold you accountable for being more forbearing, and (in the space provided) list some practical things that you can do or say to be more forbearing the next time you are irritated by that person or his idiosyncrasies.

Person	Idiosyncrasy	Forbearing actions/words

much more moderate in her appreciation for gourmet food, especially since she is the one who has to prepare it nightly, and, except for the fact that she knows it helps to recharge my emotional batteries when they are low, has absolutely no use for fly-fishing.

____________	________________	________________________
____________	________________	________________________
	________________	________________________

"All of this is really helpful, but what if I'm the one who does all the swinging? I mean, what if everything is a fire issue for the person with whom I regularly have conflicts?"

That is a great question. Up to this point, we have been speaking almost exclusively of forbearing with the *nonsinful* behavior of others. Once such a pattern develops that almost every behavior becomes a fire issue for someone who habitually demonstrates an unwillingness to yield (to be reasoned with—see James 3:17; or to be considerate of the other—see Phil. 2:4), it is no longer a matter of putting up with idiosyncratic behaviors but rather a matter of confronting the sin of being selfish (2 Tim. 3:2) or even self-willed (Titus 1:7; 2 Peter 2:10). We will take a more in-depth look at how swing and fire issues relate to conflict resolution in the next chapter.

6. Forbearance is the ability to respond lovingly to the immaturity of others without lowering ourselves to their standard of immaturity.[8]

At this very moment, every believer on earth is in a state of flux regarding his sanctification—that is, we are *all* "in process" in various stages of spiritual development. "And we all, with unveiled face, beholding the glory of the Lord, are being transformed into the same image from one degree of glory to another. For this comes from the Lord who is the Spirit" (2 Cor. 3:18 ESV). The phrase "from one degree of glory to another" means, in essence, "from one level of spiritual maturity to another."

A forbearing individual not only recognizes that we are all in various stages of spiritual development (especially because he is aware of his own need to mature in the faith) but also has compassion on his

8. The essence of this definition has been floating around my mind for more than thirty years. I have not been able to find the original source, but am sure it did not originate with me.

fellow strugglers. When he observes immaturity in others, he desires to help them grow rather than to condemn them for not yet "growing up" into his own "exalted, glorious spiritual stature." He is compassionate rather than judgmental.

If you are uncharitably judging your brother to be "immature," how much more mature are you than he? Are you not like the pot who calls the kettle black? Romans 2:1–4 is especially instructive about this point.

> Therefore you have no excuse, everyone of you who passes judgment, for in that which you judge another, you condemn yourself; for *you who judge practice the same things*. And we know that the judgment of God rightly falls upon those who practice such things. But do you suppose this, O man, when you pass judgment on those who practice such things and do the same yourself, that you will escape the judgment of God? Or do you think lightly of the riches of His kindness and *tolerance* and patience,[9] not knowing that the kindness of God leads you to repentance?

God "holds back" (forbears in exercising) his full judgment on every person who is born,[10] at least temporarily. But it is a very serious thing to think lightly of this benevolent mercy of God. We who uncharitably judge others to be immature and are thereby intolerant of them condemn ourselves because, to the extent that we are also spiritually immature (as we all are in one way or another), we are practicing "the same things."[11]

Biblically tolerant people accept the fact that others are immature. But rather than censure their immature brethren or accept their immaturity as satisfactory, they lovingly and prayerfully try to offer

9. The words for *forbearance* and *patience* in this text are cognates (in the Greek) of the same two words in Ephesians 4:2.

10. Likewise, his goodness extends to every person (see Matt. 5:45; Acts 14:16–17).

11. I'm not saying that it is wrong to judge a person to be "spiritually immature," since such a judgment is in the purview of what the Bible allows (indeed, "He who is spiritual appraises all things"—1 Cor. 2:15). What is wrong is to make an uncharitable judgment. For more on this, see my booklet *Judgments: Rash or Righteous* (Phillipsburg, NJ: P&R Publishing, 2009).

them a hand to encourage spiritual growth (see Col. 1:28), even in the midst of conflict.

7. Forbearance is the ability to demonstrate biblical love to other believers even when they are struggling with sin.

How forbearing are you with the sinful responses of those with whom you are in conflict? As I have said, it is sometimes necessary to be forbearing with others when they are sinning. After returning from the mount of transfiguration, the Lord was approached by a man who implored Him to cast out an evil spirit from his son, saying, "'I begged Your disciples to cast it out, and they could not.' And Jesus answered and said, 'You unbelieving and perverted generation, how long shall I be with you, and *put up with* you?'" (Luke 9:40–41).

Forbearance is a communicable attribute of God—one that can be, to some degree, imparted to (or shared with) man. He is forbearing (see Rom. 2:4; 3:25); therefore, we must be forbearing as well. In this case, the Lord exercised forbearance with a generation of people who were *faithless* and *twisted* (ESV). Those are two pretty serous sins! Loving forbearance is patient (the NASB translates this word as "endure" in three places). It is willing to put up with (to patiently endure) sinful behavior for a time. But being too forbearing can be problematic. Paul sarcastically uses our word twice in 2 Corinthians 11, chiding the church for being too tolerant of fools and false teachers.

> For you, being so wise, *tolerate* the foolish gladly. For you *tolerate* it if anyone enslaves you, anyone devours you, anyone takes advantage of you, anyone exalts himself, anyone hits you in the face. (2 Cor. 11:19–20)

PUTTING UP WITH SIN

When is it proper to forbear with sin? At the very least, most of the time it is proper when we know that the person who is sinning is both aware of and working on correcting the problem.[12] Change is not

12. In cases of serious sin, such as criminal misuse of company funds, ongoing interaction

easy. It usually takes time. This is especially true for someone who is trying to overcome years of life-dominating sin. When I know that my children are convicted of their sins and are really working hard to cooperate with the Holy Spirit in getting them under His control, I put up with those residues of lingering sin that still seem to be too much in control of their lives.

It is probably also necessary to show forbearance to two other types of people who may be at a slight disadvantage in regard to their own sanctification: new converts (see 1 Cor. 3:1; Heb. 5:13)—those who, because they are still immature in the faith, have not yet become fully acquainted with the sanctification process—and weak believers (see 1 Thess. 5:14)—those who, due to feebleness, are slow to comprehend the sanctification process. Try to keep these things in mind the next time you find yourself in the midst of a dispute with such individuals.

GUIDELINES FOR DEVELOPING FORBEARANCE

If, after taking the test at the beginning of this chapter and reading the descriptions of forbearance that I have just outlined, you have discovered that you are not quite as forbearing as you thought you were, here are a few suggestions to help you to become more biblically tolerant of others.

1. Learn to look for the good things in others.

Some of us see the character deficiencies in others quicker than we see their positive character traits. While being discerning is a very good thing, if we do not grow in our tolerance of others at the same time as we grow in our ability to discern their weaknesses, we will become critical, condemnatory, judgmental monsters. One of the best ways for us to become more tolerant is to make it a practice to identify the things in others that are admirable. "Finally, brethren, whatever is true, whatever is honorable, whatever is right, whatever is pure, whatever is

---

with an adulterous partner, child abuse, and the like, forbearance is not biblically indicated. Sometimes *any* continuation in sin requires intervention of the law, or the church, or both.

lovely, whatever is of good repute, if there is any excellence and if anything worthy of praise, dwell on these things" (Phil. 4:8). Have you ever thought of this passage in terms of people? "What is it about this person that is honorable, right, and so on? Let your mind dwell on these things."

Who are the people you have been most intolerant of?[13] Why not make a list of those individuals and then try to identify a dozen or so commendable things about them?

	Person's Initials: __________	Person's Initials: __________
positive traits		

You might also find it helpful to complete a worksheet like this one before you initiate a conversation with your next potential opponent.

2. Remember the degree to which God has made you dependent on others.

You may sometimes wish that you could simply snap your fingers and eliminate certain people from your life. But that would be God's prerogative, not yours. The fact is that He has designed the body of Christ to be interdependent. As members of the body of Christ, we need and are dependent on such individuals, with all their weirdness, in order to function properly.

13. I certainly hope, after what you have just read, that you grammarians are not judging me uncharitably for ending this sentence with a preposition.

> But now God has placed the members, each one of them, in the body, just as He desired. If they were all one member, where would the body be? But now there are many members, but one body. And the eye cannot say to the hand, "I have no need of you"; or again the head to the feet, "I have no need of you." On the contrary, it is much truer that the members of the body which seem to be weaker are necessary; and those members of the body which we deem less honorable, on these we bestow more abundant honor, and our less presentable members become much more presentable, whereas our more presentable members have no need of it. But God has so composed the body, giving more abundant honor to that member which lacked, so that there may be no division in the body, but that the members may have the same care for one another. And if one member suffers, all the members suffer with it; if one member is honored, all the members rejoice with it. (1 Cor. 12:18–26)

John MacArthur explains the fallacy of self-sufficiency:

> Even as Christians we sometimes fall prey to the notion that, because we are complete in Christ and because He is our sufficiency, we therefore do not really need anyone else to live a faithful Christian life. Yet the idea completely contradicts Scripture. God has made us and redeemed us not only for Himself but for each other. We would never have heard of God or of the gospel had it not been for someone leading us to Christ or providing material for us to read. We could not have grown in faith and obedience had it not been for Christian teachers and friends who helped us and guided us. We cannot possibly fulfill our own ministry, whatever it is, without being mutually dependent on others.[14]

Even the apostle Paul (who some wrongly conclude was a bit of a maverick) needed the encouragement of other believers.

14. John MacArthur, *1 Corinthians*, The MacArthur New Testament Commentary (Chicago: Moody Press, 1984), 318.

> For I long to see you so that I may impart some spiritual gift to you, that you may be established; that is, *that I may be encouraged together with you while among you, each of us by the other's faith, both yours and mine.* (Rom. 1:11–12; cf. Rom. 15:24, 32; 2 Cor. 2:1–3; 7:4–7, 13; 1 Thess. 2:17–20; 3:7–10)

There is also a sense in which we are dependent on unbelievers. From bosses and teachers to the people who service our automobiles and provide our home utilities (invisible to us though they may be), no man is an island; we are connected to others each and every day.

3. Consider that God might want to change your opinion as a result of your listening to someone else.

Could it be that the person with whom you find it so difficult to forbear could actually teach you something? Yes it could. "Iron sharpens iron, so one man sharpens another" (Prov. 27:17). Think of the scriptural examples of foolish people who, after being instructed (by those who had their best interest in mind), did not tolerate the one who reproved them. Here are a few of them.

- King Saul by Ahimelech (1 Sam. 22)
- King Asa by Hanani (2 Chron. 16:7–10)
- King Herod by John the Baptist (Mark 6:17–29)
- The People of Nazareth by Jesus (Luke 4:14–30)
- The Sanhedrin by Stephen (Acts 7)

When you find yourself struggling to be tolerant of someone, remind yourself, "If I am unwilling to put up with this person, I just might miss out on an important life lesson." The next time you find yourself going head-to-head with someone, ask the Lord to open your eyes to any lessons that He might want to teach through your opponent.

4. Don't major on minor doctrinal issues.

Since bad doctrine, in the final analysis, is sin, it is something that ought *not* to be tolerated indefinitely. To this I must add two caveats.

First, when it comes to issues that are *not* a matter of orthodox theology (things other than the inspiration of Scripture, the virgin birth of Christ, and salvation by grace alone through faith, for instance), we ought not to "break fellowship" with other professing Christians. Now, of course, I realize that technically *all* doctrinal error is sin. But by making every minor doctrinal difference a matter of contention, we will be in conflict with most of the holy catholic (universal) church, which is comprised of many diverse local churches.

This leads me to my second caveat: Within the context of the local church, even minor doctrinal differences can be problematic. Christians find unity with one another not primarily through experience but through doctrine. It is what we believe about God, how we interpret the Bible, that enables us to live in harmony with each other (see John 17:17–21; 1 Cor. 1:10; Eph. 4:13; Phil. 2:2).

Before I was ordained as an elder of my church, I took an exception to a minor doctrinal difference that was generally held[15] by my denomination, which my brothers graciously granted me. But I have never made it an issue within the church. Unless I am asked about it (or have good reason to use it to illustrate a point about minor doctrinal issues—like I am doing right now), I keep my view to myself. And when I am asked, I do not imply that those who hold the other view are way off base, but rather I explain that there may be more than one way to interpret[16] and systematize certain passages of Scripture.

5. When you find yourself passing judgment on someone or being critical of that person, pray for him.

Let me give you the quick test for intolerance: do you have a critical spirit? It's pretty much that simple. Critical people are intolerant people. One of the best ways for you to become more tolerant is to bring the person you are critical of before the throne of grace. You will find

15. Actually, it has to do with the way I *interpreted* a passage in the Westminster Confession of Faith.

16. Of course, since "no prophecy of Scripture is *a matter* of one's own interpretation" (2 Peter 1:20), if two people come up with two different interpretations of the same passage, at least one of the interpretations is wrong.

it much harder to be so judgmental of someone for whom you have been regularly praying. And, while you are at it, put in a good word for yourself, asking the Lord to help you become a more forbearing person.

6. Make it your goal to have a biblically programmed conscience.

If you realize that you are a weaker brother (see Rom. 14:1, 2, 21; 15:1; 1 Cor. 8:7, 9, 10–12), realize also that it is not good to stay that way. While it is true that the stronger brother ought to bear with the weaker brother, it is also true that the weaker brother is to do what is necessary to become a stronger brother (see 1 Cor. 16:13; Eph. 6:10; 2 Tim. 2:1). The writer to the Hebrews admonished them to grow up. He reminded them that the mark of a mature Christian is a biblically trained conscience.

> For though by this time you ought to be teachers, you have need again for someone to teach you the elementary principles of the oracles of God, and you have come to need milk and not solid food. For everyone who partakes only of milk is not accustomed to the word of righteousness, for he is an *infant*. But solid food is for the *mature*, who because of practice *have their senses trained to discern good and evil.* (Heb. 5:12–14)

7. Remind yourself frequently how forbearing God has been with you.

Maybe it would serve you well to make a list of all the sinful habits that you have yet to conquer as a Christian. If nothing else will cure you of an intolerant spirit, remembering all that God, for Christ's sake, has "put up with" in you probably will. "Or do you think lightly of the riches of His kindness and tolerance [forbearance] and patience, not knowing that the kindness of God leads you to repentance?" (Rom. 2:4).

There you have it! We have come to the end not only of this chapter but also of the four most essential biblical prerequisites for conflict resolution outlined in our text. I trust that it has been worth the wait. I cannot emphasize enough that mastering what we have just covered is more important than mastering what is to come. So I urge you to come back to these pages often to remind yourself of what is really necessary for resolving conflicts God's way. I pray that from now on, when you find yourself in the midst of conflicts, the first question you ask yourself will not be, "What shall I say next?", but rather, "Which of these prerequisite qualities am I most in need of manifesting at this point in the discussion?"

Part Two

BIBLICAL PRINCIPLES OF CONFLICT RESOLUTION

WE HAVE NOW COME to that section of the book for which you have been patiently waiting—the biblical nuts and bolts of interpersonal conflict resolution. Thank you for your patience and forbearance. In the pages that follow, you will learn many useful things about the ins and outs of biblical conflict resolution. The chapters that remain contain practical insights on a variety of topics that relate in one way or another to resolving conflicts God's way. But please keep in mind that reading alone will probably not be enough. Peacemaking is a skill that usually takes time to develop. Some of the upcoming principles you should be able to implement almost immediately (as soon as your next conflict happens). Others, because they require a level of skill and experience to perfect, will require patience as you learn to put them into practice.

From time to time, I will be suggesting various ways in which the biblical principles that I am expounding may be verbalized. These examples of how to express oneself are certainly not the only or necessarily the best ways to put things. Usually a great variety of appropriate words could be selected in order to politely communicate whatever biblical truth you wish to express (or implement) verbally—especially in the English language. "The heart of the righteous ponders how to answer" (Prov. 15:28). I urge you to consider the verbiage that I have recommended as mere templates that will need to be modified "according to the need of the moment" and according to the maturity and personality of the individuals involved in the dispute (you and your opponent). "Let no unwholesome word proceed from your mouth, but only such a word as is good for edification *according to the need of the moment*, so that it will give grace to those who hear" (Eph. 4:29).

Of course, a book of this nature cannot cover everything that the Bible has to say about conflict resolution—the topic is much too broad to be confined to one volume.[1] But, by God's grace, you will probably discover much that will enable you to be a more effective conflict resolver than you are currently.

As I have explained in another place, there is a difference between a peacemaker and a peace lover when it comes to their approaches to conflict resolution.

> A peacemaker is willing to endure the discomfort of a conflict in the hope of bringing about a peaceful resolution. (Peace not only is the absence of conflict, but is often the result of it.) A peace-lover is so afraid of conflict that he will avoid it at almost all costs. He is so concerned about "keeping the peace" with his fellow man that he is often willing to forfeit the peace of God that comes from standing up and suffering for the truth. He is essentially a coward at heart.[2]

As you work your way through the rest of the book, the biblical necessity of your involvement in conflict will become increasingly apparent. But for now, can you recall any other places where the Bible addresses or views conflict and confrontation as something not to be avoided, and therefore as a potentially good thing? After you read the remaining chapters, I think you will agree that conflicts can serve to bring people closer together, not just to tear them apart.

1. For example, the hundreds of scriptural passages that address general communication principles (all of which relate in one way or another to conflict resolution) would take several volumes to cover adequately.

2. Lou Priolo, *Pleasing People: How Not to Be an "Approval Junkie"* (Phillipsburg, NJ: P&R Publishing, 2007), 25.

5

THREE TYPES OF CONFLICT

CONFLICTS ARE NOT ALL THE SAME. Recognizing this fact is an essential element of being a good conflict resolver. In the Bible, we can identify at least three different kinds (or categories) of conflict, each one with its own rather unique solution.[1] The solution to one type of conflict will not usually work for the others and vice versa. So, as in the medical profession, if we make a mistake in diagnosing the problem, we will err in prescribing the proper medication or cure for that problem.

The first category of conflicts is those that have to do with *differentness*. As we have seen, not only has God made individuals uniquely different, but these differences sometimes cause conflicts in a world that has been cursed by sin. Paul and Barnabas's famous "sharp disagreement" is not attributed to either's sinful actions, attitudes, or motives (Acts 15:39). The same is true of the two women (Euodia and Syntyche) spoken of in Philippians 4:2, who were both exhorted to "live in harmony in the Lord." Arguably, the conflict in both of these instances was the result of issues that were not sinful, such as differences in preferences or approaches to ministry.

The second and most common form of conflict is a conflict that has to do with *sinfulness* in one or both parties. The Bible provides an abundance of examples of human conflict caused by sin. From Cain

1. I heard Wayne Mack lecture on this topic over thirty years ago and am indebted to him for introducing me to the idea that there are at least three kinds of conflicts delineated in the Bible.

and Abel (Gen. 4:1–16) to Abraham and Lot (Gen. 13) to David and Saul (1 Sam. 18–26) to Jesus and the temple moneychangers (not to mention the many religious leaders of Israel who conflicted with Him, though He never sinned—Mark 11:15–18) to Paul and Peter (Gal. 2:13–14) to John and Diotrephes (3 John 9–10), the Bible is replete with conflicts that were the result of someone's sin. We have already seen that, in addition to examples such as these, we are given specific directions about initiating confrontation with someone who sins against us.

The third category of conflict that we see in Scripture occurs when individuals have different views of what the Bible really says about a matter. To keep our outline consistent, let's call these conflicts of *righteousness*—matters of righteousness over which Christians disagree. For example, we saw in an earlier chapter the problem in Romans 14 between stronger brothers (who knew that Scripture did not forbid eating food that had been sacrificed to idols; that it wasn't necessarily a sin to partake) and weaker brothers (whose conscience prohibited them from partaking, in part because of their previous involvement with idolatry, which the Scriptures clearly say is wrong). Paul had to address both sides of the conflict. He exhorted the stronger brothers not to hold the weaker brothers in contempt ("Why don't you grow up and get over your unbiblical scruples so that the rest of us don't have to put up with your weakness?") and the weaker brothers to not judge the stronger brothers uncharitably ("How in the world can you eat something that was used to worship demons?").

THREE DIFFERENT SOLUTIONS

So what is the solution to each of these different forms of conflict? I will attempt to answer that question in depth in the next few pages, but here is the short answer for now. As I discussed earlier, the basic solution to *conflicts of differentness* is forbearance. In the final analysis, each party must learn to put up with those idiosyncratic differences that he finds tedious or irksome about the other, when they are not issues of sin. The basic solution for *conflicts of sinfulness* is repentance or change. Ultimately, conflicts of this type cannot be resolved apart from the sinning individual agreeing to repent of his sin. The basic solution for *conflicts of righteousness* involves Bible study. Both parties must study what the Scriptures (in their entirety) teach concerning the issue about which they disagree.

Sometimes these three categories overlap each other, so that implementing two or more of the aforementioned solutions will be necessary to resolve the conflict. Let's take a closer look at all three varieties of conflict.

CONFLICTS RESULTING FROM DIFFERENTNESS

I'm sure you remember Oliver and Lisa, the "mismatched" couple from chapter 4 who came from two entirely different backgrounds. We anticipated that they were going to have lots of conflicts, not because they were especially sinful, but because they were so different. The way in which they would have to solve these *differentness conflicts* is not the same as the way in which *sinfulness conflicts* would have to be resolved. Because *differentness rather than sin* is at the root of these conflicts, attempts to resolve normal marital issues will be a bit more difficult for them than for many couples whose differences are not so pronounced. And there will likely be more of them initially. (What time would they retire for the evening? Where would they purchase their clothing? What kind of car would they buy? Where would they go on a date? Where would they go on vacation? Where would they live? What kind of house would they buy? How would they furnish and decorate it? How much domestic help would they have?) If there was sin involved in their conflicts over differentness, it would be with the response (internally or externally) made by one party to the differentness of the other party. (In chapters 9 and 10 we will look in greater detail at some of these internal and external unbiblical responses.)

The solution for these conflicts, therefore, is not primarily some form of confrontation about the other person's sin,[2] but rather the

2. If anything, some form of *self*-confrontation may be in order to bring about repentance for any selfish thoughts, motives, and attitudes (if not words and actions) that have been brought to light by the differentness conflict.

application of loving forbearance. What does this look like? For one thing, it follows the seven elements of forbearance defined in chapter 4. It seeks to put the other person's interests ahead of one's own. It dies to self (and to one's own desires and expectations). It is willing to yield to the wishes of another and to put up with differences of opinion and annoying idiosyncrasies for love's sake and for the cause of Christ. It may want to discuss the matter, not with the goal of restoring a sinning brother, but rather to see if a compromise may be reached, in order to determine for whom the issue is a swing issue and for whom it is a fire issue.

Guidelines for Talking to Other Christians about Your Differences

As you read each of these guidelines, try to imagine how wonderful it would be if *both* parties in a conflict of this nature manifested these characteristics.[3] Then remember what the Bible says in Romans 12:18: "If possible, *so far as it depends on you*, be at peace with all men."

1. *Remind yourself that God made the other person with his own unique personality for His own purposes (which probably have little to do with making life easier for you).* "But they, measuring themselves by themselves, and comparing themselves among themselves, are not wise" (2 Cor. 10:12 NKJV). Guard your heart against making harsh judgments of others who have different personalities, temperaments, tastes, and values from yours (they may seem unusual but still be well within the biblical parameters for such things), those who are of a dissimilar social or educational status, those from a different race or cultural background, those who have unusual medical or physical conditions, or those who have had different life experiences.

2. *Guard against legalistic and judgmental attitudes that raise nonsin issues to the level of sin.* "I'm the standard, and if you are different from me, you are not the Christian you ought to be." This is the mind-set of those who make such rash judgments.

3. Realistically, however, in most conflicts, you will be the one (at least at first) who will have to unilaterally model these elements of loving forbearance.

As we have seen, when you judge things to be sinful that are not *clearly* delineated as such (at least in principle) in the Scriptures, you wrongly judge not only your brother who did the misjudged deed, but also the Bible for not condemning the deed, and the Author of the Bible, who apparently forgot to include it in His Book. Remind yourself how grave a matter it is to make such a presumptuous accusation against God!

3. Focus more on the interests of the other person than on your own interests.

> Do nothing from selfishness or empty conceit, but with humility of mind regard one another as more important than yourselves; do not merely look out for your own personal interests, but also for the interests of others. (Phil. 2:3–4)

Try looking at the conflict through the other person's eyes. Consider his perspective, his needs, and his interests. These may be quite different from yours but just as biblically valid.

4. Be reasonable (willing to yield to the views and desires of others). "But the wisdom from above is first pure, then peaceable, gentle, reasonable, full of mercy and good fruits, unwavering, without hypocrisy" (James 3:17). You may think that your way is the better way. Don't go into the conflict with a "my way or the highway"; "I've got to get him to do things my way" attitude. Instead, ask yourself, "Would it really be a terrible thing (a sin) if we did things his way?"

5. Be willing to put up with annoying traits of others. "Love . . . does not insist on its own way" (1 Cor. 13:5 ESV). Ask yourself, "Is it really such an intolerable trial for me to put up with this idiosyncrasy? Do not others have to put up with mine, too?"

6. Try to determine for whom it is a "swing" issue and for whom it is a "fire" issue. One way to do this in a close relationship is to ask the other person to assign a number to the issue at hand. "On a scale of one to ten, one being a 'swing issue' and ten a 'fire issue,' how important is this matter to you?" Then you can relate to him your own assessment of the matter. If his number is higher than yours, perhaps you would be willing to swing with it. If his number is lower than yours, perhaps he would be willing to swing some in your direction.

7. Allow the peace of Christ to be the referee (or umpire) of the conflict. "Let the peace of Christ rule in your hearts, to which indeed you were called in one body" (Col. 3:15). Over and over again, the New Testament emphasizes God's desire for peace and unity in the church. "Now I exhort you, brethren, by the name of our Lord Jesus Christ, that you all agree and that there be no divisions among you, but that you be made complete in the same mind and in the same judgment" (1 Cor. 1:10; cf. Rom. 12:16; 2 Cor. 13:11; Eph. 4:3; Phil. 1:27; 2:2; 1 Thess. 5:13; 1 Peter 3:8). These imperatives for believers to be at peace with each other are to be some of the ruling principles in all of our attempts at conflict resolution. Sometimes, for the sake of Christ, we must submit to the wishes of others. Be it a subordinate submitting to a superior, a stronger brother submitting to a weaker one, or one member submitting to another for the peace and purity of the church, Christ's desire for peace between His children is to guide our interpersonal relationships.

CONFLICTS RESULTING FROM SINFULNESS

All kinds of sinful behavior can cause conflict: sinful words, actions, attitudes, thoughts, and motives.[4] Often these sinful behaviors may and should be "overlooked" ("It is his glory to overlook a transgression," Prov. 19:11) or "covered" in love ("love covers a multitude of sins," 1 Peter 4:8; cf. Prov. 10:12; 12:16; 17:19).[5] But when they cannot be overlooked

4. Of course, the last two categories are usually not within our purview, since we cannot know them apart from the person with whom we are in conflict clearly revealing them to us.

5. To overlook or cover someone's sin is not to pretend that it didn't happen or wasn't wrong. To *overlook* someone's transgression is to "pass over" it in the sense of it being too small a matter to concern oneself (or the other person) with. To *cover* someone's transgression is to "hide" or "conceal" or "cloak" it (as with a shield of invisibility) so as to render it unnoticeable in terms of its impact on your relationship with that person.

(especially because they are habitual or serious), loving confrontation is necessary and conflict is often inevitable.

Be it a child who disobeys his parent, a husband who is harsh with his wife, a wife who dishonors her husband, a teacher who mistreats his student, a church member who refuses to acknowledge his divisiveness, or a "friend" who is backbiting, conflict can occur. As I touched on earlier, several key passages speak of our responsibility to confront a sinning brother. They are Matthew 18:15–18; Luke 17:3; and (by implication) Galatians 6:1. Let me develop them for you in a little more detail.

Correction of a Sinning Brother

First we are going to take another look at Luke 17:3. The operative verbal directive of this passage is to "rebuke." "Be on your guard! If your brother sins, *rebuke* him; and if he repents, forgive him."

We are to confront our sinning brother with his sin in the hope that he will repent so that we will be able to offer him forgiveness. The verb (ἐπιτιμάω) means to *rebuke, reprove, censure,* and also *speak seriously* and *warn* in order to prevent an action or to bring it to an end.[6] This is a command (an imperative)—it is not optional. The goal (or purpose) of this rebuke is to grant the sinning brother *forgiveness*: You are to rebuke your brother in the hope that he will repent and that you will therefore be able to let him know that you have forgiven him.

Restoration of a Sinning Brother

The next passage we should consider in our discussion of conflicts that come as a result of sinfulness is Galatians 6:1. "Brethren, even if anyone is caught in any trespass, you who are spiritual, restore such a one in a spirit of gentleness; each one looking to yourself, so that you too will not be tempted." The goal (or purpose) of this passage is to *restore* a sinning brother to a place of usefulness.

6. William F. Arndt and F. Wilbur Gingrich, eds., *A Greek-English Lexicon of the New Testament and Other Early Christian Literature: A translation and adaption of the fourth revised and augmented edition of Walter Bauer's Griechisch-deutsches Worterbuch zu den Schrift en des Neuen Testaments und der ubrigen urchristlichen Literatur*, 2nd ed., revised and augmented by F. Wilbur Gingrich and Frederick W. Danker from Walter Bauer's fifth edition, 1958 (Chicago: University of Chicago Press, 1996), Logos Bible Software e-book.

Please notice that the type of sin addressed by this passage is habitual sin. It says, "If anyone is *caught* in any trespass"—that is, if someone is caught as in a trap or ensnared by a sin from which he is not able to extricate himself. I mention this because, although there is much in this verse that we can apply to sin-induced conflicts that might flare up rather quickly, it underscores again the importance of graciously overlooking those sins that are of a more momentary nature if at all possible.

What exactly is this passage telling us to do to a sinning brother? We are to *restore* him. The word *restore* is a medical term used to describe the setting of a bone that has been broken. It was also used as a nautical term, describing fishermen who would repair nets that had been torn. When used of people, the idea is to repair (make useful again) a Christian who has been overpowered by a sin. In other words, your motive for confronting a sinning brother should be to *restore* him—not to expose him, not to make things easier for yourself, not to extract personal vengeance on him by humiliating him, and not to manipulate him into giving you what you want.

Another important word in this passage is one that we looked at in chapter 2: *gentleness*—we are to restore our brother "in a spirit of gentleness." You shouldn't try to talk to your brother about his sin when you are sinfully angry—when you are angrier because he has sinned *against you* than you are because he has sinned *against God*. Think about how you have felt during times when has someone has spoken to you about your sin in an angry, harsh, condescending way. How easy was it for you to take that kind of criticism? If you are too angry, cool off first. Talk to the Lord about your sin before you talk to your brother about his.

What did Paul mean when he added the words "each one looking to yourself, so that you too will not be tempted" to the restoration equation? You may remember (from chapter 2) that there is an element of humility packed into the Greek term for gentleness that does not come across in the English word. Paul was bringing out this nuance by reminding his readers that they should remember their own frailty when restoring someone—should remember that they too are capable of falling into the same sin. Moreover, they should be sure that they have dealt with (or at least are in the process of dealing with) that particular sin (or *any* sin) in their own lives before trying to restore the brother. Jesus used the word *hypocrite* to describe those who don't examine their own "log" before speaking to another about his "speck" (Matt. 7:3–5).

Winning Your Brother (or Go and Show)

The last passage I would like to consider is Matthew 18:15. "If your brother sins, go and show him his fault in private; if he listens to you, you have won your brother." This is the first step in a series of instructions that the Lord gave us to resolve conflicts resulting from sin in the church. Once again, the issue at hand is a matter of sin. And again, the person who is sinning is "your brother." The next verb in the sentence is "go." As in the Luke 17 passage, the initiative to resolve the matter is taken by the individual who has been offended (or at least who knows about the sin).

The word *show* is better translated *convict*—"If your brother sins, go and convict him of his fault." The verb form of this word was used in biblical times as a legal term to embody the idea of prosecuting a case against an individual so that he might be convicted for the crime that he had committed. It carries with it the idea of refuting an opponent to the point of *convincing* him (or if not him, then at least others who hear the evidence) of his crime. It is substantiating and proving that the charges made against someone are true.

As a biblical counselor, whose job it is on many occasions to convict people, I know that there are all sorts of ways to help people to see their sin. For example, it may be done harshly and angrily, or it may be done politely and respectfully. I've done it often with tears, and I've done it with a touch of sarcasm. But I must do it regularly.

With some people, I have found it effective to use the direct approach. I am a New Yorker by birth and early upbringing. My disposition is sort of a cross between Bill O'Reilly and (I hate to admit this) Donald Trump. "Don't waste your time sugarcoating it. Just tell me what the Bible says (hit me on the head with a brick, if you please) and get out of my way so that I can get to work on my problem." (The direct approach is not recommended for convicting people who are in positions of authority.)

With others, I use a much gentler approach. I may simply ask someone a question, which is all that is necessary to bring that person to tears.

After citing Matthew 19:8, I might ask a woman who is contemplating a divorce, "Do you really want to demonstrate to God and to others that you have a hard heart?"

"Do you really think you are going to convince your father to your way of thinking when you talk to him with such contempt and disrespect? Would you be persuaded if your parents talked to you that way?" I might ask the angry teenage son of a Christian before reading Proverbs 25:15 to him.

"Should you really expect God to help you get out of debt when you are working so many hours that it has become all but impossible for you to 'seek first His Kingdom and His righteousness' (Matthew 6:33)?"

I'm sure you can see that, despite how gently the convicting question might be worded, it is still confrontational and could potentially lead to a conflict.

Now we know that conviction of sin is primarily the work of the Holy Spirit (John 16:8) and the Scripture (2 Tim. 3:16). But the church is the body of Christ and is commissioned to do His work in the world. Matthew 18 and other passages make it clear that part of our role is (at times) to gently point out others' sin—and sometimes not so gently.

Preaching the Word is one method of conviction of sin. Paul commanded Timothy to *convict* those under his spiritual care with the Scriptures. "Preach the word; be ready in season and out of season; reprove, rebuke, exhort, with great patience and instruction" (2 Tim. 4:2). He also told him to rebuke (convict) those church leaders "who continue in sin . . . in the presence of all, so that the rest also may be fearful of sinning" (1 Tim. 5:20). In fact, one of the qualifications for being ordained as a pastor in the first place is the ability to convict those who contradict sound doctrine (Titus 1:9). In chapter 2 of his letter (verses 9–11), James uses the law to *convict* his hearers of being lawbreakers. Bringing conviction, therefore, is a part of the responsibility of the ministry of the Word.

The means by which people are convicted of sin isn't a "one or the other" scenario, either; they work in tandem. God communicates His will through Scripture, uses His people to communicate His Word, and uses His Spirit to bring conviction and apply His Word to our hearts.

Another very important conflict resolution principle found in this verse (and in the next) is the rule of privacy: keep the circle of confrontation as small as possible. This principle is taught in the book of Proverbs as well.

> Argue your case with your neighbor,
> And do not reveal the secret of another,
> Or he who hears it will reproach you,
> And the evil report about you will not pass away. (Prov. 25:9–10)

Love seeks to cover sin, not to expose it prematurely. It attempts to win an erring brother, not to publicly embarrass or shame him. And, as John MacArthur insightfully points out,

> The more a person's sin is known and discussed by others, no matter how well-meaning they may be, the easier it is for him to become resentful and the harder it may be for repentance and restoration. When he is corrected *in private*, and in a spirit of humility and love, his change of heart is much more likely. And if he does repent, a unique and marvelous bond of intimacy is established between the two believers, indicated by the phrase *you have gained your brother*.[7]

In a healthy church, biblical confrontations occur regularly, but they rarely become public because every effort is made to protect the privacy of every sinner in the family. In my church, when serious sin has occurred, people have routinely been restored with few (if any) of the leadership ever knowing about the problem. This is so because our people have been trained to follow the injunctions of Matthew 18:15–17, especially the privacy principle. Even among our elders, the mantra is "Keep the circle as small as you can for as long as you can."

7. John MacArthur, *Matthew 16–23*, The MacArthur New Testament Commentary (Chicago: Moody, 1988), 128.

The third conflict-resolution principle that we see in this passage has to do with our purpose (and even our motive) for initiating a conflict: to *win* or gain our brother. The idea is that, as a result of the confrontation, we win our brother over to our side (really, to God's side) of the argument. But winning our brother involves more than winning the argument about his sin. It is possible to win the argument but lose your brother in the process. When one person sins against another, a breach in the relationship often occurs. The way that they relate to each other is changed. Something that they had between them—something of the intimacy they shared and valued—is lost. When the reproof is "heard" (effectively received), the breach in the relationship is restored—what was lost is regained or *won* back.

Guidelines for Talking to Other Christians about Their Sin

While the use of guidelines, or biblically based directives, is profitable, it is the underlying conviction that God wants His people to dwell in unity that is to be the real driving force behind any attempts we make to resolve conflicts.

1. Get the beam out of your own eye first. It is important to begin by asking the Lord to convict you of any sins that you may have committed against the person whom you are about to convict of sin. You may have to begin the confrontation process by humbling yourself before your offender as you seek his forgiveness.

> Why do you look at the speck that is in your brother's eye, but do not notice the log that is in your own eye? Or how can you say to your brother, "Let me take the speck out of your eye," and behold, the log is in your own eye? You hypocrite, first take the log out of your own eye, and then you will see clearly to take the speck out of your brother's eye. (Matt. 7:3–5)

The last thing you will want to do is to talk to someone about his sin while he is talking to you about yours—at least not without first taking the hit (thoroughly acknowledging, repenting, and asking forgiveness) for what you have done wrong. Don't even think about trying to convict another until you have come to terms with how you may have sinned against him.

2. *Be sure that what the other person has done really is a sin (that ought not to be overlooked).* A mother, for example, can't biblically confront her adult son because he and his wife decide that they can't afford to come visit for both Thanksgiving and Christmas.[8] Luke 17:3 makes it clear that the person who is to be reproved (or convicted) must have sinned. We don't convict people just because they annoy us, upset us, disappoint us, burst our bubbles, refuse to give us what we want, or make decisions about which we disagree. They may do any and all of these in the process of sinning, but unless they have clearly sinned, we may not reprove them.[9] And, as I have said repeatedly, as much as possible we ought to cover (overlook) as many nonhabitual sins as we can.

> Love covers a multitude of sins. (1 Peter 4:8)

> A man's discretion makes him slow to anger,
> And it is his glory to overlook a transgression. (Prov. 19:11)

The idea is to cover what you can. It is when another believer continually "throws the covers off" by repeatedly committing the same sin that you must attempt to convict.

3. *Examine your motives.* Again, the goal you are trying to accomplish when dealing with a brother who is struggling with sin should be restoration, according to Galatians 6:1. "Brethren, even if anyone is caught in any trespass, you who are spiritual restore such a one in a spirit of gentleness; each one looking to yourself, so that you too will not be tempted."

8. That is, of course, unless the adult child made a promise to her about doing so (see Prov. 25:14; Matt. 5:37; James 5:12), in which case, from a biblical standpoint, they should seek to be released from a promise that was made before they had all the relevant information.

9. This is not to imply that you cannot talk to others about the nonsinful things they do that annoy you. It is only to say that your motive and approach for discussing those things is going to be something other than conviction.

4. *Use biblical terminology when talking to others about their sin.* Follow the example of Paul, who spoke "not in words taught us by human wisdom but in words taught by the Spirit, explaining spiritual realities with Spirit-taught words" (1 Cor. 2:13 NIV). To tell a person that he is "paranoid" would tempt him to anger sooner than it would bring conviction. To target his conscience (which is where conviction takes place), if you are *certain* that you have done nothing to cause the person to distrust you,[10] you would do better to use biblical terms (politely *asking* him, for example, to consider whether he is being inordinately *fearful* or *suspicious*). Telling someone that he is being pigheaded is not, as a rule, nearly as effective as politely telling him that he does not appear "open to reason" (James 3:17 ESV; in other words, that he is not being "wiling to yield"—NKJV, or even "reasonable"—NASB).

"But I'm not sure that I know the Bible well enough to do this."

Then get a hold of a Bible concordance and learn how to use it! I have included in Appendix C a chart of common, imprecise terms that people often use in conflict, along with some suggested alternatives. The list is far from comprehensive. I pray that it will at least get you started in your quest to be biblically accurate in your loving expression of truth.

You cannot effectively confront Christians about their sin without knowing and using the Bible. It's not that you will always have to cite a chapter and verse to them—in most cases, just using the appropriate biblical terminology will be sufficient to help followers of Jesus Christ realize that they really have sinned. But, since the Spirit of God brings conviction through the Word of God, you really have little hope of convicting them apart from biblical terminology.

5. *Choose the right time.* King Solomon gave us an important insight that can be properly applied to the timing of convicting others. In Ecclesiastes 3:7, he reminds us that "there is a time to keep silent and a time to speak." The best time to discuss these issues is when you can secure the other person's undivided attention. This, of course, is something

10. I cannot emphasize enough that you must be sure to get the beam out of your own eye *before* you attempt to speak to others about their sin. To be doubly sure, after examining your own actions, you may want to ask them if you have provoked the very sin of which you are planning to convict them.

that you may have to ask for explicitly, possibly by setting up a specific time in advance. If you are already in a particular conflict, it may be better to wait for another opportunity to bring up the matter if it seems that your opponent is not receptive.

6. Choose the right words. "The heart of the righteous ponders how to answer" (Prov. 15:28). It will often be necessary for you to invest extra time, effort, and thought into selecting just the right words that you will use to express to another how he has sinned. Then you must be sure that the tone of your voice, as well as your nonverbal communication, is entirely humble, gentle, and polite—not condescending, arrogant, or sarcastic. "Words from the mouth of a wise man are gracious, while the lips of a fool consume him" (Eccl. 10:12). As much as possible, go as a servant and a learner. Even as you are trying to persuade him, let him know that you are open to the fact that you may be wrong.

7. Be sure that you maintain a gentle spirit throughout the discussion. Paul warns us to go "in the spirit of gentleness." As we saw in chapter 2, the word *meekness* (or *gentleness*) combines the elements of being *humble* and being *slow to anger*. When someone sins against you, it may evoke righteous indignation in your heart. It is essential, however, that you do not express your holy passion with sinful forms of communication. Perhaps one of the best ways to keep this from happening is to remind yourself that your brother has sinned against God much *more* than he has sinned against you. The trick is to take yourself out of the picture long enough to look at the sin from His perspective. If you truly love God, you will be more concerned about helping those you convict to get back on track (i.e., restoring them) than you will be about getting them to stop making life so miserable for you by their sin. If you are too angry, it may simply be because at that moment you love yourself more than you love God (see Ex. 20:3) and your neighbor (see Lev. 19:18).

If the other person sins in the process of your ministry of conviction, seek to avoid the two sinful extremes of blowing up and clamming up that we also looked at in chapter 2. Instead, look for a way to attack the problem through biblical means of communication.

CONFLICTS RESULTING FROM "RIGHTEOUSNESS" ISSUES

The third category of conflict occurs when there is a difference of opinion about the righteous thing to do in a given situation or circumstance. One person believes that one course of action is best; the other person thinks there is another way to respond. Or one individual believes that one set of guiding scriptural principles apply, while the other individual is convinced that another guiding principle should trump the others. Basically, at the outset, both parties believe that their approaches to solving the issue are right (or even very necessarily biblical). At the very least, one individual believes that his approach is better (wiser or more biblical) than the other's approach.

As a counselor, I am called upon to help people resolve one particular "righteousness conflict" more often than any other. It is parental conflicts concerning the disciplining of children. Perhaps one parent believes that the child's behavior is really a minor offense that ought to be "covered in love" or "overlooked." But the other parent sees it not only as a serious problem but as one that is starting to become habitual and that needs chastisement. Both believe that they have scriptural support for their positions. What should they do?

You may say, "Probably the wife should submit to the wishes of her husband."

Based on 1 Peter 3:1–6, Ephesians 5:22–24, and Colossians 3:18 you are, as a rule, correct. But does that mean that she cannot try to persuade him to her way of thinking? Not at all! Sure, she should let her husband know that she has every intention of yielding to him on the matter, but, since she is also responsible before God for the upbringing of her children, she may like to have a full and frank discussion about things before she does so.

What might such a conversation look like? That is what I would like to lay out for you in the next few pages, in the form of a few guiding principles. But first let me remind you that the basic solution for "righteousness conflicts" is Bible study. Both parties ought to investigate what the Scriptures (in their totality) teach concerning the matter about which they disagree. Obviously, this third type of conflict may take longer to resolve than the first two usually do. This is where that third prerequisite—patience—is especially helpful. The guidelines that follow are stated so that both parties can follow them.

Guidelines for Talking to Other Christians about Righteousness Issues

1. *Confess and seek forgiveness for any sinful words, actions, or attitudes that may have exacerbated the conflict up to this point.* "Confess your sins to one another, and pray for one another so that you may be healed. The effective prayer of a righteous man can accomplish much" (James 5:16). Even when a disagreement is not caused by someone's sin, sinful words, actions, and attitudes often creep in and make the conflict murkier than it would have otherwise been. Sometimes the sinful responses of one or both of the parties become more of an obstacle to peace than the original difference of opinion.

2. *Try to express the problem from both perspectives.* The eighteenth chapter of Proverbs contains three very relevant verses about the importance of considering both sides of an argument.

> A fool does not delight in understanding,
> But only in revealing his own mind. (Prov. 18:2)
>
> He who gives an answer before he hears,
> It is folly and shame to him. (Prov. 18:13)
>
> The first to plead his case seems right,
> Until another comes and examines him. (Prov. 18:17)

In order for both sides to come to a mutually agreed biblical solution, the exact nature of the problem must be agreed upon up front. This is important so that *both* parties will have a clear understanding of how *the other person* views the problem. Sometimes, by stating the problem succinctly, the person who expresses the problem discovers a biblical solution that he had not previously considered. And sometimes, verbally crystallizing the problem causes the other party to realize that the disagreement is over some minor issue that is relatively easy to resolve. Occasionally you will discover that there are two (or more) different problems, each of which has a solution that is acceptable to both parties.

3. *Determine what things can be agreed upon.* Often there are elements of the conflict (and its resolution) on which both parties agree. Stating these things at the beginning of the conflict may give hope to both parties that a biblical resolution will be forthcoming, because they already have partial agreement. Here are a few general things that should apply to both parties who are having a "righteousness conflict":

- ☐ There may be more than one way to solve this conflict biblically.
- ☐ God wants us to come to a resolution of this problem as quickly as possible without either one of us sinning (any more than we already have).
- ☐ We both have a responsibility to "make every effort to maintain the unity of the Spirit in the bond of peace."
- ☐ If we cannot solve this problem between the two of us, we may have to seek the assistance of another (mature) Christian.

4. *Search the Scriptures for any biblical directives and/or principles that relate to resolving the issue.* The Bible tells us that if we *ask* and *seek* for wisdom, we will find it. In the very context of trials, James reminds us, "But if any of you lacks wisdom, let him ask of God, who gives to all generously and without reproach, and it will be given to him" (James 1:5). Speaking of wisdom, understanding, and discernment, Solomon says,

> If you seek her as silver
> And search for her as for hidden treasures;
> Then you will discern the fear of the LORD
> And discover the knowledge of God. (Prov. 2:4–5)

QUESTIONS TO CONSIDER DURING CONFLICT WITH OTHER CHRISTIANS

Have you ever wondered why the Bible says that wisdom should be sought after as silver rather than as gold? Even though gold is more valuable, it can be found without much digging. But silver must be mined—you have to dig deep for it. So it is with wisdom. To find it, you must sometimes dig deep into the Scriptures. It may take days or weeks. It may require the acquisition of certain tools (Bible concordances, dictionaries, and commentaries). It may take consultation with experts (church leaders) to determine exactly where to start excavating.

Here are a few questions to help you as you begin digging.

Question #1. Have we identified the problem (and its components) in biblical terms? A problem cannot be solved biblically until it is first diagnosed in biblical terminology. The operative phrase is found in 1 Corinthians 2:13: "Not in words taught us by human wisdom but in words taught by the Spirit, *explaining spiritual realities with Spirit-taught words*" (NIV). Force yourself to think biblically. Don't settle for less than God's interpretation of the problem. If you want to find a lasting biblical solution, keep searching for the proper diagnosis.

Question #2. Are there any other directives in Scripture that we must obey in order to resolve this conflict (or solve this problem)? Sometimes the resolution to a specific kind of conflict can be found clearly delineated in the Bible. So in order for you to resolve the matter, at least in part, specific scriptural commands must be obeyed. Up to this point you may have identified some of them, but are there others you have missed?

Question #3. Are there any principles in Scripture from which a resolution to this conflict (or a solution to this problem) can be derived? Sometimes the solution to a particular problem is not clearly delineated in the Scriptures, and it must therefore be derived from appropriate biblical principles. For example, if a husband and wife are in disagreement over whether he should take a job that puts him on the road away from home for four days a week, they probably won't find much about "how many hours a man can be away from home" or "whether it is acceptable for a married man to travel for a living." But they can find principles on the importance of a husband caring for his family financially, on the importance of a husband caring for his wife's well-being, on the father's role in parenting, on how to make decisions, and on a wife's need to submit to her husband. These are sometimes referred to as *biblically derived solutions.* A biblically derived solution is one that a Christian derives in accordance with biblical principles in order to fulfill a goal to which no specific directives are given in Scripture.[†]

More often than not, "righteousness conflicts" are resolved by implementing biblical principles rather than by obeying biblical directives. Often, both biblically directed solutions *and* biblically derived solutions are necessary in order to solve problems effectively. But remember, a *biblically derived* solution must never be elevated to the place of a *biblically directed* solution. Not to distinguish between the two, and thereby raising a biblical *principle* to the level of a *command,* runs the risk of being legalistic. As I sometimes tell those whom I counsel, "You need to read your Bible more regularly than you have been doing. Unless you have a better idea, I *suggest* that you begin with the book of Proverbs" (or the part of the Bible most relevant to their situation).

Question #4. Has anyone in Scripture ever faced the same (or a similar) situation? The Bible not only contains commands and principles that are helpful for solving problems, it also contains a wealth of examples (both good and bad) that give insight into the right and

† Jay Adams offers a helpful distinction between biblically derived and biblically directed methods of implementing truth in *What to Do on Thursday: A Layman's Guide to the Practical Use of the Scriptures* (Stanley, NC: Timeless Texts, 1995), 105.

wrong ways of solving problems. It was partly for our assistance in solving life's dilemmas that these examples have been included in Scripture. "For whatever was written in earlier times was written for our instruction, that through perseverance and the *encouragement* of the Scriptures we might have hope" (Rom. 15:4).

5. *In light of the newly discovered biblical data, propose what modifications you are willing to make in order to reach a mutually agreed solution.* By this time, perhaps one of you has discovered additional insight from Scripture that causes you to consider a slightly different approach to the issue. Maybe one of you has been convicted that your position was not totally biblical. Perhaps one of you now realizes that there actually are two or three specific biblical solutions to the problem. Perhaps you can go back to the drawing board together and come up with an entirely different, but mutually agreed upon, approach to solving the problem, based on the whole counsel of God's Word.

6. *If the problem cannot be resolved in the period of time agreed upon by both of you in advance, seek the assistance of a "true yokefellow."* The Bible speaks in several places of Christians helping other Christians to resolve interpersonal conflicts (be they the result of sinfulness, differentness, or righteousness). For example, in 1 Corinthians 6, Paul addresses the problem of believers taking their disputes to a pagan court system rather than resolving them "in house."

> Does any one of you, when he has a case against his neighbor, dare to go to law before the unrighteous and not before the saints? Or do you not know that the saints will judge the world? If the world is judged by you, are you not competent to constitute the smallest law courts? Do you not know that we will judge angels? How much more matters of this life? So if you have law courts dealing with matters of this life, do you appoint them as judges who are of no account in the church? I say this to your shame. *Is it so, that there is not among you one wise man*

> *who will be able to decide between his brethren,* but brother goes to law with brother, and that before unbelievers? (1 Cor. 6:1–6)

I am a fellow in the Association of Certified Biblical Counselors. This means that I have been certified by our parent organization not only to counsel, but also to train others to counsel and to help them become certified. I am also the founder of a new organization called Competent to Counsel International, under which I train and provide materials for pastors and counselors internationally. But in spite of this, along with thirty years of experience in helping others to resolve their conflicts, my wife and I have had conflicts that we were not able to resolve on our own. In such cases, we went to someone else (a fellow elder in our church who we agreed upon beforehand) to help us resolve the matter. I am telling you this to make the point that sometimes we *all* (even elders, Christian authors, and counselors) need true yokefellows to help us to untangle conflicts with other believers.

Before we proceed any further, I must give you a word of caution: If you are the person in the subordinate position in your conflict, you may have to make an appeal to your superior in order to rightly implement this step of involving a yokefellow. In other words, at this point, since a resolution has not been not achieved, unless your superior agrees to get someone else involved you may simply have to submit to his way of doing things. The exception, of course, would be cases in which you would truly have to violate your conscience in order to submit.[11]

A Sample Righteousness Conflict

Now, let's take that previously mentioned common "righteousness conflict" as an example and track it through our guidelines. Suppose that a couple has a daughter aged fourteen (the oldest of their three children), who was caught in a lie about using her cellular phone after the prescribed hour.

The father (Ricky) believes that the girl should be disciplined by

11. Because, in other words, you believe that the Scripture forbids you from doing what your superior has asked of you.

losing her cell phone for two weeks. Quoting Proverbs 13:24, he says, "He who withholds his rod hates his son, but he who loves him disciplines him diligently."

The mother (Lucy), on the other hand, believes that the child's behavior is a relatively minor offense—especially compared to the other teenagers she knows—and that the offense does not deserve any form of chastisement. She argues passionately that a simple "talking to" about what she did wrong is sufficient. She cites Proverbs 17:10: "A rebuke goes deeper into one who has understanding than a hundred blows into a fool."

But the father sees the offense not only as a serious problem (especially the lying), but as one that is starting to become habitual. Therefore he concludes that the child must be chastised, because a simple "talking to" will not work. They have been arguing for fifteen minutes, when Ricky decides to take the initiative to implement our conflict-resolution guidelines.

Before we go any further, let me point out that not only is there no one exact right way to solve this conflict (there is not one exclusive procedure that must be followed), but also the resolution to this problem (the end result) could differ significantly from couple to couple. This is so, once again, because there is sometimes more than one way to solve a problem biblically.

1. Confess and seek forgiveness for any sinful words, actions, or attitudes that may have exacerbated the conflict up to this point. Suppose that, after being prompted by Ricky's prayer that God would help them to solve this conflict peaceably, Lucy realizes that in the last few moments she has stepped over the line a few times by responding to Ricky in a disrespectful and condescending manner. She begins by acknowledging this to Ricky and asking his forgiveness. Ricky believes that he has handled things biblically up to this point. But, just to be sure, he sincerely asks Lucy whether he needs to seek her forgiveness. "Well, I wasn't going to mention it, but I believe that you interrupted me several times as I was trying to explain my point of view." Ricky thinks to himself, *Maybe I did, but somebody needed to put a stop to the disrespectful way you were talking to me.* But, because he is now in resolution mode, he restrains himself from throwing more fuel on the fire and instead acknowledges that he probably did interrupt her. Then he asks forgiveness for being rude.

2. *Try to express the problem from both perspectives.* Ricky suggests that they both take a few moments to write down their individual analyses of the problem in one or two sentences, and then compare notes. Lucy agrees. After a short while she presents Ricky with this assessment: "The problem is that our daughter is basically a good girl who primarily needs to be encouraged to do the right thing. She doesn't need to have her cell phone taken away from her, because she may need it in case of an emergency."

Ricky puts it this way: "The problem is that our sweet little girl has become a teenager and is starting to rebel against our authority. She has lied to us, and if we don't nip this problem in the bud with some form of discipline we are going to have a real problem on our hands in a few years."

3. *Determine what things can be agreed upon.* "Do you agree that we are dealing with two different problems?" Ricky asks.

"Do you mean breaking curfew and lying?" Lucy responds.

"Well, I would say it's more like a pattern of blatantly disregarding the rules and lying."

"She has only done it twice as far as we know."

"I think it was *three* or *four* times, *as far as we know!*"

"OK, *perhaps* a bit of a pattern is developing. But I still think she just needs to be talked to."

"I know. But right now we are supposed to be trying to see where we agree, not where we disagree."

"You're right, Ricky, but I think there is a bigger problem than just those two."

"Her rebellion?"

"Yes. There is something wrong with her heart's attitude, and I don't think that punishing her is the way to get at it."

"Sweetheart, we are still trying to determine where we *agree.*"

"Sorry—my bad. Do you agree that there is a problem with her heart that we have to deal with?"

"I do."

"Good. So we agree about both the *two* external problems and the *one* internal heart problem."

"Yeah, but I think the internal problem is a rebellion issue."

"You may be right. But there could be other things going on in her heart that are generating the rebellion—don't you think?"

"Probably so. And you think that we're not really going to get to them if we take away her cell phone."

"Exactly! I agree that you know my concern."

"Good. I wish I could get you to agree that the Bible teaches that parents should also discipline their children."

"Well, I don't disagree with that. I guess I just don't think that punishment is the best option in this case."

"Can we agree that it's time to implement the next guideline in that chapter of the conflict resolution book we are reading?"

"We can."

4. Search the Scriptures for any biblical directives and/or principles that relate to resolving the issue. "Can you think of any directives in the Bible that apply to our conflict?" Ricky asks.

"I certainly can," says Lucy, "Fathers, do not provoke your children to anger."[12]

"What does that have to do with anything?"

"I think that if our primary means of dealing with her are punitive, we will run the risk of provoking her."

"But to provoke one's children to anger means to provoke them *by sinning against them* somehow. Otherwise, everything we do that they don't like is a potential provocation in their eyes."

"I agree. But will you agree that this passage is applicable to our situation, if only to keep us from doing anything that might be perceived as sinful from her point of view?"

"But, Lucy, what if her view is wrong?"

"I guess what I'm trying to say is that we will need to be sure to

12. Ephesians 6:2.

explain to her from the Bible why we are doing whatever we decide to do, in order to help minimize the risk of exasperating her."

"Sure, I can agree to that. Can you think of any other biblical directives we need to follow?"

"How about Luke 17:3: 'If your brother sins, rebuke him; and if he repents, forgive him'? It seems to me that God expects us to talk to her about this."

"Maybe so, Lucy—but she doesn't always listen when we talk to her."

"Well, then maybe we should look at Matthew 18:15–16."[13]

"Wouldn't that be interesting? I mean, if she thought we were going to bring in someone else to help us deal with her rebellion, it just might motivate her to take us more seriously. Can you think of any other directives that we need to look at?"

"Not off the top of my head. How about you?"

"What about all those verses in Proverbs that tell us to chastise our children?"

"I've always been a bit confused about this, Ricky. Are they directives or are they principles?"

"They are truisms. But at least one of them is stated as a command: 'Discipline your son, for there is hope; do not set your heart on putting him to death.'"[14]

"Any others?"

"I can't think of any. But I know there are several other verses in the Proverbs that are relevant. And then there is the Hebrews 12 passage that essentially says that if you love your kids, you will discipline them, and that if you don't, you won't. I guess we will have to look them all up and see what we can learn?"

"That's going to be awfully time consuming. What are we going to tell our daughter in the meantime?"

"We can tell her that we are studying the Scriptures together to figure out the best way to deal with her disobedience and dishonesty.

13. "If your brother sins against you, go and tell him his fault between you and him alone. If he listens to you, you have gained your brother. But if he does not listen, take one or two others along with you, that every charge may be established by the evidence of two or three witnesses" (Matt. 18:15–16 ESV).

14. Proverbs 19:18 ESV.

And, as far as the time factor, the benefits of this study should go well beyond the application of this little crisis. My guess is that this is going to help us to get on the same page in lots of different areas as we become more 'one-flesh' in our approach to parenting."

"I know you are right."

"I can't believe that we are agreeing about so many issues!"

"Yeah, I was thinking the same thing. This is really cool."

"What about her cell phone?"

"How about if we take her cell phone away *temporarily*, except when she is en route somewhere?"

"I can live with that."

"Do you want to look up and study these passages together, or do you think we should study them individually (maybe in our personal quiet times) and then come together and compare notes?"

"I think it would be more time effective if we each did our own research and then discussed what we have learned with each other."

"Me too. How about we give it a week and plan on getting together next Saturday morning?"

"Sounds good. But if I get a really good insight before then, may I share it with you?"

"Yes; but if I don't agree, I would like to reserve the right to postpone the discussion until Saturday. Agreed?"

"Agreed!"

On Wednesday morning, Ricky calls Lucy from work. "You're not going to believe this. This morning I was tracking down the word *rod* in the book of Proverbs and I came across a verse that might help us to solve this conflict. It's Proverbs 29:15: 'The rod *and* reproof give wisdom, but a child who gets his own way brings shame to his mother.'"

"Good, honey—but I don't understand exactly how this helps us."

"Don't you see? Basically, we are both right. God encourages parents to use the rod (some type of discipline) and to use verbal confrontation (reproof). I'm not sure what that's supposed to look like, but I think we are closer to a solution."

"Great! I can't wait until Saturday. Let's keep digging!"

"Absolutely!"

5. *In light of the newly discovered biblical data, propose what modifications you are willing to make in order to reach a mutually agreed solution.* On Saturday morning, after discussing several other relevant passages, Ricky agreed that the best thing he could do was to begin spending time with all of their children in the evenings. He also needed to instruct them on the importance of obeying their parents and on the importance of being a teller of the truth. In addition, Ricky was willing to start taking their daughter on dates every two weeks in order to improve their relationship and their communication.

Lucy agreed to try to spend more one-on-one time with all the children during the day and to be an active participant in the evening as they had family time.

In light of the Scriptures that Ricky brought to the table about parental discipline, she also was willing to support him if he wanted to impose additional disciplinary measures. The only thing she asked is that, whatever disciplinary measures were decided upon, their daughter would be allowed to carry her cell phone when she was traveling from one place to another.

Since the conflict was resolved between the two of them, there was no need to implement guideline number six: seeking the help of another mature and godly believer. But let me at least give you a brief "verbatim" to help you to see what this step might look like: "Sweetheart, we have spent many hours studying the Bible for principles and directives to help us get on the same page. We have spent five or six hours discussing the matter but are still not totally in agreement. How about we call Brother ___________ and see if he can help us resolve this matter? Or is there someone else to whom you would prefer to go for assistance?"

Do you see how helpful it can be to first determine the exact nature of the conflict you are having before you attempt to resolve it? Why not think back to the last conflict or two you had with someone and see if you can identify which type it was—differentness, sinfulness, or righteousness—and then try to determine how you would handle the same conflict differently if it happened again? Knowing what kind of conflict you are dealing with is essential to resolving it.

6

LOVE COMMUNICATES

YOU'VE SEEN IT A HUNDRED TIMES. You are in the middle of trying to resolve a conflict with a family member or friend (a member of God's family), when for no apparent reason he or she shuts down right in the middle of the process. "What's going on here?" you wonder. "Is he angry?" "Is she afraid or confused?" "Is it a matter of vengeance—is she purposely shutting down in order to pay me back for something that I said earlier in the conversation?" "Has he never been taught proper biblical communication skills?" "Is she trying to avoid conflict, or is it simply a matter of her choosing not to answer because she doesn't know what to say?"

Regardless of what's behind it, refusing to communicate puts the kibosh on resolving conflicts.

In this chapter, we will discuss how you can attempt to get the discussion going again once someone has shut down. But first, let's consider the problem from the perspective of the one who has shut down. There are lots of reasons that we are tempted to improperly and prematurely end a conflict. The common denominator to all of them is usually selfishness.

SELFISHNESS: THE MOTHER OF ALL SINS[1]

Selfishness is the one sin out of which most of the others seem to flow. It is the one sin that is most common to man. Selfishness, pride,

1. Although I have written about this topic in another place, some basic truths are so essential

self-centeredness, and idolatry are different manifestations of the same sin—not putting God in His rightful place, but honoring oneself above Him.

> But realize this, that in the last days difficult times will come. For men will be lovers of self, lovers of money, boastful, arrogant, revilers, disobedient to parents, ungrateful, unholy, unloving, irreconcilable, malicious gossips, without self-control, brutal, haters of good, treacherous, reckless, conceited, lovers of pleasure rather than lovers of God, holding to a form of godliness, although they have denied its power; avoid such men as these. (2 Tim. 3:1–5)

Notice the first description of these individuals: they are lovers of self. This phrase is the overarching category under which all the other negative characteristics of this passage are classified. It is from the love of self that all the other inordinate love flows.

What is selfishness? It is the opposite of 1 Corinthians 13 love. Love is *giving*[2] (see Matt. 5:43–44; John 3:16; Gal. 2:20; Eph. 5:2, 25)—it is more concerned with what it can *give* than with what it can get. Selfishness is *taking*—it is more concerned with what it can *get* (or with what it might lose)[3] than with what it can give.

We have sinful (i.e., selfish) hearts, inclined to move away from God's command to learn how to love Him and our neighbors:

> One of them, a lawyer, asked Him a question, testing Him, "Teacher, which is the great commandment in the Law?" And He said to him, "'You shall love the Lord your God with all your heart, and with all your soul, and with all your mind.' This is the great and foremost commandment. The second is like it, 'You shall love your neighbor as yourself.' On these two commandments depend the whole Law and the Prophets." (Matt. 22:35–40)

---

to conflict resolution that they bear repeating here. For more on this problem, please see my booklet *Selfishness: From Loving Yourself to Loving Your Neighbor* (Phillipsburg, NJ: P&R Publishing, 2010).

2. It is selflessly (without having selfish motives) giving another what he needs.

3. Love is not only the antidote to *selfishness*. As we will see, love is also the antidote to *fear* (see 1 John 4:18), which selfishly focuses more on its own potential loss than on the potential gain or benefit of another.

These two great commandments, on which all the others depend,[4] are the two greatest practical antidotes for indwelling sin.[5] The more you and I love God and our neighbors, the less selfish (sinful) we will be. So, because man is sinful (because his basic problem is selfishness), God's remedy is for him to learn how to love God and love his neighbor. The New Testament emphasizes love because love is the single best antidote for sin.[6]

THE SELFISH NATURE OF NOT COMMUNICATING

Withdrawing in the midst of a conflict (without good reason) is often an unloving decision. To prematurely withdraw from a conflict because the conversation is not going your way is, in reality, selfish. "He who separates himself seeks *his own* desire, he quarrels against all sound wisdom" (Prov. 18:1). It's one thing to politely put a stop to an argument when your opponent isn't playing by the rules (i.e., God's rules) or when the discussion is going around in circles. It's quite another to abruptly run away from it out of selfish ambition, sinful anger, fear, pride (because, for example, you are losing the argument), or impatience.

The apostle Peter was guilty of selfishly (fearfully) withdrawing from the Gentiles when certain Jews were around. He sinned publicly and was publicly rebuked for his hypocrisy by his fellow apostle, Paul.

> But when Cephas came to Antioch, I opposed him to his face, because he stood condemned. For prior to the coming of certain men from James, he used to eat with the Gentiles; but when they came, he began to *withdraw and hold himself aloof, fearing* the party of the circumcision.

4. In one way or another, selfishness is at the heart of breaking each of the Ten Commandments.

5. It's not the love that comes from ourselves (the love that we may try to manifest in our own strength) that is the antidote to sin; rather, it is the love that comes from God, which has been "poured out within our hearts through the Holy Spirit" (Rom. 5:5), that enables us to deal with our sin in a way that pleases Him.

6. As a one-word definition of sin, "selfishness" is, of course, theologically inaccurate, largely because it doesn't include the idea that the transgression is committed against a holy God. But, from a practical perspective (that of progressive sanctification), this is probably as close as you can come in one word.

> The rest of the Jews joined him in hypocrisy, with the result that even Barnabas was carried away by their hypocrisy. But when I saw that they were not straightforward about the truth of the gospel, I said to Cephas in the presence of all, "If you, being a Jew, live like the Gentiles and not like the Jews, how is it that you compel the Gentiles to live like Jews?" (Gal. 2:11–14)

In addition to the four deadly character flaws that we looked at in part one (pride, anger[7], impatience, and intolerance), other selfish responses may occur in the midst of conflict, and for them we ought also to be on the alert. Let's take a look at a few more of the selfish (unloving) motives (or desires) that tempt us, like they tempted Peter, to shy away from conflict.[8]

The first two are taken from another interesting peacemaking passage.

> Who among you is wise and understanding? Let him show by his good behavior his deeds in the gentleness of wisdom. But if you have bitter *jealousy* and *selfish ambition* in your heart, do not be arrogant and *so* lie against the truth. This wisdom is not that which comes down from above, but is earthly, natural, demonic. For where *jealousy* and *selfish ambition* exist, there is disorder and every evil thing. But the wisdom from above is first pure, then peaceable, gentle, reasonable, full of mercy and good fruits, unwavering, without hypocrisy. And the seed whose fruit is righteousness is sown in peace by those who make peace. (James 3:13–18)

Jealousy or Envy

The Greek word for jealousy is *zelos,* from which we get our English word *zealous.* It means zeal, envy, or jealousy, depending on how it is used. So what's the difference between the three terms?

7. There is another point about anger I would like to mention at this juncture: even in conflicts of *differentness*, it is our idolatrous desire that (in one way or another) the other person not be quite so "different" from us, which may tempt us to respond angrily.

8. I want to thank my friend Brenda Gourley, who suggested adding these to this chapter.

To put it simply, *envy* is zeal for that which has been given to another. *Jealousy* is zeal for that which has been given to me. If I am envious, I have a selfish (covetous) zeal for that which belongs to someone else. If I am jealous, I have a zeal for protecting that which I believe is mine (more often than not because I am fearful of losing it). Envy and jealousy are like two sides of the same coin. Heads is envy—the desire to have something that belongs to another (accompanied by varying degrees of resentment). Tails is jealousy—the fear of losing to another that which you already have.

Right or wrong, when a person is jealous, he is afraid of being displaced by someone or something else. When we are jealous of *someone,* it is because we are afraid the person whom we love may prefer someone else. When we are jealous of *something,* it is because we are afraid that the thing we are jealous of is going to displace the love (or fondness, or affection, or desire, or whatever) that someone whom we love has for us. The irony is that if one is jealous, unless it is a godly jealousy, then he doesn't really love the object of his jealousy as much as he thinks he does, because the Bible says, "Love is not jealous" (1 Cor. 13:4).

Jealousy itself, like fear, may be righteous or sinful. Remember, God Himself is jealous. "You shall worship no other god, for the LORD, whose name is Jealous, is a jealous God" (Ex. 34:14). Of course, God is not fearful, but He is concerned that you and I not displace our love for Him with a love for something else. If we love anything more than we love Him, we are sinning, and we won't find ultimate satisfaction in anything but Him (see Eccl. 5:10). His jealousy, therefore, is good, loving, and holy. It has our best interest in mind.

Another example of righteous jealousy can be seen in the life of the apostle Paul. "I am jealous for you with a godly jealousy; for I betrothed you to one husband, that to Christ I might present you as a pure virgin. But I am *afraid,* lest as the serpent deceived Eve by his craftiness, your minds should be led astray from the simplicity and purity of devotion to Christ" (2 Cor. 11:2–3). Paul, as a loving and concerned spiritual father to the Corinthians, wanted his daughter, whom he promised in marriage to Christ, to remain a spiritual virgin.

In my counseling ministry I counsel more spouses of unfaithful husbands and wives than you would probably imagine. The jealousy that these faithful spouses experience is overwhelmingly of the righteous verity (with a smidgen of the sinful variety thrown in the mix). The difference between sinful jealousy and godly jealousy has to do with *motive*. You tell me what your motive is and what you're afraid of losing, and I'll tell you whether you have the right or wrong kind of jealousy.

The next time you are in conflict with someone and you suspect that you might be struggling with envy or jealousy, ask yourself these questions:

"Am I afraid of losing something that I deem important or valuable?"

"Am I afraid of losing something that God deems important or valuable?"

"Am I more afraid that those whom I love (or my opponent) will somehow displace me than I am that they will displace the Lord?"

Selfish Ambition

Since this entire section is on selfishness, I will say only a bit about this phrase. This single Greek word, *eritheia*, is sometimes translated as "strife," "contention," or "rivalry." Etymologically it means, "to work for daily hire." The term denotes the selfish, shortsighted attitude that the day laborer often has. "[Eritheia] is thus the attitude of self-seekers, harlots etc. . . . who, demeaning themselves and their cause, are busy and active in their own interests, seeking their own gain or advantage."[9] The word was used by Paul to describe those preachers who "preach Christ of contention, not sincerely, supposing to add affliction to my bonds" (Phil. 1:16 KJV). Paul uses the word again in Philippians 2:3 (KJV) to speak of motives[10] when he urges his readers to "let nothing be done through strife or vainglory; but in lowliness of mind let each esteem others better than themselves."

Here are a few self-examination questions to help to keep any selfish ambition in check during your next conflict.

9. *Theological Dictionary of the New Testament*, trans. and ed. Geoffrey W. Bromiley, vol. 2, *Δ–H*, ed. Gerhard Kittel (Grand Rapids: Eerdmans, 1964), 2:660.

10. He also uses it to describe the outward manifestations (strife and contentions) that result from this selfish attitude of the heart in Romans 2:8; 2 Corinthians 12:20; and Galatians 5:20.

"Am I seeking my own interests right now or those of Jesus Christ? (Am I making my chief ambition to please Him?)"

"In what ways can I esteem my opponent to be better (wiser, more knowledgeable, or more experienced) than I am pertaining to the matters about which we are disputing?"

"How am I going to respond if the conversation begins to go in a different direction than I would like (if things don't go my way)?"

"How willing am I to (selflessly) invest the time, effort, and energy needed to minister to my opponent should his needs become apparent?"

Empty Conceit

Paul connects this rare word (*kenodoxía*) to the previous one in Philippians 2:3 ("Let nothing be done through strife or *vainglory*"—KJV). The term seems to connote the desire to establish one's own glory (reputation) above and beyond what is in fact deserved (the word also can mean *delusion*). Here are three self-examination questions to ask yourself the next time you suspect that you may be arguing vaingloriously.

"To what extent am I exaggerating my virtues (boasting) in order to impress my opponent?"

"To what extent am I minimizing my flaws in order to impress my opponent?"

"Am I fighting more for my own reputation or for the Lord's?"

Fear

Fear is so potent that, if we let it, it will paralyze us and keep us from fulfilling our biblical responsibilities—especially our two greatest responsibilities to love God and neighbor. The apostle John develops the antithetical relationship that exists between fear and love.

> By this, *love* is perfected with us, that we may have confidence in the day of judgment; because as He is, so also are we in this world. There is *no fear* in love; but *perfect love casts out fear*, because fear involves punishment, and *the one who fears is not* perfected in love. (1 John 4:17–18)

Not only do we see an interesting connection in the Bible between fear and selfishness,[11] but we see another between *fear* and *slothfulness* (Matt. 25:24–26). The wicked and slothful slave in the parable of the talents (Matt. 25:24–26) used the fact that he was afraid to excuse his slothful work ethic. Fearful individuals are inclined to be lazy because they focus on their fears rather than on their responsibilities. What they fear distracts and often incapacitates them from faithfully doing what they ought. The proverbial sluggard is even afraid to go outside, because he says, "There is a lion outside; I will be killed in the streets!" (Prov. 22:13).

Now how can this be applied to the resolution of conflicts? Fear affects the way we relate to others. Let's contrast the selfish thoughts of the fearful individual (which are characterized by *taking*) with those of a loving (*giving*) person.

The Peace-lover (The Fearful Person)	**The Peacemaker (The Loving Person)**
"I wonder what he will think of my lack of verbal prowess."	"I wonder what his needs are."
"I'd better not reveal too much of myself to him, or he will realize that I'm not very _________ and then he'll reject me."	"What matters is not what he thinks of me but how I can minister to him."
"I've got to avoid saying anything that might make him mad—for my own protection."[†]	"I've got to try to help him see the truth of what I'm saying—for his own good."

11. People who are selfish *tend* to be fearful. People who are fearful are *necessarily* selfish. *Selfishness* is more concerned with what it can *get* than with what it can *give*. *Fear* is more concerned with what it *might lose* than with what it can *give*. For more about the correlation between these two, please see my booklet *Fear: Breaking Its Grip* (Phillipsburg, NJ: P&R Publishing, 2009).

† It isn't selfish to avoid triggering the anger of someone who is prone to getting violently out of control or to seek to keep one's distance from such a person. But to avoid ever saying anything that might bother someone or cause him to reject you might be a sinful level of self-protection.

"I feel intimidated when he looks me in the eye, so I'm going to avoid eye contact as much as possible."	"Because I want to show him how much I love him (how much I am concerned about him), I am going to give him as much eye contact as I possibly can."
"I really like this guy and don't want to risk ruining our friendship."	"Because he is my friend, I've got to speak the truth in love—even if it means risking our relationship."
"I'll probably make a fool of myself."	"If I make a fool of myself, so be it. I'm more concerned about meeting his needs than I am about what he thinks of me."
"I hate arguing with him. He is too intimidating. I just turn to mush whenever I am around him."	"There is no biblical reason for me to flee from this conflict. By God's grace, I can learn to do anything that God wants me to do. If the Lord prepared a table for David in the presence of his enemies, I can certainly face this conflict without giving in to fear."

A peacemaker (a God-pleaser) is more concerned about fulfilling his God-given responsibilities or meeting the needs of others than he is about the potential consequences of a particular action. Unlike his counterpart, the peace lover (the people-pleaser),[12] he doesn't allow the thought of unpleasant consequences to paralyze him or keep him from loving God and loving others—especially in times of conflict.

Ask yourself the following questions the next time you are tempted to walk away from a conflict because you are afraid.

"Am I in genuine danger here, or am I only uncomfortable?"[13]

12. For more insight into the difference between the two, see my book *Pleasing People: How Not to Be an "Approval Junkie"* (Phillipsburg, NJ: P&R Publishing, 2007).

13. In most cases, this question is likely to reassure you to continue the discussion and move past your fear. But if your opponent in the conflict is a real danger to you, then fear may be a signal

"Am I more concerned about what I might lose if I continue in this conflict, or with what I can give to my opponent?"

"To what extent am I reluctant to reveal myself to my opponent (or to continue discussing this matter with him) due to fear that, if I disclose certain things, I will lose his respect or face his rejection?"

"How will the information that I want to withhold from him benefit him?"

Vengeance

During a question-and-answer session at a home educator's conference where I was encouraging parents to interpret their children's problems with biblical terminology ("not in words taught by human wisdom, but those taught by the spirit, interpreting spiritual things with spiritual words"—see 1 Cor. 2:13), I was asked an interesting question. "What is the biblical term for 'passive aggressive behavior'?" Without hesitation, I said, "Vengeance." I was really surprised that my response got quite a laugh. But vengeance is no laughing matter.

Sometimes people in conflict purposely shut down[14] in order to "pay back" their opponents. But the Bible forbids us from taking our own vengeance. "Never take your own revenge, beloved, but leave room for the wrath *of God,* for it is written, 'Vengeance is Mine, I will repay,' says the Lord" (Rom. 12:19).

Why is it that God forbids us from taking our own revenge and insists on doing it for us? There are at least two reasons. First, God does not authorize any one person to take *personal* vengeance. A few verses later in chapter 13, Paul addresses the official, corporate, or governmental right of God-ordained authorities to execute His vengeance: "For he is God's minister to you for good. But if you do evil, be afraid; for he does not bear the sword in vain; for he is God's minister, an avenger to execute *wrath* on him who practices evil" (Rom. 13:4 NKJV).

So vengeance is not for us to take personally (individually). It is

---

that you need to get away and get help, *not* to risk escalating the danger by continuing in conflict.

14. Of course, refusing to talk is not the only vindictive tactic that people use in conflict. There are any number of unbiblical forms of communication that people employ in order to pay back those with whom they are offended (or displeased).

a judicial issue, not a personal one. God Himself will (directly or indirectly) right all wrongs in His time and in His way. Vengeance does not recognize the lawful and righteous execution of God's judgment.

Vengeance does not belong to us. It belongs to God. "'Vengeance is Mine, I will repay,' says the Lord." If God were to say to you, "This is my crown," would you walk up to Him and take it off His head? Well, every time you take your own revenge, you are *stealing* from God.

The second reason that God forbids us from executing our own vengeance is the fact that we really don't have the *ability* to do it properly.[15] Since we don't have all the facts necessary to make the proper judgment, we are incapable of making the right kind of judgment necessary to execute vengeance justly. So we are told to wait in such cases. "Therefore do not go on passing judgment before the time, but wait until the Lord comes who will both bring to light the things *hidden in the darkness* and disclose the *motives of men's hearts*; and then each man's praise will come to him from God" (1 Cor. 4:5).

We don't always know the full circumstances of why a person acts the way he does; only God knows. Perhaps he has an undiagnosed brain tumor or has been unable to sleep for the past two nights because he recently discovered that his wife is being unfaithful to him. Perhaps he was fed misinformation by someone. While understanding the full circumstances still might not absolve him from culpability, it would necessitate his being shown more mercy than you would be disposed to give if you didn't have all the necessary information. On the other hand, suppose that he has committed the same offense fourteen additional times this year to half a dozen other people. Would not a more severe judgment than you would think to give him be required in that case? Perhaps more importantly, you do not know his motives. They might be better or worse than you realize. Only God knows what they are. "Man looks at the outward appearance, but the LORD looks at the heart" (1 Sam. 16:7). The proper amount of vengeance that is in accordance with God's justice is predicated on His knowledge of man's motives, to which we have not been given total access.

15. See Jay E. Adams, *How to Overcome Evil: A Practical Exposition of Romans 12:14–21* (1977; repr., Phillipsburg, NJ: P&R Publishing, 2010), 135–39, for a more thorough explanation of this concept.

Here are a few questions with reference to vindictive motives that you may find helpful when in a conflict:

"Has my opponent really sinned against me, or am I just upset because things aren't going my way?"

"Did I do anything wrong that might have provoked my opponent's improper response?"

"Am I harboring bitterness or resentment in my heart toward my opponent?"[16]

"How can I bless[17] my opponent even in the midst of our disagreement? (What are his needs? What resources do I have with which to meet them?)"

The Love of Pleasure[18]

When a family member or friend with whom we are conversing needs our undivided attention but we selfishly do not want to be distracted (or delayed) from some pleasurable activity (even if it is only some mental activity), we can become quite impatient with the person simply because we don't want to make the effort right then and there to stop what we are doing and talk. Such impatience can take many forms. We may become inattentive (because our thoughts are focused miles away, on our pleasures), we may hastily rush to a premature termination of the conflict, or we may resort to harshness in order to pressure the other person "not to bother" us with what we believe is trivial (in comparison to what we would rather be doing or thinking about). When tempted to think that way, perhaps we should consider how much pleasure God receives when two of His children resolve their differences so that they can dwell together in unity.

> Behold, how good and how pleasant it is
> For brothers to dwell together in unity!
> It is like the precious oil upon the head,
> Coming down upon the beard,

16. If you are, your ability to effectively resolve conflicts with him will almost certainly be hindered until you resolve the issues relating to your bitterness.

17. See Romans 12:14; see also Matthew 5:44; 1 Peter 3:9.

18. See Proverbs 21:17; 2 Timothy 3:4.

Even Aaron's beard,
Coming down upon the edge of his robes.
It is like the dew of Hermon
Coming down upon the mountains of Zion;
For there the LORD commanded the blessing—life forever. (Ps. 133)

Self-evaluation questions:

"Does God really want me to focus my attention right now on what I would like to, or does He want me to give this person my undivided attention?"

"Would it be best for me to politely ask for a 'rain check' until such a time as I will be able to give this person a greater portion of my undivided attention?"

The Love of Control

We previously saw that Diotrephes "*loved to be first* [or *loved to be the chief*] among them" (i.e., his peers—3 John 9). Sometimes people want to gain (or maintain) control of their opponents, so they resort to all manner of manipulative ploys in order to have the upper hand during a conflict. They raise their voice, hurl insults, put on a fierce countenance, abuse their authority, withhold information, make false accusations, cry, sulk, pout, make obligatory statements, or use flattery or cajolery, all in a selfish attempt to make their opponent feel guilty, ashamed, anxious, or any number of other unpleasant emotions that will give them what they want.

Self-evaluation questions:

"Have I asked my opponent for precisely what I want, or am I selfishly pressuring him into giving me what I want?"

"Am I prepared to take 'no' for an answer should I not be able to persuade him to give me what I want?"

"Am I content in not having persuaded him to my way of thinking because I refused to resort to sinful ways of doing so?"

Laziness

As you are hopefully beginning to see, there is much in the Bible about solving conflicts (not to mention about how to communicate). It takes a considerable amount of time, effort, and thought to study and implement the many passages of Scripture that will make one into a proficient communicator / conflict resolver. But some people are just too lazy to learn. Others are so lazy that they won't even exert the energy required to bring a conflict to a satisfactory resolution.

> The sluggard buries his hand in the dish;
> He is weary of bringing it to his mouth again.
> The sluggard is wiser in his own eyes
> Than seven men who can give a discreet answer. (Prov. 26:15–16)

This is in sharp contrast to Paul's admonition to make every effort to "maintain the unity of the Spirit" (Eph. 4:3 ESV). Resolving conflicts can be hard work. It requires determination and effort.

Self-evaluation questions:

"Have I really made every effort to resolve this conflict biblically?"

"Am I being active or passive in this process? (Does God want me to take the initiative to say something to help bring about a resolution to the conflict?)"

"Do I need to invest extra time to research how I might best handle this conflict for the glory of God?"

Contempt for Authority

God has given authorities the right and responsibility to inquire about (search out) and acquire certain relevant data. "It is the glory of God to conceal a matter, but the glory of kings is to search out a matter" (Prov. 25:2). Willfully withholding such information from someone in a "need to know" position is not only disrespectful, it is insubordinate—if not rebellious.

Self-evaluation questions:

"Does this person have a biblical right to the information I want to conceal from him?"

"What is making me hesitate to provide him with that information?"

"Is my contempt for this individual tempting me to be unnecessarily provocative?"

Malice

Some people are just intent upon doing evil. One of the Greek words for evil (κακία; meaning not just the doing of it, but the internal disposition to it) is also translated *malice* six times in the New Testament.

> Therefore, laying aside all *malice*, all deceit, hypocrisy, envy, and all evil speaking, as newborn babes, desire the pure milk of the word, that you may grow thereby. (1 Peter 2:1–2 NKJV)

It may be hard for you to imagine, but some people find evil pleasure in hurting, belittling, and humiliating others.

Wisdom personified, in the book of Proverbs, "cries aloud in the streets." She is a clear communicator. She takes the initiative. She speaks truth and does not withhold it (1:20–23; 8:1–11; 9:1–6). Her counterparts, however, Madam Folly and the Adulterous Woman, also take initiative. And although they may be loud (7:11; 11:13), they also keep secrets. They are seductive and deceptive. They lie and withhold the truth (7:21, 23; 9:17–18). Sometimes people do not communicate, or they withhold information (deceive by concealment), because they are laying a trap for their victims. They have ulterior motives. Full disclosure would foil their plans.

Self-evaluation questions:

"Am I taking any malevolent pleasure in not actively participating in this conversation?"

"If so, what is it?"

- ☐ I want to embarrass my opponent.
- ☐ I want to frustrate my opponent.
- ☐ I want to provoke my opponent into a sinful response that I can later exploit.
- ☐ I want to intimidate my opponent.
- ☐ I want to gain the upper hand over my opponent (to control him).
- ☐ I want to annoy my opponent.
- ☐ I want to see my opponent squirm.
- ☐ I want to ________________ my opponent.
- ☐ I want to ________________ my opponent.

A Condescending, Critical, Unkind Spirit

"You are not worth it." "You wouldn't understand anyway." "I am smarter, shrewder, and holier than you. I can't trust you with this information; you would just mess it up, and you are certainly not worth my time explaining it."

These thought patterns (and dozens like them) could rightly be categorized as unloving. They are antithetical to 1 Corinthians 13.

Let's consider the selfish nature of these kinds of thoughts. Notice how contrary they are to the description of love given in 1 Corinthians 13:4–7.

Love	Vs.	Selfishness (says or thinks before it stops talking)
is patient		"I don't have time for you." "It would take too long to explain (and you'll probably want to ask me a dozen follow-up questions)."
is kind		"You are not worth my time." "You wouldn't understand." "I know that you want the information, but I'm going to withhold it from you just because I want to."
is not jealous (or envious)		"If I give you this information, you will know what I know and may use it to displace me in the eyes of my peers." (If I told you everything, it would foil my plans to get the things that you have and I don't!)

does not brag	"I have some information that you don't have. I know something that you don't know. I have a secret, and I'm not going to share it with you."
is not arrogant	"You wouldn't understand." (I know better than you.) "You're not worthy of my time (or of this knowledge)."
does not act unbecomingly	"I don't have to answer (or respond to) you." "Don't expect me to be polite or to carry this conversation. I'm going to speak only when spoken to."
does not seek its own	"I've got more important things to do right now than to talk to you." "I am not going to give you this information, because it would spoil my plans to manipulate you or to otherwise get what I want. I am going to maintain control of you and this situation."
is not provoked	"Because I'm upset with you, I'm not going to give you this information." "How dare you ask me to tell you that? That's none of your business!"

does not take into account a wrong suffered	"The last time I gave you this kind of information, you used it against me. So I'm not going to disclose another thing to you."
does not rejoice in unrighteousness	"It's such a good feeling to know that I have something that you want and are not going to get (at least not from me)." "You can just keep on being in the dark about that! I'll never tell you what you want to know."
rejoices with the truth	"You may have a piece of the truth, but I'm not going to let you have all of it. You'll have to be content with what little you have."
bears all things	"I can't bear the thought that you would know as much as I do about this matter." "You are so irritating. Why do you ask so many foolish questions?"
believes all things	"If I give you this information, you will figure out a way to use it against me."
hopes all things	"Why should I bother opening up to you? You won't know how to handle it."

endures all things	"I'm tired of trusting you with my heart anymore. From now on, I am going to keep my thoughts and feelings locked inside."

Self-evaluation questions:

"Am I more interested in what I can give to this person or in what I can get from him?"

"Am I taking the posture of a superior or a servant?"

In the final analysis, if we do not understand that we have a biblical responsibility to communicate in the midst of conflicts—if we are not convicted that in most circumstances it is unbiblical[19] to refuse to communicate (even if the communication is only to politely ask for a "rain check")—then we will be slow to change our style of communication.

Change is difficult. Therefore our conscience—programmed by the Word of God and by the Spirit of God—must be the greatest driving force behind that change. Of course this involves more than just the awareness that not to change would be sinful. It also involves knowing that God will be pleased for us to do that which is biblically necessary to bring about change. So it is our love for God as well as our love for our neighbor that impels us to speak when we don't want to.

"But isn't it better to keep silent in many cases?" you may be wondering. "Besides, what about those verses in Scripture that basically tell us that it's better to keep our mouths shut than to sin, such as Proverbs 17:27–28?

> He who restrains his words has knowledge,
> And he who has a cool spirit is a man of understanding.
> Even a fool, when he keeps silent, is considered wise;
> When he closes his lips, he is *considered* prudent."

19. It is at best a sin of omission.

Sure, but there are times when we must speak if we want to please God. Christians, as a rule, are to be active rather than passive in the communication process. They may not sit passively by, expecting those with whom they are supposed to be conversing to take all the initiative. Inactive individuals, on the other hand, expect their counterparts to drag out of them all but the most basic information, rather than volunteering data that is necessary for the dialogue.[20]

BIBLICAL PRINCIPLES INVOLVED

Here are a few biblical communication principles, along with some corresponding Scripture passages from which the principles have been extrapolated. It is my hope that unpacking them may help you to reprogram your conscience (if necessary) and thereby help you find more freedom to communicate when and as you ought.

1. Sometimes, not to speak is a sin.

There are many situations when we are obligated to speak. There is "a time to be silent[21] and a time to speak" (Eccl. 3:7). When we refuse to do what God tells us we are required to do, we are sinning. "When I say to the wicked, 'O wicked man, you will surely die,' and you do not speak to warn the wicked from his way, that wicked man shall die in his iniquity, but his blood I will require from your hand" (Ezek. 33:8).

Sometimes we are required to speak, for example, when others are in danger.

> Then Mordecai told them to reply to Esther, "Do not imagine that you in the king's palace can escape any more than all the Jews. For if you remain silent at this time, relief and deliverance will arise for the Jews from another place and you and your father's house will perish. And

20. Sometimes their silence is due to the fact that they are convinced that the other person knows exactly what they are upset about and why. This is often not the case and is usually an uncharitable judgment of the other's motive.

21. There are indeed times when it is necessary to remain silent, even when questioned (see Matt. 15:23; Mark 14:60–61; 15:4).

> who knows whether you have not attained royalty for such a time as this?" (Est. 4:13–14; see also 7:4)

Or sometimes we must speak because we know of another's sin and are in a place to rebuke him: "Be on your guard! If your brother sins, rebuke him; and if he repents, forgive him" (Luke 17:3).

Sometimes we are obligated to speak by virtue of biblical injunctions that require the use of communication to carry out the biblical directions. For example, when you know that a fellow believer is burdened and you do not say anything to help him carry that burden, you are sinning by omitting your responsibility to "bear one another's burdens, and thereby fulfill the law of Christ" (Gal. 6:2). Although it is possible to fulfill this verse by *doing* something and *saying* absolutely nothing, it is difficult to imagine (apart from doing something anonymously) how that could be done practically. It is similarly hard to imagine how someone could fulfill verses such as these without opening his mouth (or opening his arms[22]).

> But *encourage* one another day after day, as long as it is still called "Today," so that none of you will be hardened by the deceitfulness of sin. (Heb. 3:13)

> And let us *consider how to stimulate* one another to love and good deeds, not forsaking our own assembling together, as is the habit of some, but *encouraging* one another; and all the more as you see the day drawing near. (Heb. 10:24–25)

> Pursue peace with all men. (Heb. 12:14)

> Therefore, confess your sins to one another, and pray for one another so that you may be healed. The effective prayer of a righteous man can accomplish much. (James 5:16)

22. Nonverbal forms of communication, such as kisses, handshakes, and hugs, are valid ways to express oneself. In certain circumstances, they may be preferred—especially if one is not sure what to say. They certainly are better than not saying anything.

2. Because love does not act unbecomingly (it is not rude—1 Cor. 13:5), it does not impolitely become unresponsive but rather gives an appropriate answer.[23]

Sometimes it is not possible, or not appropriate, to provide requested information. In such a case, you can explain why you cannot—or at least *that* you cannot—currently respond as expected to the request.[24] Most Americans consider it quite rude not to respond to a direct question. Similarly, some statements, while not interrogatives, implicitly obligate the receiver to a response that, if not given (or at least acknowledged), will be taken as rudely offensive.

> Give no offense either to Jews or to Greeks or to the church of God. (1 Cor. 10:32)

> Let your speech always be with grace, as though seasoned with salt, so that you will know how you should respond to each person. (Col. 4:6)

> Outdo one another in showing honor. (Rom. 12:10 ESV)

Of course, there may be times when one has to risk the potential of being considered rude, as for example when the question is clearly intended to be manipulative.

3. Love takes the initiative to express itself—even when it may "hurt" the person being loved.

Love gives another person what he needs, not necessarily what he wants.[25] It follows, then, that it is not *necessarily* a sin to "hurt someone's feelings"—as long as what "hurt" him is the fact that he did not

23. See Ephesians 4:15, 25.

24. This is the rule. There are, however, exceptions to the rule—as, for example, when Jesus refused to answer questions from certain individuals (see Matt. 15:23–26; Mark 11:29–30).

25. The disciples, as one example, wanted Jesus to stay on earth to establish His kingdom. But He knew they *needed* something else—something more important (the coming of the Holy Spirit and His advocacy with the Father). So, at the cost of making them temporarily sorrowful, He didn't give them what they wanted but rather what they needed (cf. John 16:1–16).

receive what he wanted but rather received what he needed.[26] If we get our feelings hurt by something that someone said that didn't offend God, we are the ones who have to repent (change our thinking) rather than the one who "offended" us.

> For out of much affliction and anguish of heart I wrote to you with many tears; not so that you would be made sorrowful, but that you might know the love which I have especially for you. (2 Cor. 2:4)

> For though I caused you sorrow by my letter, I do not regret it; though I did regret it—for I see that that letter caused you sorrow, though only for a while. (2 Cor. 7:8)

4. Those in superior positions (parents, bosses, teachers, rulers) have a right and responsibility to request information from their subordinates. Those in subordinate positions have a responsibility to open up to (communicate with) their superiors.

When someone in a position of authority has a biblical "need to know" or a biblical right to know something, and we conceal that information from him, we are sinning. (Concealment is a form of lying.)[27]

> It is the glory of God to conceal a matter,
> But the glory of kings is to search out a matter. (Prov. 25:2)

> Since the word of the king is authoritative, who will say to him, "What are you doing?" (Eccl. 8:4)

> Our mouth has spoken freely to you, O Corinthians, our heart is opened wide. You are not restrained by us, but you are restrained in your own affections. Now in a like exchange—I speak as to children—open wide *to us* also. (2 Cor. 6:11–13)

26. Actually, our feelings don't really get hurt. Rather we interpret what is said to us as somehow offensive and our internal response to that interpretation produces unpleasant feelings.

27. For more on this, see my booklet entitled *Deception: Letting Go of Lying* (Phillipsburg, NJ: P&R Publishing, 2008).

5. It is sometimes proper to respond with a totally different answer than what might be expected.

Sometimes wisdom dictates that a foolish question not be answered but rather rebuked. There may also be circumstances where a partial answer (or even an evasive one) may be appropriate (as in the case when the individual asks for information he has no biblical need to know).[28]

> Do not answer a fool according to his folly,
> Or you will also be like him.
> Answer a fool as his folly deserves,
> That he not be wise in his own eyes. (Prov. 26:4–5)

> When He entered the temple, the chief priests and the elders of the people came to Him while He was teaching, and said, "By what authority are You doing these things, and who gave You this authority?" Jesus said to them, "I will also ask you one thing, which if you tell Me, I will also tell you by what authority I do these things. The baptism of John was from what source, from heaven or from men?" And they began reasoning among themselves, saying, "If we say, 'From heaven,' He will say to us, 'Then why did you not believe him?' But if we say, 'From men,' we fear the people; for they all regard John as a prophet." And answering Jesus, they said, "We do not know." He also said to them, "Neither will I tell you by what authority I do these things." (Matt. 21:23–27)

6. Sometimes we must speak even when we are asked to keep quiet.

God doesn't give anyone absolute authority. No one has the authority to give a gag order to a Christian who is required to speak (i.e., no one has the authority to command a believer to disobey God).

> And when they had summoned them, they commanded them not to speak or teach at all in the name of Jesus. But Peter and John answered and said to them, "Whether it is right in the sight of God to give heed to

28. For example, I am sometimes asked (by nosey Christians) to provide confidential information about individuals I am counseling. My typical (first) response is, "That's not a fair question."

> you rather than to God, you be the judge; for we cannot stop speaking about what we have seen and heard." (Acts 4:18–20)

7. It is not necessarily wrong to communicate when one is angry (as long as the anger is righteous rather than sinful[29] and is transmitted through biblical means of communication).

Admittedly, righteous indignation is hard to come by, and, as noted earlier, most of the hundreds of "anger" verses in the Bible speak of the sinful variety, but there is a time and a place for holy passion in the life of the Christian.

> Now Elihu had waited to speak to Job because they were years older than he. And when Elihu saw that there was no answer in the mouth of the three men his anger burned. So Elihu the son of Barachel the Buzite spoke out. (Job 32:4–6)

> [There is] a time to love and a time to hate;
> A time for war and a time for peace. (Eccl. 3:8)

> After looking around at them with anger, grieved at their hardness of heart, He said to the man, "Stretch out your hand." And he stretched it out, and his hand was restored. (Mark 3:5)

> Now while Paul was waiting for them at Athens, his spirit was being provoked[30] within him as he was observing the city full of idols. So he was reasoning in the synagogue with the Jews and the God-fearing Gentiles, and in the market place every day with those who happened to be present. (Acts 17:16–17)

But we must always keep in mind that when righteous anger is expressed with sinful forms of communication, it will likely be perceived

29. I mention this because many Christians believe that if they are angry (even if righteously so) they must remain silent rather than speak. Consequently, out of fear of committing one sin (a sin of commission), they commit another (a sin of omission) by remaining silent when they should speak.

30. The word παροξύνω is a term that implies indignation or anger.

as sinful anger. More important, such expressions indeed will be sinful in the eyes of God. So, it is usually best to wait until your anger (righteous as it may be) has subsided before attempting to proceed with discussing the issue about which you are angry.

As we conclude this chapter, let's again consider the instructions of the apostle Paul to the Corinthians:

> We have spoken freely to you, Corinthians, and opened wide our hearts to you. We are not withholding our affection from you, but you are withholding yours from us. As a fair exchange—I speak as to my children—*open wide your hearts also.* (2 Cor. 6:11–13 NIV)

In this very intimate epistle, Paul reminds the Corinthians of his love, affection, and concern for them. He has opened his heart to them and urges them to open their hearts to him. You cannot open up and clam up at the same time. Love communicates!

7

RESPONDING TO REPROOF[1]

SOLOMON SAID, "Do not reprove a scoffer, or he will hate you, reprove a wise man and he will love you" (Prov. 9:8). As you read through this chapter, please try to keep in mind that under certain circumstances your brothers and sisters in Christ may have a duty to reprove you (to show you your fault). "If your brother sins, go and show him his fault in private; if he listens to you, you have won your brother" (Matt. 18:15).

What does it mean to show someone his fault?[2] As we saw in chapter 5, the verb for *show* (which is the same word, used in its noun form, in 2 Tim. 3:16[3]) is better understood as *convict*, which is the way I use it throughout this book as an alternative to the word *reprove* or *reproof*. This is the way it appears in the most popular English Bible translations of 2 Timothy 3:16, and I believe that it better describes the essential meaning of the original word.

What comes to mind when you hear the word *conviction*? Jesus used this word when addressing the Laodicean Church in Revelation 3.

> I know your deeds, that you are neither cold nor hot; I wish that you were cold or hot. So because you are lukewarm, and neither hot nor

1. The material in this chapter has been adapted from my article entitled "A Biblical Alternative to Criticism," which first appeared in the *Journal of Pastoral Practice* 10, no. 4 (1992): 15–25.

2. For more about this concept, please see Jay Adams's helpful book *How to Help People Change: The Four-Step Biblical Process* (Grand Rapids: Zondervan, 1986), 111–18.

3. "All Scripture is inspired by God and profitable for teaching, for reproof, for correction, for training in righteousness."

> cold, I will spit you out of My mouth. Because you say, "I am rich, and have become wealthy, and have need of nothing," and you do not know that you are wretched and miserable and poor and blind and naked, I advise you to buy from Me gold refined by fire so that you may become rich, and white garments so that you may clothe yourself, and so that the shame of your nakedness may not be revealed; and eye salve to anoint your eyes, that you may see. Those whom I love, I reprove [*convict*] and discipline; therefore be zealous and repent. (vv. 15–19)

The convicting that He was speaking of in this passage was akin to that of a prosecuting attorney. He was *prosecuting His case* against them. The lukewarm church had deceived itself into believing that it was rich when, in fact, it was poor. It had grown self-sufficient ("I . . . have need of nothing," it said). It was in need of being convinced and convicted of its sin because it did not know that it was "wretched and miserable and poor and blind and naked."

The Laodicean Church did not realize either the extent to which it was sinning or the degree to which it needed to change. As sinful men and women, we do not always realize the extent to which we are sinning. Neither do we always realize the extent to which we must change. So God sends others to help us comprehend these things.

RESPONDING TO REPROOF[4]

Few people realize the abundance of instruction that is contained in Scripture about responses to reproof. Even fewer seem to possess the humility and discipline necessary to develop skills that are commensurate with the instruction. Let's begin by looking at some of the sinful responses to reproof. The book of Proverbs illustrates at least three foolish reactions to reproof. The first is to *spurn* reproof. Wisdom personified, warning about the consequences of not listening to her reproof, says in Proverbs 1:30, "They would not accept my counsel, they

4. Much of the material in this section originally appeared in my book *Teach Them Diligently: How to Use the Scriptures in Child Training* (Stanley, NC: Timeless Texts, 2000).

spurned all my reproof." The word for *spurn* means "to despise" or "to treat with contempt." Many foolish individuals not only despise reproof, they also despise the reprover (see Prov. 9:8; 15:12).

Another sinful response to reproof is to *forsake* it. "He is on the path of life who heeds instruction, but he who ignores reproof goes astray" (Prov. 10:17). The Hebrew word (*azab*) means to leave or abandon (see Prov. 28:13: "He who conceals his transgressions will not prosper, but he who confesses and *forsakes* them will find compassion"). The general attitude of someone who has forsaken reproof is typically that of prideful rejection: "I don't want to have anything to do with being corrected anymore."

The third foolish response to reproof in the book of Proverbs is found in verse 10 of chapter 15. "Grievous punishment is for him who forsakes the way; he who *hates* reproof will die." According to one Hebrew scholar, the verb *to hate* "expresses an emotional attitude toward persons and things which are opposed, detested, despised and with which one wishes to have no contact or relationship. The hated and hating person are considered foes or enemies and are considered odious and utterly unappealing."[5] This proverb says that the person who hates reproof "will die" (will be destroyed). Another proverb (12:1) exclaims the insensibility of the one who hates reproof: "Whoever loves discipline loves knowledge, but he who *hates* reproof is stupid [as dumb as an ox]."

If we do not train our ears to hear God's reproofs, we run the risk of responding to them incorrectly. Examine the following unbiblical but all-too-common approaches to reproof. How many of them have you used in recent weeks?

1. Assuming that, since your reprover has his own personal deficiencies, God will not use him to point out your deficiencies.

Isaiah 9 gives an interesting account of God using the ungodly nation of Assyria to chastise His people . . . and then turning around and punishing Assyria for its own sins.

5. R. Laird Harris, *Theological Wordbook of the Old Testament* (Chicago: Moody Press, 1980), 2:880.

The nation of Israel forgot whom it served, and it pridefully asserted its own power and authority. God got ready to step in and remind His people that He is in control (Isa. 9:8–17).

Assyria, after defeating Israel, turned around and insisted that it was stronger than Israel, Judah, Samaria, and all the nations and their gods—including the true God, who was, of course, watching all of this play out, and who said,

> Woe to Assyria, the rod of My anger
> And the staff in whose hands is My indignation,
> I send it against a godless nation
> And commission it against the people of My fury
> To capture booty and to seize plunder,
> And to trample them down like mud in the streets.
> Yet it does not so intend,
> Nor does it plan so in its heart,
> But rather it is its purpose to destroy
> And to cut off many nations.
> For it says, "Are not my princes all kings?
> Is not Calno like Carchemish,
> Or Hamath like Arpad,
> Or Samaria like Damascus?
> As my hand has reached to the kingdoms of the idols,
> Whose graven images were greater than those of Jerusalem and Samaria,
> Shall I not do to Jerusalem and her images
> Just as I have done to Samaria and her idols?" (Isa. 10:5–11)

But God will not be silent. He may use sinful nations (or people) to rebuke His own people, but that doesn't mean that He doesn't see their sin too.

> So it will be that when the Lord has completed all His work on Mount Zion and on Jerusalem, He will say, "I will punish the fruit of the arrogant heart of the king of Assyria and the pomp of his haughtiness." For he [Assyria] has said,

"By the power of my hand and by my wisdom I did this,
For I have understanding;
And I removed the boundaries of the peoples
And plundered their treasures,
And like a mighty man I brought down their inhabitants,
And my hand reached to the riches of the peoples like a nest,
And as one gathers abandoned eggs, I gathered all the earth;
And there was not one that flapped its wing or opened its beak or
chirped."

Is the axe to boast itself over the one who chops with it?
Is the saw to exalt itself over the one who wields it?
That would be like a club wielding those who lift it,
Or like a rod lifting him who is not wood.
Therefore the Lord, the God of hosts, will send a wasting disease
among his stout warriors;
And under his glory a fire will be kindled like a burning flame.
And the light of Israel will become a fire and his Holy One a flame,
And it will burn and devour his thorns and his briars in a single day.
And He will destroy the glory of his forest and of his fruitful garden,
both soul and body,
And it will be as when a sick man wastes away.
And the rest of the trees of his forest will be so small in number
That a child could write them down. (Isa. 10:12–19)

For a short time, at least, it seemed that Israel would learn the lesson that relying on themselves or on the false gods of other nations would not be to their benefit. God can use anyone He chooses to deliver a lesson or a message. He decides the messenger; what matters is whether the message aligns with God's will for us.

In 1 Kings 13, we read of an unnamed prophet who was commanded by God to ride into Bethel and deliver a message to King Jeroboam, and the prophet was given a rather unusual instruction: "You shall not eat bread, nor drink water, nor return by the same way you came" (v. 9 NJKV). The prophet obeyed and refused more than one invitation to partake of food.

On his way back, the man of God stopped to rest under an oak tree. There another, older prophet, who had heard what happened in Bethel, sought the man of God and invited him home for a meal. The invitation was declined, as the man of God cited the divine declaration. But the older prophet was more persistent: "I too am a prophet as you are, and an angel spoke to me by the word of the LORD, saying, 'Bring him back with you to your house, that he may eat bread and drink water'" (v. 18 NJKV). But, the text continues, "He was lying to him" (v. 18 NIV).

Think about that. Here is a man of God lying to another man of God with a lie that misrepresented God Himself—a deliberate, premeditated, blatant deception that was designed to contradict the Word of God and to lead another man into disobedience. Do you think that God would resort to using such a scoundrel to communicate a rebuke? First Kings 13:20–24 shows the rest of the story: God chose to rebuke the man of God through the lying prophet, and a lion killed him for his disobedience to the clear word of God.

God certainly did use a nation with major character flaws to reprove His people, along with a man who was dishonest to chastise one of His prophets, and there is no reason to believe that He would not use such a person, or another type of imperfect source, to do this today.

"But didn't you explain earlier that we should first take the beam out of our own eye before we attempt to remove the speck from our brother's eye?" I did. But that instruction is given to the reprover, not to the reproved. You may not use character flaws in your reprover's life as an excuse for despising, rejecting, or hating reproof.

2. Thinking that if your reprover has a poor attitude when he reproves you, you don't have to listen.

Do you remember the account of Shimei, who cursed King David?

> When King David came to Bahurim, behold, there came out from there a man of the family of the house of Saul whose name was Shimei, the son of Gera; he came out cursing continually as he came. He threw stones at David and at all the servants of King David; and

> all the people and all the mighty men were at his right hand and at his left. Thus Shimei said when he cursed, "Get out, get out, you man of bloodshed, and worthless fellow! The LORD has returned upon you all the bloodshed of the house of Saul, in whose place you have reigned; and the LORD has given the kingdom into the hand of your son Absalom. And behold, you are *taken* in your own evil, for you are a man of bloodshed!" (2 Sam. 16:5–8)

David took this foul-mouthed, disrespectful insult seriously. When one of his men even offered to do away with this scoundrel—"Then Abishai the son of Zeruiah said to the king, 'Why should this dead dog curse my lord the king? Let me go over now and cut off his head'" (2 Sam. 16:9)—David not only took Shimei seriously, but in fact he actually saw the rebuke as coming directly from God Himself.

> But the king said, "What have I to do with you, O sons of Zeruiah? If he curses, and if the LORD has told him, 'Curse David,' then who shall say, 'Why have you done so?'" Then David said to Abishai and to all his servants, "Behold, my son who came out from me seeks my life; how much more now this Benjamite? Let him alone and let him curse, for the LORD has told him. Perhaps the LORD will look on my affliction and return good to me instead of his cursing this day." So David and his men went on the way; and Shimei went along on the hillside parallel with him and as he went he cursed and cast stones and threw dust at him. (2 Sam. 16:10–13)

You must learn to look beyond the reprover's poor attitude and to determine from Scripture whether the reproof is legitimate. Again, this is not to say that you cannot convict your reprover for his poor attitude after examining his reproof in light of Scripture. The basic issue, however, is that God may be sovereignly using the rebuke (poor attitude notwithstanding) to drive you back to His Word. With Bible in hand (or at least in your heart), you must prayerfully consider the legitimacy of each admonition.

3. Viewing the reproof as too small a concern.

Some of the most intense conflicts occur over the most seemingly inconsequential matters.

God is concerned with how we handle the little things: "He who is faithful in what is least is faithful also in much; and he who is unjust in what is least is unjust also in much" (Luke 16:10). Therefore, you should consider not the smallness of the offense but its sinfulness. If what you are being reproved for is a transgression of God's law, regardless of how small it is, the reproof is valid. You cannot rightly overlook it on the basis of relative insignificance.

4. Failing to focus on the attitude to which your reprover is reacting.

For all of Job's critical analysis of what the Lord was doing to him, he failed to see (as Elihu ultimately explained) that his self-justifying attitude was the real problem.

> Then these three men ceased answering Job, because he was righteous in his own eyes. But the anger of Elihu the son of Barachel the Buzite, of the family of Ram burned; against Job his anger burned because he justified himself before [or "more than"] God. (Job 32:1–2)

When the prophet Samuel was delayed after a battle, he came into the camp of Israel and was surprised to discover that King Saul had not had all the spoil destroyed, but had kept the best of the livestock. When questioned, King Saul self-righteously explained that he had kept some to offer sacrifices to God. Not bothering to question whether the excuse was a last-minute, self-protecting lie (in other words, not being distracted and focusing on a superficial but secondary issue), the prophet rebuked him for a deeper matter: thinking that he could buy off God. "Samuel said, 'Has the Lord as much delight in burnt offerings and sacrifices as in obeying the voice of the Lord? Behold, to obey is better than sacrifice, and to heed than the fat of rams'" (1 Sam. 15:22; cf. Mark 12:33).

Matthew 7:21–23 shows us that more important than the action is the motive behind the action, when Jesus explained,

> Not everyone who says to Me, "Lord, Lord," will enter the kingdom of heaven, but he who does the will of My Father who is in heaven will enter. Many will say to Me on that day, "Lord, Lord, did we not prophesy in Your name, and in Your name cast out demons, and in Your name perform many miracles?" And then I will declare to them, "I never knew you; depart from Me, you who practice lawlessness."

When a wise person is reproved for things he has said or done, he will examine his life and will look beyond the surface problem to determine whether there are underlying habit patterns or attitudes that ought to be replaced with biblical ones. Sadly, this concept is perhaps practiced least often in the home, between husband and wife and between parent and child.

DETECTING UNDERLYING ATTITUDES

Our minds have been compared to computers in some ways—they are constantly storing information and classifying it into categories. As we saw with Juliet and the spoiled dinner, when a certain number of unpleasant or painful actions are inflicted upon us by a particular member of our family, a buzzer in our head goes off and our computer displays the file of offenses that are each categorized under their corresponding headings. There, the updated offense pops up in full color on the screen of our minds. But the Bible forbids us to keep lists such as these, even in our minds, for 1 Corinthians 13:5 states that love "does not impute [keep a running account of] evil."

This dynamic—to remember past offenses categorically—is all too "common to man" (see 1 Cor. 10:13). A document dump of past offenses isn't a good way to approach a relative or friend; but, if someone does it to us, even their bad approach should motivate us to look for those kinds of sinful attitudes in us that may have triggered such a display in the mind of our reprover—especially if that reprover is someone who lives with us and knows us better than most others do. See if you can identify the underlying attitudes behind the following sets of reproofs (i.e., if you can tell what problem the items in each set have in common).

A. Set number one (husband):
   1. Regularly "forgetting" to take the kitchen trash out to the bin in the garage
   2. Spending hours in front of the television (or some other screen) night after night instead of attending to the spiritual needs of his children
   3. Making excuses to avoid or to unnecessarily postpone the conversation that his wife has been wanting to have about her ongoing depression

B. Set number two (wife):
   1. Including personal purchases in an expense report
   2. Failing to report all of her income from her part-time job to the IRS
   3. Buying organic grapes but choosing the code for a cheaper variety at the self-checkout

C. Set number three (preteen son):
   1. A pattern of finding fault with every teacher
   2. Sarcastic rejoinders when his mother tells him to clean up his room
   3. Determining that he is not going to join the new church that his family is attending because it believes in church discipline

The husband's underlying attitude, in the first set of reproofs, is *laziness*. The wife in the second set has a problem with *stealing*. The third set of behaviors shows a consistent *problem submitting to authority*. By learning to "read between the lines" in this manner, you will be better prepared to respond to your reprover and will save yourself from having to face similar reproofs in the future.

5. Justifying (excusing) your behavior.

Perhaps one of my most important tasks as a biblical counselor is to identify and correct the many excuses that counselees offer to justify their irresponsible, unbiblical behavior. Here are a few of the most common ones, accompanied by a typical remedial comeback:

> Counselee: "I can't."
> Counselor: "You can't say 'can't' as a Christian. The Bible says that you can do all things through Him who strengthens you. Please don't say, 'I can't'; say, 'I will' or 'I won't.'"
>
> Counselee: "You can't teach an old dog new tricks."
> Counselor: "That may be true of dogs, but you are not a dog. You are a Christian, and God says that you can change at any age. You therefore must change any behavior that is inconsistent with the character of the Lord Jesus Christ."
>
> Counselee: "If I told my parents the truth, it would hurt them too much."
> Counselor: "Telling your parents the truth may very well hurt them, but not nearly as much as if they caught you telling a lie. Telling the truth may hurt for a while, but telling a lie will hurt longer and more intensely and will have more consequences. That is one reason why God forbids you to do it."
>
> Counselee: "You can't expect me to do that, because I didn't have a role model growing up."
> Counselor: "You may not have had a role model as you were growing up, but now that you are a believer you have *the* role model: the Lord Jesus. God expects you to learn how to do this because He has commanded you to do it. God has not asked you to do anything without first promising [in Philippians 2:13] to provide you with the wisdom, the ability, and even the desire to do it."
>
> Counselee: "I know that I should have done my counseling homework, but I was so busy this week that I just didn't have time to do it."

> Counselor (opening the file drawer of his desk and reaching in as if to grasp a handful of something): "I don't have any 'whiffle dust' to sprinkle on you that will instantly transform you into the image of Christ. God doesn't work that way. God changes your behavior from the inside out as you work on your own salvation with fear and trembling. Change is hard for you and for me; but there is something harder than changing, and that is not changing! The way of the transgressor is hard. The choice is yours: hard work for a while, or a hard way for life. Which will it be?"

What kinds of excuses do you use when people attempt to convict you of sin? Perhaps there were extenuating circumstances, perhaps you had a "logical reason" for your sin, perhaps someone provoked you, but your reprover will likely not be interested in understanding these things until after you've acknowledged your own culpability. These "reasons" will be seen as "excuses" until you fully take the hit for your sin.

6. Resorting to an instinctive act of revenge.

Here are some of the most common retaliatory responses to being reproved.

- Pouting (allowing your hurt feelings to prevent you from responding properly)
- Giving your reprover "the silent treatment"
- Reminding your reprover that he is not perfect either
- Blame-shifting (blaming your reprover for provoking you into a sinful response)
- Blowing up (yelling, screaming, stomping, and so on)
- Threatening (blackmailing your reprover into "dropping the charges" by means of fear and intimidation)
- Throwing a temper tantrum
- Other: ________________________________

Next let's consider some righteous responses to reproof. The book of Proverbs gives a vivid picture of the wise person who responds correctly to reproof. In like manner, we'll look at three snapshots of this individual. Wisdom personified again begins by imploring (in verse 23 of chapter 1), "*Turn* to my reproof, behold, I will pour out my spirit on you; I will make my words known to you." The word translated *turn* is the foremost Old Testament term for "repent." It involves the same concept that we looked at earlier in our discussion of repentance: the idea of turning away from evil and turning toward good. A wise man not only turns away from the sin for which he is being reproved, he also turns favorably toward the one who reproves him and, like David, says, "Let the righteous strike me; it shall be a kindness. And let him reprove me; it shall be as excellent oil; let my head not refuse it" (Ps. 141:5 NKJV).

The second proper response is to *regard* reproof. "Poverty and shame will come to him who neglects discipline, but he who *regards* reproof will be honored" (Prov. 13:18). To regard something is to "exercise great care over" it[6] (or to pay careful attention to it). The word may also be translated "to wait upon" or "attend to" someone or something. The clear idea, then, is that a wise person will carefully consider both the charges made against him and any advice about correcting the problem in his life for which he is being reproved. He will not react with defensive pride or dismiss the charges without thorough deliberation.

The third appropriate response to reproof is *listening to* (or *hearing*). "He whose ear *listens* to the life-giving reproof will dwell among the wise" (Prov. 15:31). The word denotes more than the mere ability to comprehend what is being said. Hearing reproof involves not only attending *to* what is being said but also intending to *obey* or *heed* what is being said. Here are some suggestions to improve your hearing.

1. *Thank God.* Your first response should be acknowledging that you are aware of His sovereignty by giving thanks to Him: "In everything give thanks for this is the will of God in Christ Jesus for you" (1 Thess. 5:18).

2. *Ask yourself, "What is my reprover really saying to me?"* This is the biblical alternative to sinful response number four, from earlier in

6. Ibid., 393.

the chapter: failing to focus on the attitude lying behind the words and actions to which your reprover is reacting. "Rebuke is more effective for a wise man than a hundred blows on a fool" (Prov. 17:10). Looking for the truth in what your reprover is saying, whether it involves your wrong attitude or your God-dishonoring habit pattern, is a practical way to put on humility. Unless you are absolutely certain that your reprover is mistaken, it is best to leave "the door ajar" for the possibility that your sinful heart has blinded you from seeing the truth.

3. *Thank your reprover for his reproof (or at least for his willingness to reprove you).* This step not only will communicate your receptivity to the reproof, but also will prepare your brother for more open communication. Keep in mind that when a wise man is reproved, he responds in love: "Rebuke a wise man, and he will love you" (Prov. 9:8). Remember also that an appropriate response on your part enhances the radiance of your character: "Like an earring of gold and an ornament of fine gold is a wise rebuker to an obedient ear" (Prov. 25:12).

4. *Ask yourself, "What message might God be trying to get through to me?"* If your focus is on the attitude of the one who reproves you, you may miss any truth that is apparent in the reproof. If you prayerfully look beyond your reprover's bad attitude and ask God to show you from Scripture whether or not the reproof is valid, you may walk away with new insight into how you can become more Christlike. One of the strongest verses in the whole Bible concerning God's sovereignty addresses the fact that no one can say that anything comes about without God allowing it to happen: "Who is he who speaks, and it comes to pass, when the Lord has not commanded it?" (Lam. 3:37).

5. *If the reproof is legitimate, take steps to correct the problem.* At this point, your responsibility is to implement whatever scriptural solutions are necessary to bring about biblical change. Having heard it, you must become a "doer of the Word" (James 1:22). As we have seen, a biblical solution usually involves replacing the sinful behavior with the biblical alternative to that behavior (putting off and putting on). In other words,

it will not be enough for you simply to stop practicing the wrong you have done. You also must make it your goal (through the enabling of the Holy Spirit) to practice the right that you have not done, so that doing right becomes "second nature" for you (see Eph. 4:22–24).

6. If you have sinned against someone, seek his forgiveness. When we sin, we must take responsibility (including taking the initiative) to make things right.[7] If conflicts are not resolved quickly (especially because someone has not made past offenses right), there is a great potential for both parties to become bitter.

HAVING A GOOD CONSCIENCE

The Bible has much to say about our obligation to strive for a clear conscience. Paul told his Jewish hearers, "I . . . do my best to maintain always a blameless **conscience** both before God and before men" (Acts 24:16, cf. 2 Tim. 1:3). He twice warned Timothy in the same letter about the potential danger of not having a clear conscience.[†]

> But the goal of our instruction is love from a pure heart and a *good conscience* and a sincere faith. For some men, straying from these things, have *turned aside to fruitless discussion.* (1 Tim. 1:5–6)

> This command I entrust to you, Timothy, my son, in accordance with the prophecies previously made concerning you, that by them you fight the good fight, keeping faith and a *good conscience*, which some *have rejected and suffered shipwreck* in regard to their faith. Among

† Several other references to the conscience are mentioned in the book of 1 Timothy, including a sober warning in chapter 4, verses 1–2: "But the Spirit explicitly says that in later times some will fall away from the faith, paying attention to deceitful spirits and doctrines of demons, by means of the hypocrisy of liars seared in their own conscience as with a branding iron."

7. Even when the conflict is not the *result* of our own sin, we often sin *in the process* of resolving the conflict.

> these are Hymenaeus and Alexander, whom I have *handed over to Satan*, so that they will be taught not to blaspheme. (1 Tim. 1:18–20)

It has been said that the essence of a clear conscience is being able to look everyone whom you have ever known in the eye and truthfully say, "I have never knowingly offended you without at least trying to make it right." When we realize that we have sinned against another, we are to "make it right." How do we do that?

Some people believe all that is necessary to "make things right" after sinning against someone is to apologize by saying "I'm sorry." I disagree. Simply saying "I'm sorry" does not thoroughly deal with the offense. You say, "I'm sorry for lying to you." I may respond with, "You sure are sorry! You're one of the sorriest people I've ever met!"

The ball is still up in the air if you only say, "I'm sorry." The loose ends are not tied up biblically. You and the person whom you offended may walk away not knowing whether the issue is resolved (never to be brought up again). But by asking those you have sinned against to forgive you, you secure certain commitments from them that will truly put the offenses behind you both and tie up any loose ends.

When we ask for forgiveness (rather than simply apologizing) and are granted it, we secure for ourselves those three aforementioned promises of forgiveness: (1) "I promise not to bring up the offense again to you." (2) "I promise not to bring up the offense again to anyone else." (3) "I promise not to bring up the offense again to myself (not to dwell on it in my heart)."

I'd like to suggest one approach that you can use when seeking forgiveness from a person you have offended—especially one with whom you are trying to resolve a conflict.

First: Acknowledge that you have sinned.

Let the offended party know that you realize that what you did was wrong.

Example: "I was wrong for the way I spoke to you."

Second: Identify your specific sin by its biblical name.

Using biblical terminology lets the offended party know that you realize that your offense was also a violation of God's Word and therefore a sin against Him.

Example: "When I rudely interrupted you, I answered a matter before I heard it and judged your motives uncharitably."

Third: Acknowledge the harm that your offense caused.

Show remorse for the hurt that your sin has caused.

Example: "I really am sorry that I upset you. It must be frustrating not to be able to finish your thoughts."

Fourth: Identify an alternative, biblical behavior to demonstrate repentance.

One of the best ways to demonstrate that you have repented (changed your mind) is by letting those whom you have offended know that you have thought through a more biblical option than the one for which you are about to ask forgiveness.

Example: "I should have waited until you finished your thoughts before I interrupted you, and then, if I had any questions about your motives, I should have asked you about them rather than presuming to know what they were."

Fifth: Ask for forgiveness.

This step puts the ball in your offender's court and *secures* forgiveness.

Example: "Will you forgive me?"

Since some problems are the result of (or are exacerbated by) our own sins, our ability to thoroughly resolve them biblically is predicated on our humbling ourselves, confessing our faults to those we have sinned against, and securing the promise of forgiveness from them. Think back to your last conflict. To what extent was its resolution hindered because either you or your opponent was not willing (or not quick enough) to seek forgiveness? Now think ahead to your next potential conflict. How much more willing will you be to ask for forgiveness? (How much more swiftly will you do so?)

7. *If you are convinced from Scripture that you have not sinned as the reproof has claimed, wait until your reprover knows that you have spent some time thinking it through, then consider explaining your viewpoint to him in a reasonable fashion.* The apostle Paul had a rather lengthy answer to the Corinthians, who were aware of an accusation that some had made against him: "My answer to those who examine me is this . . ." (1 Cor. 9:3).[8]

If you come to the conclusion that you have not sinned, it *may*[9] be appropriate to communicate this conclusion to your reprover. It may sometimes be wise to suggest going to a biblical mediator, just in case you are mistaken about your culpability in the matter. (At least one of you probably is.) Perhaps something along the lines of the following would be appropriate:

> "I have thought long and hard about your reproof, and, although I would likely do things differently in the future, I honestly cannot see how I've sinned against you. I realize that I may be deceiving myself about this matter, so, if you would like, I would be more than willing to discuss it with Brother So-and-So. Perhaps he could persuade me. Would you be willing to go with me to see him?"

> "Sister, I wanted to get back with you about our conversation last Tuesday. I have been praying for the Lord to convict me about the sin that you believe I have committed against you. I am not yet convinced that I have done anything that requires me to ask for your forgiveness, but

8. Paul's motive here was to vindicate himself not because he cared what people thought about him personally (see 1 Cor. 4:3; 10:33; Gal. 1:10; 1 Thess. 2:4), but rather because he knew that the message of the gospel could be hindered if the false allegations made against him were not refuted. He was concerned more about protecting God's reputation than about protecting his own.

9. I say "may" because you sometimes have the option of "taking it on the chin" or "turning the other cheek" when falsely accused (see Matt. 27:12–14; 1 Cor. 6:7).

> I am very sorry that you were hurt by what I did (or said). I regret not showing you more ____________ in the matter. If I had to do it over again, I would have ____________. Is there anything short of asking forgiveness that I can do to make things right between us? Perhaps if we spoke to Pastor ____________ about it, he would be able to help me to see more clearly how I've sinned."

If the reprover, however, is an authority over you (like a parent, school official, or boss) you may still be biblically obligated to change your behavior, even if the behavior for which you were reproved is not a sin.

Now that you have some guiding principles for receiving reproof, what will you do with them? Could it be that, by virtue of reading this, you have been convicted of not following these precepts in your dealings with others? If so, do not act like the proverbial fool whose chief characteristic is to not listen to instruction. Rather, make a commitment to prayerfully change your habitual miscommunication skills by practicing these biblical communication skills until you are able to speak them fluently.

And, if you are not sure how to evaluate yourself, why not ask those who are closest to you to help you to evaluate how you typically respond to correction or reproof? Ask them if you are more like the wise person who welcomes it or like the fool who despises it. Consider asking them to review this chapter with you in order to help you understand exactly where you do and do not respond biblically when reproved.

8

GETTING TO THE HEART OF CONFLICT

AS WE THINK ABOUT CONFLICT, we are often tempted to consider only who is right, who is wrong, who started it, and so on. But biblically the roots go deeper. We have to look at the heart of our desires—what we want and why. Do we find our greatest pleasure in loving God and loving other people (the two greatest commandments)?

James 4 asks a question and then provides the answer.

> What is the source of quarrels and conflicts among you? Is not the source your pleasures that wage war in your members? You lust and do not have; so you commit murder. You are envious and cannot obtain; so you fight and quarrel. You do not have because you do not ask. You ask and do not receive, because you ask with wrong motives, so that you may spend it on your pleasures. You adulteresses, do you not know that friendship with the world is hostility toward God? Therefore whoever wishes to be a friend of the world makes himself an enemy of God. Or do you think that the Scripture speaks to no purpose: "He jealously desires the Spirit which He has made to dwell in us"? But He gives a greater grace. Therefore it says, "God is opposed to the proud, but gives grace to the humble." Submit therefore to God. Resist the devil and he will flee from you. Draw near to God and He will draw near to you. . . . Humble yourselves in the presence of the Lord, and He will exalt you. (vv. 1–8, 10)

If the focus of our delight is on anything other than God, the object that we are focusing on is likely an idol. If we focus our delight on the object itself, seeing God only with our peripheral vision if at all, then our focus is wrong and we turn an otherwise lawful desire into an idolatrous one. If, on the other hand, we can use our peripheral vision to see and enjoy secondary things that we delight in while keeping our focus "on God, who richly supplies us with all things to enjoy" (1 Tim. 6:17), and if we can use those objects as means to praise our gracious Creator, then we are worshiping God rather than the idolatrous desires in our hearts.

Our ability to discern our desires while we are experiencing intense conflict is difficult. But recognizing the sinful desires of our hearts is a prerequisite to bringing them "captive to the obedience of Christ" (2 Cor. 10:5; cf. Deut. 15:9; Ps. 15:2; Isa. 55:7; Jer. 4:14; Matt. 15:19). "The heart is deceitful more than all else" (Jer. 17:9) and cannot be known apart from the Word of God, which is able to discern its thoughts and motives (Heb. 4:12). The heart's voice is often camouflaged by its own lawful desires. In other words, it's hard to detect wrong thinking because the desires that drive our thoughts often seem legitimate to us, because they are lawful desires that become unlawful only when we long for them *inordinately* (James 1:12–16; 4:1–2).

WHEN DESIRE BEGETS SIN

"Desire when it has conceived," James says, "gives birth to sin" (1:15 ESV). It is one thing to want something but to be content without it. It is quite another to sinfully pressure others into giving us what we want. When we are in the midst of a conflict, however, this is exactly what we are most tempted to do. Our desires give birth to all manner of sinful tactics for pressuring people into doing what we want them to do. We make demands of our opponents, manipulate them by various means (we try to evoke guilt, anger, fear, or some other emotion in their hearts), uncharitably judge their motives, interrupt them, intimidate them, insult them, purposely exaggerate (or otherwise misrepresent) their arguments, attack their character (whether accurately or inaccurately), stall, divert, ignore or avoid answering their questions (or responding to their arguments), falsify or conceal important information (through deception or double-talk), or prematurely terminate the conflict.

If we practice these sinful tactics long enough, they become habits—behaviors that are done regularly, effortlessly, and for the most part unconsciously. But these external "conflict resolution busters" often[1] have their roots in sinful desires. Therefore, before we attempt to improve our conflict resolution skills (to replace our unbiblical approaches to conflict with biblical alternatives), we must identify and begin to dethrone our inordinate desires.

It is often not until you stop and ask yourself specific questions concerning your motives that you can put your finger on exactly what they are. If you have difficulty identifying them, try asking yourself these questions right after your next botched conflict:[2]

What Was I Willing to Sin in Order to Get?

What was it that I wanted so much that I was willing to sin (by using unbiblical forms of communication) in order to get it? The short test for idolatrous desires is how willing I am to sin against God in order to get what I want (or what I do when I am prevented from having it). Ask yourself, "Is there some idolatrous desire in my heart that might tempt me to use sinful approaches to conflict resolution?"

Is it *respect* or *control* or *pleasure*? Does it have to do with your *time* or *money* or *reputation*? Think about the last few conflicts you had that weren't resolved. See if you can retroactively identify what unbiblical desire might have contributed to your part of the dilemma.

What Did I Believe That I Couldn't Be Happy Without?

Discontentment fuels many a conflict. A contented person realizes that God has already provided him with everything necessary to

1. I say "often" but not "always." Sometimes we develop these habits not as a result of specific sinful desires but simply because we have learned them from others—especially those with whom we have regularly had conflicts or whom we have regularly observed in conflict (like our parents).

2. Several in the biblical counseling movement have put forth various self-examination questions in order to help us look into our hearts. Perhaps the most notable is David Powlison, whose book *Seeing with New Eyes: Counseling and the Human Condition Through the Lens of Scripture* (Phillipsburg, NJ: P&R Publishing, 2003) is especially helpful (see esp. 132–40).

be happy.[3] According to 1 Timothy 6:8, we should be content with food and covering. Any temporal gifts above and beyond these are a bonus for which we should be especially grateful. When we are discontent, we not only murmur and complain against God (whose providential dealings with us we disapprove of), but often do so against others—especially against those instruments (or secondary causes) whom He places between us and what we want. The discontentment in our hearts often finds its way out of our mouths (and onto our faces) in various forms, which in turn tempts others to resist our attempts to persuade them to our way of thinking. We, in turn, are tempted to respond to their "unreasonable" resistance with angry incredulity. And the fight is on! A contented heart would prevent many a conflict.

What Was It That I Craved?

An *appetite* is a desire to satisfy some bodily need or craving.[4] The word is also used to describe a strong desire or fondness for something. Our misguided attempts to get others to satisfy our appetites are often the greatest cause of contention in conflict.

What Did I Believe I Had to Have?

Was it really a need, or was it a want? Most people can't distinguish between the two because our culture has synchronized them. We have progressed from saying "I want you to respect me," through "I need you to respect me," to "I have a need for you to respect me." But we don't have as many needs as we typically think we do. Our greatest need, of course, is forgiveness. Beyond this, it is hard to make a case for many other scriptural *needs* besides food and covering.[5] But we often convince ourselves that we need something that we just

3. For a further explanation of this principle, see my booklet *Discontentment: Why Am I so Unhappy?* (Phillipsburg, NJ: P&R Publishing, 2012).

4. The New American Standard Bible translates the common Greek word for desire (*epithumeo*) as *crave* in 1 Corinthians 10:6: "Now these things happened as examples for us, so that we would not crave evil things as they also craved. Do not be idolaters, as some of them were; as it is written, 'The people sat down to eat and drink, and stood up to play'" (vv. 6–7).

5. If we die in an unforgiven state as a result of not having food or covering, we will be in a much worse condition than if our sins were eternally forgiven at the time we died from starvation or exposure.

intensely want. When we convince ourselves that something we *want* is something that we really *need*, we can end up fighting for it with more passion than is warranted and, in so doing, evoking responses from our counterparts (who may not see it as a need) that further frustrate or provoke us.

What Was I Most Worried about (Or Afraid of) Losing?

Fear is another driving force that negatively affects our ability to resolve conflicts God's way. In addition to tempting us to withdraw from conflict, it tempts us to overly protect our territory—to possessively and emotionally defend against the loss of whatever we inordinately love.[6] Fear is often the flip side of idolatry.

Just as there are two sides to a coin, so there are typically two sides to idolatry. The "heads" side says, "Inordinate Desire for Something." The "tails" side of the coin says, "Inordinate Fear of Losing Something." The more that we want something, the greater will be our fear of losing it. People who love money fear losing their wealth. Those who love to be in control fear being unable to control the circumstances and people that surround them. The person who loves pleasure is often afraid of missing out on opportunities to gratify his fleshly desires. Those who "love man's approval" are typically afraid of losing approval (or respect, or favorable opinion) and/or fear being rejected. They are also very afraid of conflict.

Which of My "Rights" Did I Believe Were Being Violated?

It is sometimes difficult for us to see the sinfulness of our desires when we are fighting for what we believe are our "rights." "It's a matter of justice and fairness—of right and wrong," we reason. "I have a *right* to life, liberty, and the pursuit of my own happiness." Is that really what the Bible teaches are the rights of a slave of Christ? John MacArthur describes what it meant to be a slave in biblical times.[7]

6. This exaggerated response often evokes a counter response from our opponent, which hinders a biblical resolution to the dispute.

7. John MacArthur, *Slave: The Hidden Truth about Your Identity in Christ* (Nashville: Thomas Nelson, 2010), 27–28.

> To be a slave was to be in someone else's possession, totally subjugated to one's master in everything. Greek philosopher Aristotle defined a slave as a human being who was considered an article of property, someone who belonged completely to another person.[8] Ancient Rome viewed slaves the same way: "The slave had, in principle, no rights, no legal status whatsoever; he was a chattel owned by his master."[9] As a result, a slave "could be owned and dealt with like any other piece of property. He was [completely] at the mercy of his owner, without rights."[10]

As Christians we are to defend and protect the rights of others;[11] but when it comes to our personal rights, we may sometimes have to surrender them because, as slaves of Christ, we really gave them up when we were redeemed by Him.[12]

Even when we do believe it is biblically appropriate to defend our God-given rights (or our good name, or our theological position), we must be careful not to do so in an ungracious manner. So, in conflict, it is often a good thing to determine what "rights" we think may be at stake, so that we can be sure it is proper to defend or protect them and so that we can be sure that our motives are right before we attempt to do so.

What Was It That I Loved More Than I Love God and My Neighbor?

Love is not always a good thing. Love is the ultimate Christian virtue, but it can also be a vice. There are four different Greek words for *love*. There is the 1 Corinthians 13 *agapao* kind of love, which is the pure and highest kind of self-sacrificing love (although it *is* possible to

8. Aristotle, *Politics*, 1.254a7. W.W. Buckland, in *The Roman Law of Slavery*, noted that "the Roman slave did not possess the attributes which modern analysis regards as essential to personality. Of these, capacity for rights is one, and this the Roman slave had not" ([Union, NJ: Lawbook Exchange, 2000], 3); quoted in MacArthur, *Slave*, 27n5.

9. Pierre Grimal, *The Civilization of Rome*, trans. W. S. Maguinness (London: George Allen, 1963), 499; cited in MacArthur, *Slave*, 27n6.

10. Michael Grant, *The World of Rome* (New York: World Publishing, 1960), 116; cited in MacArthur, *Slave*, 28n7.

11. Even when we are fighting for the rights of others, we can do so with secondary sinful motives (to acquire or maintain a reputation for being a defender of justice, for example). And, of course, we can also resort to all manner of unbiblical forms of communication when we have the best of motives.

12. Of course, this must be balanced with the truth that we do have certain rights as adopted children of God (see 1 Cor. 9:4–12).

corrupt[13]). Then there is the word *phileo*, which is a fond affection for someone or something. The word *storge*, which does not appear in the New Testament except in the alpha privative form (i.e., the negated form: "*un*loving"),[14] is the love that family members have for each other. The word for romantic love, *eros*, does not appear in the New Testament, but it does show up several times in the Septuagint[15] (a Greek translation of the Old Testament from which Jesus quoted).

Both James and John identified loving the world as an evidence of idolatry (1 John 2:15; James 4:4[16]). But the Scriptures also identify a number of other things that a person may love, or desire, or delight in too much. Let's take a look at four of the most common inordinate loves mentioned in the Bible: the love of money, the love of pleasure, the love of approval, and the love of power.

The Love of Money.

> But those who *want to* get rich fall into temptation and a snare and *many foolish and harmful desires* which plunge men into ruin and destruction. For the *love of money* is a root of all sorts of evil, and some by *longing* for it have wandered away from the faith and pierced themselves with many griefs. (1 Tim. 6:9–10)

13. For example, in John 12:43, the word *loved* in the term "loved the approval of men" is *agapao*, as it is in the injunction "Do not *love* the word" in 1 John 2:15.

14. In Romans 1:31 and 2 Timothy 3:3, Paul uses ástorgos (ἄστοργος), "without family love," to describe certain types of unbelievers. According to *Wuest's Word Studies in the Greek New Testament*, "This is the Greek word denoting natural affection, with Alpha, which when prefixed to a word negates its meaning" (Kenneth S. Wuest, *Word Studies in the Greek New Testament* [Grand Rapids: Eerdmans, 1984], Logos Bible Software e-book). Benjamin B. Warfield defines it as follows: it designates "the quiet and abiding feeling within us, which resting on an object as near to us, recognizes that we are closely bound up with it and takes satisfaction in this recognition" ("The Terminology of Love in the New Testament," *The Princeton Theological Review* 16, no. 1 [January 1918]: 4). It is a love that is "a natural movement of the soul—as something almost like gravitation or some other force of blind nature" (ibid., 5). "This is precisely what children and parents feel to one another" (ibid., 7). It is a love of "obligatoriness—if we may use that term in a quasi-natural rather than an openly moral sense; its 'necessity' under the circumstances . . . constitutes the cement by which any natural or social unit is bound together" (ibid., 7–8).

15. As, for instance, in Proverbs 7:18.

16. "You adulteresses, do you not know that friendship with the world is hostility toward God? Therefore whoever wishes to be a friend of the world makes himself an enemy of God." The word *friendship* in this passage is *philia*, a term that can also be translated *love*.

The love of money is not *the root*, as the KJV translators inaccurately translated the anarthrous noun in the original text, but rather *a root*. It is one of a number of root desires identified in the Bible that men inordinately long for (or excessively desire), to their own harm.

The Love of Pleasure.

> He who *loves pleasure* will become a poor man;
> He who loves wine and oil will not become rich. (Prov. 21:17)

> But realize this, that in the last days difficult times will come. For men will be lovers of self, lovers of money . . . *lovers of pleasure* rather than lovers of God. (2 Tim. 3:1, 2, 4)

The root word *pleasure*, from which this rare Greek word is derived, may be a good pleasure or one that is inherently evil. In other words, the term may denote those pleasures that are in and of themselves sinful, or it may indicate those pleasures that become criminal only due to excess and abuse.

The ability to enjoy pleasure is a blessing from God, who "richly supplies us all things to enjoy" (1 Tim. 6:17). But, if we are not careful, we will set our hearts on pleasure to the point of becoming hedonistic (an English word taken from the same Greek word for *pleasure*), not unlike those who are "enslaved to various lusts and pleasures" (Titus 3:3).

The Love of Approval.

> For they [the Pharisees] *loved the approval of men* rather the approval of God. (John 12:43)

> But they [the scribes and the Pharisees] do all their deeds *to be noticed by men;* for they broaden their phylacteries and lengthen the tassels of their garments. They *love the place of honor* at banquets and *the chief*

> *seats* in the synagogues, and *respectful greetings* in the market places, and *being called Rabbi by men.* (Matt. 23:5–7)

It is not necessarily wrong to desire the approval of others; otherwise, for a parent to praise or commend his child would be to necessarily tempt him to sin. But, as with money and pleasure (or anything else that is not intrinsically evil), to long for approval to such an extent that it develops into a love for approval turns a lawful desire into a sinful desire. The scribes and the Pharisees were approval addicts. That is, their desire for the approval of others was so inordinate that they were in bondage to it (see 2 Peter 2:19). They wanted approval so much that they spent much of their time and effort doing things that would bring them glory from people. Even acts that were religious in nature (like praying and fasting and giving) were done in order to gain man's approval (Matt. 6:1–16.).

The Love of Power (or Control). We have many examples in Scripture of those who exercised idolatrous desires for power or control. The apostles themselves were not above such attempts, when they asked Jesus to rain down fire from heaven to destroy a city that had rejected them, or when they wrangled over which of them would sit at Jesus' right or left hand in eternity—or even when they smugly waited for Him to declare Himself King, figuring that they would be His vice-regents. Simon the magician was so amazed by the apostles' power that he offered money for a share in the Holy Spirit (Acts 8:9–24).

For a church leader to have the desire to manage those individuals over whom the Lord has given him ecclesiastical authority is not a sin, nor is it improper to take one's authority as a parent or a supervisor seriously. But when the desire to oversee that which has been duly entrusted to you by God turns into "*lording it over* those allotted to your charge" (1 Peter 5:3), then that desire has turned into an idolatrous love of power.

Other inordinate loves are identified in the Bible.[17] So we must not

17. For example, the Bible speaks of those who love sleep (Prov. 20:13), those who love food (Prov. 21:17), those who love silver and abundance (Eccl. 5:10), those who love darkness (John 3:19), and those who love their own lives (John 12:25).

be deceived into thinking that we are free from idolatrous lust simply because we don't struggle with any of the aforementioned items. John Calvin said that the heart is "a perpetual factory[18] of idols."[19]

I like the way that Puritan pastor Richard Baxter expresses the danger of loving things too much.

> Remember that too much love hath the *present* trouble of too much care, and the *future* trouble of too much grief, when you come to part with what you love. Nothing more createth care and grief to us than inordinate love. You foreknow that you must part with it; and will you *now* be so glued to it that *then* it may tear your flesh and heart?[20]

As we have seen, one of the best evidences that we love something more than we love God is our willingness to sin against God either *in order to acquire what we want,* or *because we cannot acquire it,* or even *to keep it.* When the latter occurs, we may become angry. By identifying biblically the specific sinful desire that is associated with our anger, we can correct our anger not only *externally* (as seen in temper tantrums, sarcasm, vengeance, and so on), but also *internally,* in our hearts where the anger resides (as seen in idolatry such as the love of pleasure, love of money, love of praise, and so on).

In What Did I Trust More Than I Trusted in God?

Depending on yourself more than on God when you are in conflict is a foolish and dangerous thing to do. The arrogance that disposes you to trust in your own wisdom more than in God's may be displayed before your opponent in ways unbeknownst to you. There is already a fine enough line between confidence and arrogance. The former is often misinterpreted for the latter. When we enter conflicts depending more on our own intellect or verbal prowess than on God's enabling

18. The word that he used was *forge*—that is, a place where idols of all sizes and shapes could be hammered out.

19. John Calvin, *Institutes of the Christian Religion,* ed. John T. McNeill, trans. Ford Lewis Battles (1960; repr., Louisville: Westminster John Knox Press, 2006), 108.

20. Richard Baxter, *Baxter's Practical Works,* vol. 1, *A Christian Directory* (Ligonier, PA: Soli Deo Gloria Publications, 1990), 277, emphasis added.

power, we invariably tip the scales in the minds of our opponents, who conclude not that we are confident but rather that we are proud (and are in need of being humbled).

In What Did I Most Delight?

To delight in something is to seek one's happiness in that something. "Delight yourself [seek your happiness] in the LORD; and He will give you the desires of your heart" (Ps. 37:4). We often enter conflicts seeking to walk away from them with our delights still intact. It is our will (what we want) that is preeminent. But we should delight to do God's will (what He wants) when we are in conflict. The psalmist David wrote, "I delight to do Your will, O my God" (Ps. 40:8). Again, we should assume that, as a general rule, what God wants from us when in conflict with other believers is that a peaceful resolution be found in a relatively short period of time without our sinning in the process. When we lose sight of this, our wants come to the forefront of our hearts, and we increase our likelihood of dishonoring God because we are delighting (seeking our happiness) in the wrong thing.

In What Did I Seek My Refuge (Relief)?

Where we turn for relief and comfort when we are under stress may be another indication of the level of our idolatry. It is certainly not wrong to enjoy or take a certain amount of comfort in the lawful pleasures that God has freely given us to enjoy. The book of Ecclesiastes makes this clear—in light of the vanity of this sin-cursed world, Solomon encourages us to stop and smell the roses that God has provided to encourage us along the way.

> Go then, eat your bread in happiness and drink your wine with a cheerful heart; for God has already approved your works. Let your clothes be white all the time, and let not oil be lacking on your head. Enjoy life with the woman whom you love all the days of your fleeting life which He has given to you under the sun; for this is your reward in life and in your toil in which you have labored under the sun. (Eccl. 9:7–9)

Richard Baxter also explained the extent to which God gave us these temporal enjoyments.

> Remember to what ends all worldly things were made and given you. . . . They are the provender of our bodies; our traveling furniture and helps; our inns and solacing company in the way; they are some of God's love-tokens, some of the lesser pieces of his coin, and bear his image and superscription. They are drops from the rivers of the eternal pleasures; to tell the mind by way of the senses how good the Donor is, and how amiable; and what higher delights there are for souls; and to point us to the better things which these foretell. They are messengers from heaven, to testify of our Father's love, and duty; and to bear witness against sin and bind us faster to obedience. . . . They are the tools by which we must do much of our Master's work. They are means by which we may refresh our brethren, and express our love to one another, and our love to our Lord and Master in his service. They are our Master's stock, which we must trade with. . . . These are the uses to which God gives us outward mercies. Love them thus, and delight in them, and use them thus, and spare not; yea, seek them thus, and be thankful for them. But when the creatures are given for so excellent a use, will you debase them all by making them only the fuel of your lusts, and the provisions for your flesh? And will you love them, and dote upon them in these base respects; while you utterly neglect their most noble use?[21]

So, while it is fine to gratefully enjoy lawful temporal pleasures with a heart that is filled with gratitude to God for His gracious provision, we must take care not to look to these things, in and of themselves, as the source of our delight or to use them as the primary means through which we comfort ourselves in the midst of life's pressures. In other words, if they serve as a mechanism that focuses our minds on the One who has freely given us all things to enjoy, so that we ultimately worship God in the process of enjoying these things, that is well and

21. Ibid., 220.

good. But if our focus is fixed on these *created things* so that we seek our respite or comfort in them rather than in the *Creator*, we will be guilty of idolatry.

"What does this have to do with conflict resolution?" you may be wondering. To those who would rather not face the stress of conflict, the thought of avoiding (or prematurely terminating) a conflict in the hope of finding comfort elsewhere can be a real temptation. "I would rather be eating (or fishing or golfing or shopping or sleeping or watching the game) than arguing with so and so" is often the thought driven by such a lust for comfort or relief. On the other hand, if we are looking to God as the primary source of our consolation and respite, we will not tend to avoid certain conflicts because we know and anticipate the satisfaction that results from doing God's will (if His will is for us to participate in them). We know, in other words, that after the conflict our consciences will be at rest and that we will have peace and rest as a result of doing God's will even if the conflict is not effectively resolved—but especially if it is resolved in a God-honoring way.

What Did I Hope to Accomplish During the Conflict?

What exactly were you fighting for? Try to put it in biblical terms. Was it your honor—your good name and reputation—or God's (or your neighbor's)? Was it *your* will you were fighting for or *God's* will? Was it something temporal or something eternal? Was it the acquisition of money, pleasure, power, or praise? Was it to humiliate or embarrass your opponent? Was it to "teach him a lesson"? Was it to thwart him somehow? If so, why did he need thwarting? Were you attempting to change your opponent's mind? Did it really need changing? Were you trying to appeal your opponent's unwise decision (asking him to change his mind based on further information)? Was it right for you to do so? If it was, did you prolong the appeal process beyond what you should have? Did you simply refuse to accept a "no" answer? Were you more troubled about your own sins or about those of your opponent? By answering these questions, you may discover that you had both sinful and righteous reasons for fighting (or for running away from the fight).

On Whose Stage Was I Performing?

"Was I more concerned with the internal thoughts and motives of my heart, which only God saw in the midst of the conflict, or with how my opponent was going to judge me based on what I said, how effectively I argued, and whether or not I persuaded him to my way of thinking?" "Did the words that I spoke and the posture that I took during the conflict glorify God or embarrass Him?" As I have said, in another place, about the person whose goal is to please God rather than man,

> He is performing on God's stage for an audience of One. Though many others may be watching, he considers the applause of God to be better and sweeter, more thunderous and more glorious than the applause of all the kings and rulers, celebrities, and dignitaries he will ever hope to meet. He knows that mere humans can only evaluate him subjectively and superficially by what they see with their eyes, but God will evaluate him righteously by what He sees in his heart.[22]

How Much Did Fear, Jealousy, Selfish Ambition, Hatred, or Bitterness Enter the Picture?

For the moment, try to answer this question based primarily on what you have already read. I will address these more thoroughly in the next chapter, as *responses* to conflict, but they are certainly also (if not first and foremost) motives.

The preceding questions were all designed to help you to evaluate past conflicts. The Bible says, "The heart of the righteous ponders how to answer" (Prov. 15:28). This involves pondering not just our words, but also our motives, in light of the Word of God, which is able to discern the "thoughts and intentions of the heart" (Heb. 4:12 ESV). Remember what Jesus said about what is in our hearts: be it good or bad, it will sooner

22. Lou Priolo, *Pleasing People: How Not to Be an "Approval Junkie"* (Phillipsburg, NJ: P&R Publishing, 2007), 141.

or later make its way to our tongues and out of our mouths. So here are the questions reworded for use *prior to your next conflict.*[23]

- ☐ Is there something that I want so much that I might be willing to sin (by using unbiblical forms of communication) in order to get it?
- ☐ Is there something that I believe I cannot be happy without? (With what am I discontent?)
- ☐ What is it that I am craving? (What appetite might tempt me to sin?)
- ☐ Is there something that I believe I have to have? (Is there some "want" that I might be misinterpreting as a need?)
- ☐ Is there something that I am worried about (or afraid of) losing?
- ☐ Which of my rights do I believe are being violated?
- ☐ Is there something that I love more than I love God and my neighbor?
- ☐ Do I trust (am I putting my hope in) something other than (or more than) the Lord?
- ☐ Is there something that I am delighting in (seeking my happiness in) more than I am in the Lord?
- ☐ In what am I seeking more refuge, comfort, or relief than in the Lord?
- ☐ What am I hoping to accomplish as a result of the conflict?
- ☐ On whose stage am I intending to perform?
- ☐ To what extent might fear, jealousy, selfish ambition, hatred, or bitterness be clouding my judgment in this matter?

You may want to consider other common motives as you prayerfully examine what was in your heart during conflict. Those on the left (some of which we have looked at before) are desires that are inherently wrong. Those on the right are desires that, although not inherently

23. Of course, not all conflicts are planned. Being familiar with these questions may help you to evaluate your motives on the fly during future spontaneous conflicts.

wrong, may be desired too intensely and consequently may sabotage your peacemaking efforts.

Unlawful Desires	**Lawful Desires**
I wanted to control (manipulate) my opponent.	I wanted to defend the truth.
I wanted to intimidate my opponent.	I wanted to convict my opponent.
I wanted to disgrace my opponent.	I wanted to biblically silence my opponent.
I wanted to get even.	I wanted to have a fair hearing.
I wanted something that belonged to my opponent.	I wanted to be respected.
I wanted to hurt my opponent.	I wanted to be understood.
I wanted to "teach my opponent a lesson."	I wanted to be properly appreciated.
I wanted to protect my own selfish interests.	I wanted to protect another.
I wanted to divert my opponent's attention.	I wanted to protect myself from my opponent.

GOOD MOTIVES

"Beyond glorifying God," you may be wondering, "are there any other proper motives to have during interpersonal conflicts?" Sure there are—lots of them—too many to explore in this chapter. I will mention only a few. These should probably be considered "submotives," because they are subordinate to the ultimate one of honoring and pleasing the Lord. Here are just a dozen.[24] There is some overlapping in these moti-

24. These are in addition to some of the "lawful desires" mentioned above.

vations. They all belong under the same roof of "glorifying God," but the walls between some of the rooms of this house do not go all the way to the ceiling.

I want to obey a particular scriptural directive that requires the initiation of a confrontation on my part. Jesus said, "If you love Me, you will keep My commandments" (John 14:15). He has given us several commandments that have to do with confrontation (see Matt. 18:15–18; Luke 17:3; Gal. 6:1).

I want to find a biblical (God-honoring) resolution to the conflict as quickly as possible with a minimum amount of sin on the part of either contestant (see Prov. 17:14; 20:3; Rom. 12:18; Eph. 4:3, 25–32; Col. 3:15; James 3:17–18). Conflicts are inevitable, but followers of Jesus Christ must contend according to His rules. For us, it is a matter of not only whether we win or lose but how we play the game (or fight the battle).

I want to demonstrate the love of Christ to an opponent (see 1 Cor. 10:31–33; 13:4–7). Paul exhorted the Corinthians, "Let all that you do be done in love" (1 Cor. 16:14). This applies to having interpersonal conflicts as well. Win or lose, we must endeavor to leave a memorable mark on the minds of our opponents that will hopefully draw them to the Savior (or, if they already are believers, will cause them to glorify God because of our manner of contending).

I want to be like my heavenly Father, who is kind to sinful men (see Matt. 5:38–48). As our Heavenly Father shows love to His enemies (sending His sun to shine on them), so we are to show love to our enemies—even when we are in conflict with them.

I want to win an opponent to Christ (see Acts 6:24–29; 13:43; 18:4–6; 1 Cor. 9:19–23). Biblical evangelism can take many forms. Apologetics (the science and skill of defending one's faith) often involves conflict. The erroneous notions and presuppositions that unbelievers hold are to be winsomely and persuasively challenged.

I want to persuade someone to a more biblical way of thinking (see Acts 13:43; 18:4–6; 19:8; 2 Cor. 5:11–15). "Iron sharpens iron, so one man sharpens another" (Prov. 27:17). Sparks usually fly when iron clashes with iron, but the intended result is the sharpening of both parties.

I want to provoke someone to love and good works (see Heb. 10:24). To provoke someone is not necessarily a sin. "Let us consider how to stimulate [provoke] one another to love and good deeds." The word *provoke* also connotes sharpening—perhaps to suggest the idea of prodding or spurring someone on who might be a bit sluggish.

I am provoked to say something in response to someone's sin (see Job 32; Acts 17:16–17). Paul was provoked (to righteous indignation) as he observed the city of Athens given over to idolatry, so he opened his mouth and reasoned (argued his case for the gospel) with the Jews and God-fearing men in the synagogue and in the market places.

I want to defend the Truth (see Acts 9:21; 18:28; 1 Thess. 2:2; Jude 3). Standing up for the gospel can be dangerous. But it is sometimes necessary. In 1 Thessalonians 2:2, Paul reminded the church that "after we had already suffered and been mistreated in Philippi, as you know, we had the boldness in our God to speak to you the gospel of God amid much opposition." The word for *opposition* is a favorite word of Paul's (see Phil. 1:29–30; Col. 2:1; 1 Tim. 6:12; 2 Tim. 4:7). It means strife, contention, a contest for victory, or the mastery of an athletic skill such as running, boxing, or wrestling. Paul applies the word to the evangelical contest against the enemies of man's salvation.[25]

I want to defend or protect another (see 1 Sam. 19:4–7; 20:32; 22:14–15; Est. 4:13–14; Prov. 24:11–12; 31:8–9; John 7:51; Acts 7:22–25; 1 John 3:16–17). Although we risk upsetting those who abuse or unjustly accuse others,

25. Spiros Zodhiates, *The Complete Word Study Dictionary: New Testament* (Chattanooga: AMG Publishers, 2000), Logos Bible Software e-book, Strong's number G73.

it is sometimes necessary for us to speak up on their behalf. Indeed, not to do so is cowardly.

I long to obtain more heavenly rewards (see Luke 6:22–24; Col. 3:23–24). It may *seem* selfish, but it's not necessarily wrong for us to be motivated by the prospect of reward. Indeed, something is wrong if we're *not* motivated by reward. To resist wanting rewards is pseudospiritual. It goes against the grain of the way God created us and the way He sometimes motivates us.[26]

I delight (take pleasure) in the Lord and in doing His will (see Pss. 37:4; 40:8). Christians experience a certain pleasure (a joy or happiness) when they know that they are doing what God asks them to do. Of course, they know it is only His grace that enables them to do it, but it is still a marvelous thing that they are able to accomplish His will in a given circumstance.

It is not always easy to be a peacemaker, but those who are willing to do so are blessed (see Prov. 12:20; Matt. 5:9). Much more could be said about what impels us to fight. But here's the bottom line: as a rule, we are wrongly motivated when we fight primarily because we aren't getting what we want, and we are rightly motivated when we fight because God isn't getting what He wants. We know what He wants in many circumstances because He has revealed His will to us in Scripture. So, the next time you are up for a fight (or are in the midst of one), ask yourself, "For whom am I fighting?"

26. For more about this, see Randy Alcorn's helpful book *In Light of Eternity: Perspectives on Heaven* (Colorado Springs: WaterBrook Press, 1999).

9

UNBIBLICAL RESPONSES TO CONFLICT: INTERNAL

THE EFFECT OF SIN on our minds is great. It permeates our thoughts, desires, volition, reasoning ability, and emotions—and even our sense of humor. Consequently, in innumerable ways, our wicked and deceitful hearts can sabotage our attempts to resolve conflicts in God-honoring ways. In this chapter we will take a look at some of the internal issues that hinder the conflict resolution process.

You will see a check box (☐) in front of each attitude described in this chapter. As you continue reading, place a check next to any attitude that you believe you routinely manifest when you are in a conflict with others. Think especially about the conflicts that you have with those closest to you (your spouse, parents, children, working associates, close friends, and so on).

Let's begin with some of the unbiblical postures and mind-sets that people sometimes take as they approach a problem.[1]

☐ The first one is that of a *Conqueror*. This is the mind-set that is most like a cocky lawyer. It says, essentially, "You have no case. The sooner you acknowledge this, the sooner your misery will end. Just

1. When we repeatedly resort to the same unbiblical approaches to conflict resolution, we habituate ourselves to them over time. They become locked into our thought patterns and can become a dominant part of our character.

admit that you are wrong and I am right, and the conflict will be over." This person may resort to intimidation and manipulation in order to win the argument. Diotrephes, the proud, punitive man in 3 John 9–10 who loved preeminence, rejected authority, and presumptuously assumed authority over others, is exemplary of this approach to resolving conflict.

☐ Akin to the Conqueror is the *Dominator*. This is the person who selfishly controls the conversation by talking incessantly. Like the proverbial fool who "does not delight in understanding, but only in revealing his own mind" (Prov. 18:2), he is quick to speak and slow to listen. His opinions are what matter most—and they protrude from his conversations like a small animal protrudes from the body of the otherwise sleek python that just swallowed it whole.

☐ Another posture that some people take is the *Peace Lover* (see John 12:42–43).[2] This is a person who hates conflict so much that he yields to the other side not because he is persuaded by sound reason but because he is afraid. The essence of this mind-set is, "Whatever you want is fine with me. Please don't get upset or do anything to reject or embarrass me."

☐ Then there is the *Dismisser*. This style of conflict resolution manifests a dismissive attitude about the issue at hand. "You are making a mountain out of a molehill. This issue isn't worth fussing about. In fact, it's so trivial that I'm not going to waste my time discussing it." Paul told Titus, "Let no one disregard you" (Titus 2:15). The word for "disregard" is περιφρονέω (*periphroneo).* It literally means to "think around" someone. Paul exhorted Titus not to allow others to have a dismissive attitude toward him. The Dismisser disregards (thinks around, or thinks lightly of) the opinions, values, and feelings of those with whom he is in a conflict.

2. As mentioned previously, the peace lover should not be confused with the peacemaker, who, rather than avoiding necessary conflicts, is willing to initiate them when biblically required to do so.

☐ Some people are *Evaders*. They don't necessarily have a dismissive attitude, but through a variety of means (trying to change the focus of the conversation,[3] answering questions with questions,[4] redefining terms so as to promote ambiguity,[5] and so on), they selfishly attempt to dodge important issues. Abraham neglected to tell both Pharaoh and Abimelech that Sarah was his wife (Gen. 12; 20:1–18) in order to avoid what he thought would be deadly conflicts.

☐ Others are *Blame Shifters*. This is literally the oldest trick in the Book. "The woman whom You gave to be with me, she gave me from the tree, and I ate" (Gen. 3:12). This posture attempts to dodge personal culpability by fallaciously shifting the blame from oneself to another person or thing.

☐ And let's not forget the *Manipulator*. He uses a variety of techniques (and postures)[6] to make you feel guilty. Even if your arguments are sound, he will do his best to make you believe that you are wrong for wanting him to see things your way. A number of people attempted to manipulate Christ (see Matt. 20:20–23; Luke 2:41–49; 6:1–5; 10:38–42; 20:19–26). No one ever succeeded! We will take a closer look at manipulation (and blame shifting) in the next chapter.

PROBLEMATIC PEOPLE FROM THE PROVERBS

The book of Proverbs identifies several types of individuals who are especially prone to mishandling conflict. (The common denominator across the lives of these individuals is found in several Hebrew words generally rendered as *strife* or *contention*.) When an individual

3. See John 4:17–19.
4. See Genesis 4:9.
5. See Genesis 3:1.
6. It is not only the Conqueror who manipulates. The Surrenderer, the Evader, and the Dismisser can all use manipulation in their various selfish approaches to conflict resolution. For more information about this problem, see the author's booklet *Manipulation: Knowing How to Respond* (Phillipsburg, NJ: P&R Publishing, 2008).

continually gives himself over to a particular sin, he eventually becomes bound by that sin. At some point the individual may rightly be categorized according to the name of the sin that he allows to master him.[7] The sin penetrates into and affects other areas of his life.

Knowing when you are up against one of these individuals in conflict will be advantageous to you.[8] For the most part, you will know up front that your chances of bringing your conflict with such a person to a peaceful resolution are very slight. As a rule, the best thing you can do is to warn him of the consequences of his actions and stay out of his way.[9] But more importantly, you do not want to be like any of these characters. For, if you are, your ability to resolve conflict will be greatly diminished.

☐ *The hot-tempered person.* "A hot-tempered man stirs up strife, but the slow to anger calms a dispute" (Prov. 15:18). The root of this Hebrew word means "to be hot." It is typically used to convey the concept of an inner emotional heat that rises and is fanned to varying degrees.[10] This person is often passionate about many things, but his intense passion frequently expresses itself in sinful anger. We sometimes refer to him as a "hothead." The problem with this character is that he *stirs up* strife. What comes to mind when you hear the phrase "stir up"? I like to imagine a beaker filled with water and sand that has been lying perfectly still for twenty-four hours. All the sand is lying peacefully at the bottom of the glass. The water that lies above the sand looks good enough to drink. All of a sudden, Mr. (or Ms.) Hothead approaches the container, sticks in a glass stirrer, and with two or three swishes kicks up the sand so that it is once again a homogenized mess of muck. This is what happens when you argue with a "man of fury." The waters

7. For example, a person who continually gives himself over to folly is properly referred to as a *fool.* The biblical name for the person who habitually lies is *liar.* The Bible refers to the person who drinks excessively as a *drunkard.*

8. Learning how to respond to such problematic people would require a book in and of itself. Please keep in mind that they are included here for our purposes primarily to help you, by God's grace, to determine whether you have any of these tendencies yourself and to repent of them.

9. Of course, if they are professing believers you may very well have to take them through the Matthew 18:15–17 process.

10. R. Laird Harris, Gleason L. Archer Jr., and Bruce K. Waltke, *Theological Wordbook of the Old Testament* (Chicago: Moody Press, 1999), 374.

get muddy, and it is difficult to see clearly through the contention to a biblical solution.

☐ *The perverse person.* "A perverse man spreads strife, and a slanderer separates intimate friends" (Prov. 16:28). Like a perverse computer hacker who sends forth viruses across the internet, this person releases strife into his relationships. One of his tactics is to slander (or whisper about or backbite) his victims in the hopes of sabotaging their close friendships (see Prov. 17:9).

☐ *The lover of transgression.* "He who loves transgression loves strife; he who raises his door seeks destruction" (Prov. 17:19). Rather than loving life and wisdom and God and righteousness (and a dozen other lawful pleasures), this rebellious person[11] loves both sin and strife. Who else would love strive besides a person who also loves sin? He enjoys a good fight, whether he is in the ring himself or is coaching from the corner. By raising his door (opening his mouth in pride) he finds what he is looking for—someone getting annihilated.

☐ *The obstinate fool (the stupid person).* "A fool's lips bring strife, and his mouth calls for blows" (Prov. 18:6). At least three types of fools are identified in the Proverbs. This one is someone who is stupid (or dull) not because of mental deficiency but simply because of his propensity to make wrong choices.[12] He is stubborn. Like one of those small fruit-drink containers that has a mini-straw attached to it, this person brings contention along with him. It is part of the package. When he moves his lips, contention will shortly emerge. His words are provocative, "calling for blows"—in effect, asking for a beating.

☐ *The morally deficient fool.* "Keeping away from strife is an honor for a man, but any fool will quarrel" (Prov. 20:3). This fellow is one

11. "Pasha' (פָּשַׁע) signifies *to revolt* or *to refuse subjection to rightful authority*. It is very generally rendered transgression" (Robert Baker Girdlestone, *Synonyms of the Old Testament: Their Bearing on Christian Faith and Doctrine* [London: Longmans, Green, and Co., 1871], 133, italics in original).

12. Harris, Archer, and Waltke, *Theological Wordbook*, 449.

grade below the obstinate fool. *The Theological Wordbook of the Old Testament* has a nice summary of the way this type of fool (*ev·eel*) relates to others.

> The *'ĕwîl* identifies himself as soon as he opens his mouth. He would be wise to conceal his folly by keeping quiet (Prov. 17:28). When he starts talking without thinking, ruin is at hand (Prov. 10:14). While a wise man avoids strife, the fool quarrels at any time (Prov. 20:3). He cannot restrain himself and will "display his annoyance at once," whereas a wise man overlooks an insult (Prov. 12:16 NIV). A fool has no balance in his relations with others. The wisdom instructor indicates that while stones and sand are most burdensome, a fool's anger is even more intolerable.[13]

☐ *The scoffer.* "Drive out the scoffer, and contention will go out, even strife and dishonor will cease" (Prov. 22:10). This person makes a good number of appearances in the book of Proverbs.[14] We are warned of the potential dangers of crossing swords with him. "He who corrects a scoffer gets dishonor for himself, and he who reproves a wicked man gets insults for himself. Do not reprove a scoffer, or he will hate you" (Prov. 9:7–8).

Solomon provided us with other interesting insights into his character.

- He doesn't listen to rebuke (13:1).
- He isn't able to find wisdom, although he attempts to (14:6).
- He doesn't love those who reprove him (15:12a).
- He will not consult with those who are wise (15:12b).
- He is proud (21:24).
- He is "hated" by (an abomination to) mankind (24:9).

13. Ibid.

14. This schismatic individual also appears in Titus 3:10, where he is similarly encouraged to be driven out. "As for a person who stirs up division, after warning him once and then twice, have nothing more to do with him, knowing that such a person is warped and sinful; he is self-condemned" (Titus 3:10–11 ESV).

- He suffers a variety of consequences for his scoffing (9:12; 19:29; 21:11).

☐ *The contentious man.* Although most Christian men are aware of the distress associated with being married to a *contentious woman* (Prov. 19:13; 21:9; 25:24; 27:15), few have considered that there is such a thing as a *contentious man* (a man of contention or quarrels). But, whether man or woman, this person is vexing to encounter—especially in the midst of conflict. To restrain him "is to restrain the wind or to grasp oil in one's right hand" (Prov. 27:16 ESV). "Like charcoal to hot embers and wood to fire, so is a contentious man to kindle strife"(Prov. 26:21).

Have you ever tried to picture this passage?[15] If you put a piece of charcoal next to a couple of embers, it is only a matter of time before a fire will ignite. If you place a piece of dry wood in close vicinity to a blazing fire, the wood will ultimately burst into flames. If you stay too long in the presence of a contentious person, it is just a matter of time before your conversation will detonate into a quarrel. I think the point that Solomon is making here is that you shouldn't stay in this person's presence longer than is absolutely necessary.

☐ *The arrogant man.* Here is another kind of "stirrer upper" to be wary of. There is a clear-cut correlation between pride and contention. "An arrogant man stirs up strife" (Prov. 28:25). It is very unlikely that you will resolve a conflict effectively when it is with this character. Proverbs 13:10 puts it this way: "Through insolence comes nothing but strife."

☐ *The angry man.* "An angry man stirs up strife, and a hot-tempered man abounds in transgression" (Prov. 29:22). The "stir up" concept is here again, applied to the person whose life is characterized by anger. In chapter 2 we saw how difficult it is to resolve conflicts when we are angry, because anger tempts us to erupt into a volcanic fury or to prematurely

15. I once heard Jay Adams describe the book of Proverbs as "portable truth." Pregnant with meaning, these pithy passages paint pictures in your mind that you can easily take with you wherever you go.

withdraw before the conflict has been successfully terminated. But imagine how difficult it would be to solve conflicts with an individual who is characterologically angry—that is, with someone whose anger has taken control of his live to such an extent that God now classifies him as an "angry man." The Bible cautions us not to get too close to this person lest his angry ways rub off on us.

> Do not associate with a man *given* to anger;
> Or go with a hot-tempered man,
> Or you will learn his ways
> And find a snare for yourself. (Prov. 22:24–25)

But we are not only in danger of being influenced directly by getting too close to him; like an "arrogant man," an angry person can also "stir things up" between others. He can walk up to the relational beaker of his friends (who are at peace with each other), stick in his little glass wand, and muck up their friendship.

SINFUL INTERNAL ATTITUDES

In addition to problems with unbiblical postures and problematic people, our internal attitudes can hinder and thwart our ability to resolve conflicts God's way.

☐ *Fear.* Apart from anger, fear is quite possibly the greatest hindrance to effective conflict resolution. Fear can keep us from *physical* danger (like taking foolish risks while driving). It can keep us from *spiritual* danger (like exposing ourselves to temptation, or being brought into bondage by a life-dominating sin)—Solomon said, "By the fear of the LORD one keeps away from evil" (Prov. 16:6). But fear can be destructive in many ways also. In a previous book, I outlined some of the ways in which fear can be destructive.[16] Let me unpack a couple of these as they relate to resolving conflicts.

16. Lou Priolo, *Fear: Breaking Its Grip* (Phillipsburg, NJ: P&R Publishing, 2009).

Fear is destructive (sinful) when that which produces our fear is attributed more power than the Bible allows. When we are more afraid of the person with whom we are in a conflict than we are of displeasing God, then we are struggling with sinful fear. Jesus said,

> I say to you, My friends, do not be *afraid* of those who kill the body and after that have no more that they can do. But I will warn you whom to fear: *fear* the One who, after He has killed, has authority to cast into hell; yes, I tell you, fear Him! (Luke 12:4–5)

> The LORD is my light and my salvation;
> *Whom* shall I fear?
> The LORD is the defense of my life;
> *Whom* shall I dread?
> When evildoers came upon me to devour my flesh,
> My adversaries and my enemies, they stumbled and fell.
> Though a host encamp against me,
> *My heart will not fear;*
> Though war arise against me,
> In spite of this I shall be *confident.* (Ps. 27:1–3)

> The fear of man brings a snare,
> But he who trusts in the LORD will be exalted. (Prov. 29:25)

Sometimes God places us in relationships (even close relationships—such as marital, parental, or vocational ones) with people who appear to have much greater arguing power than we do—be it due to their vast knowledge, vocabulary, reasoning ability, or dominating personalities. Our tendency in such circumstances is to cower under the assumption that we are no match for such people. But if God has indeed brought us into such a close relationship, should we not rather assume, for both the Lord's sake and the sake of that person, that it is His will for us to learn how to be a more persuasive biblical arguer? I can learn to do all things through Him who strengthens me. How much more is this the case when we are dealing with fellow believers in Jesus Christ (who profess to play by the rules of Scripture) than when we are dealing with unbelievers (who do not)?

Ask yourself, the next time you are afraid of your counterpart in conflict, "What is it that I am afraid of? Do I *really* believe that God is bigger and stronger than my opponent? Can I not trust God to give me the courage and wisdom to glorify Him in this conflict? Can I not trust Him to protect me from harm?" Fear is also destructive (sinful) when it keeps us from fulfilling our biblical responsibilities, such as loving God and neighbor as the Bible commands. And, as we have seen, our biblical responsibilities sometimes involve participation in conflict.

☐ *Bitterness.* One of the biblical terms for bitterness (see Eph. 4:31) was used to describe the bitter taste of certain foods and drinks. The verb translated "to be bitter" literally means "to cut" or "to prick." We sometimes think of bitterness as a self-inflicted, internal wound. But a resentful, unloving attitude will cut and prick others as well. As we saw in chapter 2, bitterness is the result of not forgiving. If we are bitter at someone, it means that we haven't truly forgiven him. Bitterness is the result of not responding biblically to an offense.

Bitterness is especially destructive to conflict resolution. It spawns many other sinful attitudes such as suspicion and distrust, disrespect, rebellion, critical spirits, and dismissive attitudes.

Trying to resolve conflicts with someone you are unwilling to forgive is like trying to erect a skyscraper without first laying a solid foundation. This is one of the reasons why, when I am doing marriage counseling (or parent/child counseling), my very first homework assignment involves having each person make a list of the ways in which he or she has sinned against the other. This is accompanied with either a booklet or a recording delineating the biblical basics of forgiveness. Then, in our very next meeting (the second counseling session), I typically have the parties confess their sins to each other and ask for forgiveness.[17] Removing bitterness by granting forgiveness clears the way for

17. At this point I have them exchange their lists and then add to and put in order of priority the offenses that each would like to see the other rectify. These prioritized lists become my counseling agenda for the duration of my time with them.

conflicts to be resolved effectively. Allowing the bitterness to continue sabotages the process. Humbling oneself by confessing sin and seeking forgiveness often sets the stage for lasting resolution by disposing the other person to be conciliatory.

☐ *Defensiveness.* Rooted in pride, defensiveness does not want to face the uncomfortable emotions (e.g., shame, embarrassment, humiliation, and so on) that are typically associated with being wrong about something. Rather than appreciating the validity of Proverbs 15:33, "Before honor comes humility," and 1 Peter 5:5, "God is opposed to the proud, but gives grace to the humble," a defensive person hates being reproved and refuses to take the hit (with all of its painful emotional discomfort) for his mistakes. So he resorts to a variety of conflict-resolution killers, such as justifying or extenuating his behavior, shifting the blame to someone or something else, arrogantly claiming to have already considered his opponents' point, or ridiculing the person who is pressuring him to take responsibility for his actions (or to assume the culpability for his sin).

☐ *Deceitfulness.* Honesty is arguably *the* primary principle of biblical communication (see Eph. 4:15). There are dozens of ways to practice deception,[18] but they can essentially be broken down into two basic categories. We perpetrate deception by falsifying information or by concealing information. *Falsification* distorts the truth (*changes* the essential facts of a matter). *Concealment* withholds vital elements of the truth (*omitting* the essential facts). This is why, when we are sworn in before taking the witness stand, we are required *not only* to tell the truth, but also to tell the *whole truth* and *nothing but the truth*. The three elements of this oath cover just about every form (and combination) of lying.

While not everyone with whom we are in conflict may have a biblical need to know everything that goes through our minds, to purposefully withhold from them the vital information that they need in order to

18. In my booklet entitled *Deception: Letting Go of Lying* (Phillipsburg, NJ: P&R Publishing, 2008), I categorize more than twenty biblical lies and offer guidance on how to become a teller of the truth.

rightly resolve an issue is dishonest. Likewise, to knowingly exaggerate, minimize, or otherwise distort information that is essential to a resolution is similarly disingenuous. It is usually pride, sinful fear, and, as we have seen, selfishness that tempt us to be less than truthful with those with whom we are in conflict. We will look at the external expression of dishonesty in the next chapter.

☐ *Dismissiveness.* Titus was not the only person who the apostle Paul exhorted not to allow others to despise (think lightly of). He used a different Greek word for "despise" when addressing Timothy. He said, "Let no one despise your youth" (1 Tim. 4:12 NKJV). The Greek word for despise here is *kataphroneo*, "to think down," or, as the New American Standard Bible renders it, "look down on." In either case, whether one is "thinking down on" someone or, as in the Titus passage, "thinking around" him, to despise someone is to dismiss what he has to say as unimportant. This is the direct opposite of the "with humility of mind, regard one another as more important than yourselves" attitude of Philippians 2:3.

☐ *Contempt.* Another interesting (and similar) term[19] is the word for *contempt. Exoutheneo* can also mean to despise someone or something on the basis that it is worthless or of no value[20]—to consider him (or it) as nothing. It ranges in meaning from thinking too lightly of someone all the way to treating him with scorn or contempt. In Romans 14 (the text that deals with differentness, if not righteousness, issues—the kind of food that is consumed and the kind of holy days that are celebrated), the word is used twice (vv. 3, 10). In Luke 18:9–12, *contempt* is associated with having a self-righteous attitude.

> And He also told this parable to some people who trusted in themselves that they were righteous, and *viewed others with contempt*: "Two men

19. Paul uses this word (which the NASB translates "despise") in his first letter to the Corinthians in reference to Timothy. "See that he is with you without cause to be afraid, for he is doing the Lord's work, as I also am. So let no one *despise* him" (16:10–11).

20. Johannes P. Louw and Eugene A. Nida, *Greek-English Lexicon of the New Testament: Based on Semantic Domains*, 2nd ed. (New York: United Bible Societies, 1989), Logos Bible Software e-book.

> went up into the temple to pray, one a Pharisee and the other a tax collector. The Pharisee stood and was praying this to himself: 'God, I thank You that I am not like other people: swindlers, unjust, adulterers, or even like this tax collector. I fast twice a week; I pay tithes of all that I get.'"

A prideful, self-righteousness attitude communicates that "I am (or I can think and reason) better than you." It typically accompanies contempt and is an enormous hindrance to effective conflict resolution.

Perhaps one of the most interesting connotations of this word is that of rejection. In Matthew 21:42, the word *rejected* in the phrase "the stone [i.e., Jesus] which the builders rejected [and which] became the chief corner stone"[21] is translated from this term.[22] The sense of rejection that often accompanies being held in contempt by another is a harsh and painful emotion that makes resolving conflicts very difficult. Add to the mix the aforementioned arrogant, condescending (self-righteous) attitude that is associated with contempt, and you have a recipe for disaster.

☐ *Suspicion.* Baseless suspicion can be a very destructive force in conflict resolution. Saul's distrust of David (and God) made him very difficult to deal with. When David returned from killing Goliath, the women came out of all the cities of Israel and began to sing and dance, saying, "Saul has slain his thousands, and David his ten thousands" (1 Sam. 18:7). The biblical account expresses what happened next in these terms.

> Then Saul became very angry, for this saying displeased him; and he said, "They have ascribed to David ten thousands, but to me they have ascribed thousands. Now what more can he have but the kingdom?" *Saul looked at David with suspicion from that day on.* (vv. 8–9)

21. See Psalm 118:22.

22. And, in 1 Samuel 8:7, the Septuagint (LXX) uses this same word for *rejected*: "They have not *rejected* you, but they have *rejected* Me from being king over them."

Charles Spurgeon had this to say about the danger of suspicious minds:

> Suspicion makes a man a torment to himself and a spy towards others. Once [you] begin to suspect, [the] causes for distrust will multiply around you, and your very suspiciousness will create the major part of them. Many a friend has been transformed into an enemy by being suspected.[23]

☐ *Hatred.* "Hatred stirs up strife, but love covers all transgressions" (Prov. 10:12). This is the opposite of biblical love[24]—especially in terms of one's feelings. Hatred is active ill will that manifests itself in words and conduct or in a persecuting spirit.[25] "For we also once were foolish ourselves, disobedient, deceived, enslaved to various lusts and pleasures, *spending our life in malice and envy, hateful, hating one another*" (Titus 3:3). The last phrase of this verse is sobering. This is the description of what we did (how we spent our lives) before Christ. Is it really any wonder that learning to resolve conflict is so difficult for us?

☐ *Harshness.* A classic example of harshness can be seen in the conflict between Abram's two wives.

> After Abram had lived ten years in the land of Canaan, Abram's wife Sarai took Hagar the Egyptian, her maid, and gave her to her husband Abram as his wife. He went in to Hagar, and she conceived; and when she saw that she had conceived, her mistress was despised in her sight. And Sarai said to Abram, "May the wrong done me be upon you. I gave my maid into your arms, but when she saw that she had conceived, I was despised in her sight. May the LORD judge between you and me." But Abram said to Sarai, "Behold, your maid is in your power; do to

23. Charles Spurgeon, *Lectures to My Students* (Grand Rapids: Zondervan, 1979), 325.
24. If hatred stirs up the beaker, love covers it so that the peace will remain undisturbed.
25. Spiros Zodhiates, *The Complete Word Study Dictionary: New Testament* (Chattanooga: AMG Publishers, 2000), Logos Bible Software e-book, Strong's number G3404.

> her what is good in your sight." So Sarai treated her harshly, and she fled from her presence. (Gen. 16:3–6; cf. 1 Kings 12)

The root of this Hebrew term for *harsh* speaks to the effect exerted by an overly heavy yoke, which is hard to bear.[26] It is associated with the characteristics of one who is hard, stubborn (stiff-necked), rough, rude, and cruel. Would the people who typically go up against you in conflict see you as harsh? Would God?

Listed below are some common ways that we can be harsh in dealing with our opponents. Even though some of the items on the list may not directly involve speech, the harsh attitude behind them is usually communicated very clearly. As you read over the list, ask yourself, "How might I be communicating these attitudes of harshness to those with whom I am in disagreement?"

- Unwillingness to consider requests (or appeals) made by your opponent
- Responding to your opponent in a discourteous or condescending manner
- Having a critical, condemnatory, judgmental attitude toward your opponent
- Having unrealistic expectations of your opponent[27]
- Being intolerant of your opponent's (non-sinful) idiosyncratic behaviors
- Being unjustly suspicious of your opponent (rather than trusting him)
- Insulting your opponent (especially when you know that you don't have a persuasive argument)
- Refusing to make eye contact with your opponent or smile at him
- Interrogating your opponent in an unsympathetic or uncaring manner

26. Harris, Archer, and Waltke, *Theological Wordbook*, 818.

27. If the opponent is a subordinate, harshness may be shown in exacting too many demands from him.

- Speaking to your opponent with a gruff (or intimidating) tone of voice or an angry expression on your face
- Using biting sarcasm against your opponent
- Having an impatient attitude with your opponent

What is the antidote to harshness? It is gentleness[28] and patience. Does that sound familiar? The material that we looked at in chapters 2 and 3 should be of great help if you are one who routinely manifests this attitude.

☐ *Unreasonableness.* God's wisdom is easily entreated (willing to yield). "But the wisdom from above is first pure, then peaceable, gentle, *reasonable*, full of mercy and good fruits, unwavering, without hypocrisy" (James 3:17). If I were to ask your last opponent how reasonable you were during your last conflict (on a scale of 1 to 10), what would he tell me?

There are actually two words in this passage that connote reasonability and a willingness to consider the viewpoint of another. The word for *gentle*[29] means "ready to yield." It has no exact English equivalent but speaks of one's readiness to give up his will (in things that are not essential). Gentleness is willingness to be taught and to even have one's mind changed by the engrafted Word, which is able to save one's soul (see James 1:21).

The term that follows it is *reasonable*.[30] It again implies being open to reason, willing to listen, and easily persuaded. Is this the mind-set you typically take into your conflicts? Or would the people with whom you clash say that you are stubborn, pigheaded, or even self-willed?

☐ *Lack of Compassion:* We spoke of compassion briefly in chapter 4, but it deserves greater attention here. The wisdom that James describes is also full of mercy and good fruits. It is not the only word that can be translated as *compassion*.[31] Although there is a distinction in meaning

28. "A gentle answer turns away wrath, but a harsh word stirs up anger" (Prov. 15:1).
29. ἐπιεικής (*epieikēs*)
30. εὐπειθής (*eupeithēs*)
31. This word is ἔλεος (*éleos*). Two other words are οἰκτιρμός (*oiktirmós*) and σπλαγχνίζομαι

between them, they overlap enough to suffice for our purposes. The big idea about mercy or compassion is that it not only *feels* the pain associated with the problems of others, but it also *takes action* to help solve those problems if possible. It doesn't harden its heart to the concerns of its opponent. Instead it looks for a way to biblically deal with them.[32] It shows kindness and concern for those in serious need.[33]

A merciful person does not lose sight of the fact that mercy triumphs over judgment and that he will be shown mercy to the extent that he shows mercy (James 2:13).

On the lines below, please list the specific internal attitudes that you have checked off in the process of reading this chapter. Next to each one, prayerfully record what you can do to correct these problem areas.

My Sinful Attitude (Problem attitudes with which I struggle)	**What I Can Do to Change My Sinful Attitude** (What I can do to replace these problem attitudes with their biblical alternatives)
☐	__________ __________ __________
☐	__________ __________ __________
☐	__________ __________ __________

(*splagchnízomai*). Both are also used in relation to peacemaking. The former is used in Philippians 2:1 as a grounds to appeal to the saints at Philippi to be likeminded. The latter is used of the father of the prodigal son (and his self-righteous older son) when he sees the prodigal returning home.

32. For more on this subject, see Joshua Mack's excellent resource *Compassion: Seeing with Jesus' Eyes* (Phillipsburg, NJ: P&R Publishing, 2015).

33. Louw and Nida, *Greek-English Lexicon of the New Testament.*

☐	
☐	
☐	
☐	
☐	
☐	
☐	
☐	

10

UNBIBLICAL RESPONSES TO CONFLICT: EXTERNAL

CERTAIN FORMS of communication are sinful and therefore should be avoided. Such ways of conversing hinder our ability to resolve conflicts.

UNBIBLICAL CONFLICT RESPONSES

It is sometimes difficult to distinguish between our heart attitudes and our patterns of speech. What comes out of our mouth (and shows up on our face) is indicative of what is going on in our heart. As you work through some of the most common conflict-resolution killers identified in this chapter, keep in mind that some unsavory thought or motive might very well be generating these responses.

Interruption

Whether it is in the middle of a sentence or of a dialogue, when you interrupt your counterpart before he finishes his thoughts, you may violate several scriptural principles.[1] In conflict it is useful to keep James

1. This is not to imply that interruption is always wrong (rude). Indeed, as a counselor, I have become quite adept at politely interrupting someone's flow of speech in order to redirect our discussion in a direction that is more beneficial than the one I'm interrupting. Perhaps I will interrupt to ask a clarifying question. The trick is to do it politely and in a way that helps the other person to understand that it is in his best interest (and God's) to be interrupted. After patiently waiting for a pause in the flow of the conversation, I may say, "Forgive me for interrupting, but in order

1:19 at the forefront of your mind: "Let everyone be quick to hear, slow to speak and slow to anger." When you rudely interrupt your opponent, you will likely be perceived as being quick to speak and slow to hear. Another verse that I like to keep in mind when in conflict is Proverbs 18:13: "He who gives an answer before he hears, it is folly and shame to him." Take care to avoid arguing your position (or point of view) before you have heard out your opponent. Thoughtless interruption is a provocative (if not rude) way to handle disputes. Not only is it inconsiderate, but it may also communicate a "know it all" attitude that essentially says, "I know where you're going with that, and you are either wrong or are not focusing on the right issue. Let me tell you how it really is."

Rash Judgments[2]

A rash judgment is jumping to hasty and unfounded negative conclusions without having sufficient cause. As Christians, we must be careful to make judgments on proven facts rather than on superficial appearances. Jesus said, "Do not judge according to appearance, but judge with righteous judgment" (John 7:24).

Conflict can be a breeding ground for such uncharitable judgments—from imputing evil motives to one's opponent to making judgments of him based on insufficient evidence, from judging without having the proper authority to judging based on suspicion. It is especially tempting in the midst of conflict to make rash judgment about one's rival based on outward appearances (his countenance, body language, or dress).

Judging Motives

This is a particular kind of rash judgment (imputing evil motives to someone) that deserves special attention, because it is commonplace among people in conflict. It can bring peacemaking efforts to

---

to help you with the issue at hand, may I remind you of the question I asked you a moment ago?" There are times when a counselee is sinning by what he says, and then I may be more abrupt and say, "Whoa" or "Hold on," and then proceed with a biblical exhortation or reproof.

2. This problem is so great that I have written an entire booklet about it, entitled *Judgments: Rash or Righteous* (Phillipsburg, NJ: P&R Publishing, 2009).

a screeching halt and actually make matters worse. First Corinthians 4:5 forbids us to judge the motives of others. "Therefore do not go on passing judgment before the time, but wait until the Lord comes who will both bring to light the things hidden in the darkness and disclose the motives of men's hearts; and then each man's praise will come to him from God."

Only God knows another person's heart fully—we do not. (This is true even of our own hearts.) While we may rightly judge another's words, attitudes, and actions (because they are apparent), we may not presume to do what only God can do: to judge the heart of another. "God sees not as man sees, for man looks at the outward appearance, but the Lord looks at the heart" (1 Sam. 16:7; cf. 1 Kings 8:39; 1 Chron. 28:9; Luke 16:15).

Love requires us to believe the best about others (see 1 Cor. 13:7).

Here are a few examples of motive judgments that occur during conflict:

> "You just want to have things your own way."
> "You only said that because you want me to feel guilty."
> "You did that just to spite me!"
> "You don't care about what I want (or think, or feel)."
> "You're not trying to understand my point of view."
> "Why don't you stop thinking only of yourself?"

Unless the individuals in question have clearly stated their motives or thoughts, we simply don't have the right (or ability) to presume to know them.

Blame Shifting

Pride not only blinds us to our own sin, but, as we saw with Adam and Eve, it also looks for someone other than ourselves to blame. Jesus said, "First take the log out of your own eye, and then you will see clearly to take the speck out of your brother's eye" (Matt. 7:5). When someone reproves you, don't immediately look for another person to blame. Rather, be willing to assume 100 percent of the responsibility for your own sin (even if you believe you are only 5 percent wrong and your reprover is 95 percent wrong).

Imagine what would happen if, the next time you were on the receiving end of an opponent's blame shifting, you responded with something along these lines: "Why don't you tell me exactly what you think I've done wrong? When you do, I promise to be attentive, to acknowledge where I've sinned, to ask your forgiveness, and, by God's grace, to repent of my sin. The only thing I ask is that, after we've dealt with my sin, you let me talk to you about how I believe you've sinned."

Such a response not only sets a good example of humility, but, because humility begets humility, it also makes it easier for your opponent to lower his resistance and humble himself. Don't be surprised if, after you've finished acknowledging and repenting of your faults, your opponent voluntarily acknowledges his faults even before you've had a chance to articulate them.

Sweeping Generalizations

What is the problem with using the following phrases in conflict?

"You *never* . . ."
"You're *always* . . ."
"The *only* time you . . ."
"*Nothing* that I (or you) do . . ."
"You are the *worst* (or *most,* or *last,* or *biggest,* or *stupidest,* or *clumsiest,* or *ugliest*) . . ."

Statements that contain these phrases are, more often than not, dishonest. They are almost always perceived as false accusations.

At best, a rash generalization is a violation of 1 Corinthians 13:7 (not believing the best about others) and is thus an uncharitable attitude. At worst, it is a violation of the ninth commandment: "You shall not bear false witness against your neighbor" (Ex. 20:16).

The historic Heidelberg Catechism asks and answers the following question:

What is required in the ninth commandment?

> That I bear false witness against no man; wrest no one's words; be no backbiter or slanderer; *do not judge, or join in condemning, any man rashly or unheard*; but that I avoid all sorts of lies and deceit as the proper works of the devil, unless I would bring down upon myself the heavy wrath of God; likewise, that in judicial and all other dealings I love the truth, speak it uprightly, and confess it; and that, as much as I am able, I defend and promote the honor and reputation of my neighbor.[3]

"Laying aside falsehood," the Bible says, "speak truth each one of you with his neighbor, for we are members of one another" (Eph. 4:25). It is almost certainly not true that your opponent is *always* or *never* or *only* as bad as you make him out to be when you use such inaccurate language. Using such imprecise terminology can lead to arguments over the frequency of the problem and thus sidestep the real issue (e.g., "That's not true! I haven't left my socks on the floor since last Tuesday!").

If you truly believe there is some sinful snare into which your opponent regularly falls, then, rather than making a statement, consider asking a question along the lines of: "Do you think you have developed *a tendency* to . . . ?" or "Have you noticed how *frequently* you . . . ?" or "Are you aware that this is the fourth time this week that you . . . ?" or "Am I seeing a *pattern* of ___________ developing?"[4]

Multiplying Words

Is loquaciousness[5] a sin? It certainly can be. Here's why.

As Solomon put it, "A fool's voice is known by his many words"

3. G. I. Williamson, *The Heidelberg Catechism: A Study Guide* (Phillipsburg: P&R Publishing, 1993), 201, emphasis added.

4. These are merely suggestions that will have to be personalized according to the need of the moment and the people involved in the dialogue.

5. *Loquacious* is an adjective meaning a tendency to talk too much or too freely. It is akin to the word *garrulous*, which means pointlessly if not annoyingly talkative—especially in a rambling sort of way.

(Eccl. 5:3 NJKV), and, "When there are many words, transgression is unavoidable, but he who restrains his lips is wise" (Prov. 10:19).

Some people "hog the stage" while in conflict. They dominate the conversation in a variety of ways. They incessantly interrupt their counterparts. They make superfluous comments and arguments. They don't stay on task. They speak only of what interests them—purposefully changing the focus of the conversation to pursue their private agendas. They do not easily yield the floor to their opponents. They show little consideration for the views of their opponents. They seem to be "intoxicated by the exuberance of their verbosity." And, of course, they don't listen. By the time the conflict is over, they have done more than 75 percent of the talking.

So to multiply words in conflict is selfish, inconsiderate (if not rude), and a manifestation of pride and foolishness. It is often a manipulative attempt to control the conversation. "A fool does not delight in understanding but only in revealing his own mind" (Prov. 18:2).

As followers of Jesus Christ, we ought to be persuasive. But our speech, especially when we are trying to persuade others to a more biblical way of thinking, ought to be characterized by love (not selfishness), by thoughtfulness (not inconsideration), by grace (politeness and good manners, not rudeness), by humility (not pride), by wisdom (not foolishness), and by sincerity (not manipulation). At the end of the conflict, it doesn't matter who got the floor most of the time as much as it matters who manifests the character of Christ in the process.

Biting Sarcasm

Is it or isn't it? That is the question—is it necessarily sinful to use sarcasm? In light of the numerous examples of sarcastic humor used by godly people in Scripture (and by God Himself), there are times when it is legitimate, if not necessary. Take as one example Elijah's hysterical (and humiliating) comments to the prophets of Baal in 1 Kings 18:27: "Cry aloud, for he is a god. Either he is musing, or he is relieving himself, or he is on a journey, or perhaps he is asleep and must be awakened" (ESV).

A valid figure of speech employed repeatedly in the Bible, called irony, is the category under which sarcasm rightly falls. E. W. Bullinger, in his classic book *Figures of Speech Used in the Bible*, describes this figure, *Eironeia*, as speaking in such a way as "to convey a sense contrary to the strict signification of the words employed: not with the intention of concealing his real meaning, but for the purpose of adding greater force to it."[6] The clear implication of a contrary meaning takes irony out of the realm of lying, because the "deception" is understood (or apparent—sort of like, when you watch a play or a movie, you are not being lied to by the actors, whom you understand are not really who they pretend to be).

Perhaps the single best example of sarcasm can be seen in Paul's very intimate and self-disclosing second letter to the Corinthians. He is trying to undo the damage to his reputation that was perpetrated by his detractors. Notice the sarcastic nature of his remarks in italics.

> *I have become foolish;*[7] you yourselves compelled me. Actually I should have been commended by you, for in no respect was I inferior to *the most eminent apostles,*[8] even though I am a nobody. The signs of a true apostle were performed among you with all perseverance, by signs and wonders and miracles. For in what respect were you treated as inferior to the rest of the churches, *except that I myself did not become a burden to you? Forgive me this wrong!*[9] Here for this third time I am ready to come to you, and I will not be a burden to you; for I do not seek what is yours, but you; for children are not responsible to save up for their parents, but parents for their children. I will most gladly spend and be expended for your souls. If I love you more, am I to be loved less? But be that as it may, I did not burden you myself; nevertheless, *crafty fellow that I am, I took you in by deceit.*[10] (2 Cor. 12:11–16)

6. Ethelbert William Bullinger, *Figures of Speech Used in the Bible* (New York: E. & J. B. Young, 1898), 807.

7. Paul is obviously not trying to lose credibility with his readers by convincing them that he has suddenly become foolish.

8. That is, "super-apostles," in the Greek.

9. Paul really didn't offend them by not being a burden to them. And he certainly didn't think that he was really in need of their forgiveness for his generosity.

10. He was not an unscrupulous liar, as the terms *crafty* and *deceit* imply.

But the context of this letter is not a personal conflict as much as it is a teaching opportunity—one that is entirely for the benefit of his hearers and for God's glory, as Paul makes clear in verse 19.[11] It is didactic. He is using sarcasm to make a point, to be persuasive, but not to hurt or be combative with his beloved Corinthians.

On the other hand, in Acts 13, after reasoning with a mixed crowd (of Jews and Gentiles), Paul resorted to sarcasm after it was clear that some in his audience were so hostile that they would no longer hear him. He used it not to win the argument, but rather to put an end to it.

> The next Sabbath nearly the whole city assembled to hear the word of the Lord. But when the Jews saw the crowds, they were filled with jealousy and began contradicting the things spoken by Paul, and were blaspheming. Paul and Barnabas spoke out boldly and said, "It was necessary that the word of God be spoken to you first; *since you* repudiate it and *judge yourselves unworthy of eternal life*, behold, we are turning to the Gentiles. For so the Lord has commanded us,
>
> 'I have placed You as a light for the Gentiles,
> That You may bring salvation to the end of the earth.'"
>
> When the Gentiles heard this, they began rejoicing and glorifying the word of the Lord; and as many as had been appointed to eternal life believed. (Acts 13:44–48)

Using mild forms of sarcasm (or other ironic figures of speech) when trying to solve conflicts may be useful in some cases, but employing biting sarcasm (sarcasm that is intended to vindictively demean, humiliate, embarrass, or otherwise wound your opponent) is hardly ever useful when trying to bring about a peaceful resolution to an argument. Resorting to such vitriolic rhetoric may indeed help you to win an argument, but it will keep you from winning your brother (see Matt. 18:15).[12]

11. "All this time you have been thinking that we are defending ourselves to you. Actually, it is in the sight of God that we have been speaking in Christ; and all for your upbuilding, beloved."

12. Most of us have witnessed debates in which one of the contestants scored a technical win

Disrespect

Fundamentally, disrespect is an attitude of the heart that is rooted in the sins of pride and selfishness. Like the root of a live oak tree that sprouts other trees, it is a sin that sprouts all manner of other sins (e.g., resentment, abusive speech, and hatred). Disrespect is the sin of not esteeming others more highly than you do yourself (Phil. 2:3). It is the conceited conviction that you are wiser, smarter, cooler, or otherwise better than others. Beyond this, it is not giving others the honor that they are due and, in some cases, showing contempt for them. Because it flows from a proud heart, disrespect despises the thought of humbling itself in the presence of others by treating them as if they were in any way superior.

There may be nothing that provokes people to anger quicker and more often than disrespect. To make matters worse, there are dozens (if not hundreds) of ways in which disrespect can be communicated. The *words* that you choose, the *tone* of your voice, and what you say with your *body*—especially your *face*—all have the potential (individually and collectively) to communicate all sorts of bad attitudes that can shut down a conflict in a heartbeat.

How do people disrespect their opponents during conflict? Here are some common examples. Which ones have you most often been guilty of doing?

- ☐ By refusing to converse
- ☐ By ridiculing my opponent
- ☐ By rolling my eyes
- ☐ By raising my voice
- ☐ By using biting sarcasm
- ☐ By using profanity
- ☐ By putting my opponent down
- ☐ By threatening my opponent
- ☐ By looking at my opponent with contempt

---

on points but, because of the uncharitable way he conducted himself, clearly lost not only the debate but also much of his credibility and respect.

- ☐ By scoffing at or mocking my opponent
- ☐ By cursing my opponent
- ☐ By being rude and unmannerly
- ☐ By interrupting my opponent when he is speaking
- ☐ By not being attentive to what my opponent is saying
- ☐ By prematurely or improperly walking away from the conflict
- ☐ By having a condescending attitude
- ☐ By making my opponent out to be ridiculous or contemptible

Exhumation

If something from the past has been buried by virtue of forgiveness being sought and granted, the matter ought not to be disentombed. As a counselor, I find myself reminding those to whom I minister that one of the promises of forgiveness is that the forgiver will not use the forgiven offense in a pejorative way.

As we saw in chapter 2, if someone sins against you, either you may "overlook the transgression" and "cover" it in love (see Prov. 19:11; 1 Peter 4:8), or you must pursue (confront) him with the intent of granting him forgiveness (Luke 17:3) once he has acknowledged his sin. Once you have granted forgiveness, you ought not to dig his sins up. If you have truly forgiven your offender, you may not use those offenses as a weapon against him ever again. Biblical love "does not take into account a wrong suffered" (1 Cor. 13:5—or, in the NIV, "it keeps no record of wrongs").

Scolding

One of the Greek words from which the term *scolding* was derived means "to snort with anger."

> While He was in Bethany at the home of Simon the leper, and reclining at the table, there came a woman with an alabaster vial of very costly perfume of pure nard; and she broke the vial and poured it over His head. But some were indignantly remarking to one another, "Why has this perfume been wasted? For this perfume might have been sold for over three hundred denarii, and the money given to the poor." And they were scolding her. (Mark 14:3–5)

It is easy to fall into a rapid-fire, machine-like rant when our adrenaline runs high in the midst of conflict. When you are tempted to multiply words in your anger, it is usually best to wait until you can speak with careful, measured words. Two passages of Scripture have helped me to calm down (at least when I have been able to call them to mind while my heart was rapidly pounding and tempting my mouth to rapidly scold someone). They both have to do with *patiently instructing* those who are oppositional.

> The Lord's bond-servant must not be quarrelsome, but be kind to all, *able to teach, patient when wronged,* with gentleness *correcting*[13] those who are in opposition, if perhaps God may grant them repentance leading to the knowledge of the truth, and they may come to their senses and escape from the snare of the devil, having been held captive by him to do his will. (2 Tim. 2:24–26)

> Preach[14] the word; be ready in season and out of season; reprove, rebuke, exhort, *with great patience and instruction.*[15] (2 Tim. 4:2)

Manipulation

The essence of manipulation is using unbiblical means to control (or influence) another. To be more specific, it involves inciting an *emotional reaction* instead of a biblical response from that individual. This is typically (and selfishly) accomplished by coercing someone *to* or inhibiting someone *from* a particular course of action by causing him to sense some kind of threat, directly or indirectly.

13. The Greek word *paideúō* may also be translated as "instructed."

14. These verses are from two of the Pastoral Epistles but have application to all. When dealing with family members and friends, I think not in terms of preaching but proclaiming (or teaching) the truth to those with whom I am frustrated. It also helps me to remember as the head peacemaker of my family, it should not be a matter of me versus them (my wife or children), but rather what they are doing or saying versus what God's Word says. The trick is to take myself out of the equation and look on my family members as their shepherd rather than as someone in the boxing ring with me.

15. The *New International Version* renders this "careful instruction." This rendition helps me slow down and think through what I am about to say. Otherwise, in my haste to get the words out of my mouth, I know that I am not being *careful.*

The particular emotions that manipulators attempt to evoke within their victims range from anxiety and fear, to shame and humiliation, to anger. But the greatest of these weapons is the emotion of guilt.

Various tactics may be employed in the process of manipulation. Sulking, pouting, crying, accusing, making obligatory statements, asking "why" questions (a favorite of those who attempted to manipulate Christ), withholding affection and friendship, flattering, and cajoling are some of the more effective ones.

In evaluating yourself, keep in mind that it isn't always obvious when one is being manipulative. At this point it may not be a conscious action at all. But, from childhood on, you may have known how to push certain people's buttons (albeit ever so sweetly) to get what you want, to the point that you aren't even choosing to do it but are just doing it naturally. If you trained yourself to get what you wanted by using manipulative tactics and practiced and practiced those manipulative behaviors, you perhaps did not even know until later (if you have ever realized at all) that you have become manipulative.

I have written a little booklet entitled *Manipulation: Knowing How to Respond*,[16] which can help you to better understand the degree to which you use manipulation in your relationship with others and can help you to stop being victimized by manipulative individuals.

Unbiblical Prophetic Speculations

Making prophecies about the other person's future sinful activities is another unbiblical response to conflict.

> "You'll never amount to anything."
> "You'll never change."
> "I know you will not follow through on that commitment."
> "You've been a worrier since you were a little girl, and you're probably going to die prematurely of a stomach disease."
> "I guess I'd just better get used to your discontentment, because you'll never be satisfied no matter how much money I make!"

16. Lou Priolo, *Manipulation: Knowing How to Respond* (Phillipsburg, NJ: P&R Publishing, 2008).

As I often tell my counselees who speculate about such things, "You are not a prophet or the son (or daughter) of a prophet, so please stop your unbiblical prophesying. If you must speculate about the future, you really should do so in the light of Philippians 4:8. 'Finally, brethren, whatever is true, whatever is honorable, whatever is right, whatever is pure, whatever is lovely, whatever is of good repute, if there is any excellence and if anything worthy of praise, dwell on these things.'"

Additionally, 1 Corinthians 13:7 says that love "believes all things." That is, it interprets people's actions in the best possible light (unless of course there is hard evidence to the contrary).

Hastiness (Speaking before Thinking)

Solomon wrote, "Do you see a man who is hasty in his words? There is more hope for a fool than for him" (Prov. 29:20). He also penned these words: "There is an appointed time for everything. And there is a time for every event under heaven . . . a time to be silent, and a time to speak" (Eccl. 3:1, 7). Conflicts can't always be planned. They often pop up when you least expect them. But, when in conflict, we should take care not to say something prematurely. The temptation to blurt out something that ought to be held in until a more opportune occasion arises is greater once our adrenaline has kicked in. It requires self-control, patience, and continual prayer to not give full vent to one's spirit, but rather to quietly hold it back (see Prov. 29:11; also 28:26) in the midst of a conflict—as hard as it is, though, this should be our aim.

There are, of course, times when we must initiate a confrontational conversation with someone. Timing is also important then. Here are a few questions for you to ask yourself to help ensure that the timing is right for the discussion.

- ☐ Have I spent enough time praying about this?
- ☐ Have I spent enough time thinking though my arguments and wording (see Prov. 15:28)?
- ☐ When will I have this person's undivided attention?
- ☐ Would it be best if I made an appointment (see Est. 5:1–8)?

☐ Have I spent enough time thinking through possible resolutions to the conflict?

Dishonesty

If you are like most people, you sometimes struggle with telling the truth—especially in the midst of conflict. As a Christian, you not only *know* the truth but are *commanded to speak* the truth (in love).

Even if you are not a practicing liar, deceit is in your heart. Indeed, "The heart is deceitful above all things . . . who can understand it?" (Jer. 17:9 ESV). David said, "The wicked are estranged from the womb; they go astray from birth, speaking lies" (Ps. 58:3 ESV). The ninth commandment—"You shall not bear false witness against your neighbor"—is one of the most basic biblical directives for living the Christian life (see Ex. 20:16).

I have previously mentioned that there are basically two ways to lie. Deception can be accomplished either by falsifying information (distorting the truth—*changing* the essential facts of a matter) or by concealing information (withholding vital elements of the truth—*omitting* the essential facts). I have personally identified two dozen kinds of lies practiced by various biblical characters (not dozens of lies, mind you, but dozens of varieties of lies—almost every variety of which making numerous appearances in Scripture).[17] From the "I don't know" lie used by Rahab the harlot, to David's incredible insanity act before King Achish, to the apostle Peter's threefold denial of Christ (with a bit of profanity thrown in for effect), the Bible is filled with examples of deception (most of which at least temporarily succeeded).

The greatest impact of deception on the resolution of interpersonal conflicts is the loss of trust that inevitably comes with it. Nothing causes others to lose trust in us quicker than our telling a lie. In fact, in the scores of marital infidelity cases that I've had the privilege to work with, the faithful partners invariably found it more difficult to believe that their spouses would never lie again than that their spouses would never cheat

17. Most of these have been catalogued in my little booklet *Deception: Letting Go of Lying* (Phillipsburg, NJ: P&R Publishing, 2008).

again. Once trust is lost between two people, conflicts become much more difficult to resolve. The ensuing suspicion slows down the peace process and makes the need for a mediator more likely. The promises and commitments that are necessary for resolution, and which heretofore would have been taken at face value, are now devalued and doubted.

It should be noted again that there is a distinction between forgiveness and trust. If I were to sin against you and then ask for your forgiveness, it would be incumbent upon you as a Christian to forgive me (Matt. 18:21–35; Luke 17:3–10). It would not, however, be required for you to give me the trust that I may have lost as a result of my sin. Rather, it is my job to earn back the trust that I have lost as a result of my sin. In most circumstances, forgiveness should be granted immediately. The rebuilding of trust, however, is typically a more time-consuming venture.

Defensiveness

This problem was briefly mentioned as an unbiblical internal attitude in chapter 9. Because it can be observed by others, however, and because it is such a common problem whose effects upon conflict resolution are so great, I have devoted the entire next chapter to one of its most effective remedies.

As mentioned previously, the driving force behind this "circuit jammer" is pride. Defensiveness is manifested in many ways. We just took a look at one of the most common ways: *blame shifting*. Other forms of defensiveness include the following:

☐ Refusing to acknowledge failure or sin
"I didn't do anything wrong."

☐ Refusing to accept responsibility
"It's not (it wasn't) my job to take care of that."

☐ Overreacting to criticism (feeling a pinprick like a knife wound)
"I can't believe you would do/say such a thing!"

☐ Rationalizing
"There is a good reason for me to say/do that."

☐ Extenuating
"The circumstances were beyond my control."

☐ Pulling rank
"Who do you think you are, talking to your superior that way?"
☐ Denying the existence of wrong motives
"I was not trying to manipulate you!"
☐ Bringing up a similar fault in your counterpart
"You did the very same thing to me last weekend!"[18]
☐ Refusing even to consider the need for change
"That's just the way I am."

Let's do a quick review before we continue. The fifteen unbiblical forms of communication that we have looked at in this chapter are certainly not the only forms of speech that hinder our ability to resolve conflicts God's way, but they are some of the most common ones. On the worksheet below, put a check next to the items with which you struggle most. Then prayerfully search the Scriptures to identify the biblical alternative for each sinful response. Record what you will endeavor to do, in cooperation with the Holy Spirit, to facilitate change.

DEALING WITH MY UNGODLY RESPONSES

My Unwholesome Speech (Sinful patterns of speech that I must correct)	**What I Can Do to Change My Sinful Communication** (What I can do to replace my sinful speech patterns with their biblical alternatives)
☐ Interruption	______________________ ______________________ ______________________

18. While this response can be legitimate in pointing out hypocrisy, and others of these responses may be biblically legitimate in certain situations, we are concerned at present about tactics used to justify sin, blame shift, or otherwise divert/deflect attention away from the issue at hand: one's personal culpability.

☐ Rash Judgments	
☐ Judging Motives	
☐ Blame Shifting	
☐ Sweeping Generalizations	
☐ Multiplying Words	
☐ Biting Sarcasm	
☐ Disrespect	
☐ Scolding	

☐ Exhumation	
☐ Manipulation	
☐ Prophetic Speculations	
☐ Hastiness	
☐ Dishonesty	
☐ Defensiveness	

11

CONFLICT-RESOLVING QUESTIONS

ONE OF THE MOST basic passages in the Bible regarding conflict resolution is Proverbs chapter 18. In it we find no less than three important truisms about conflict resolution.

Verse 2 says, "A fool does not delight in understanding, but only in revealing his own mind."

Verse 13 says, "He who gives an answer before he hears, it is folly and shame to him."

Verse 17 says, "The first to plead his case seems right, until another comes and examines him."

All three of these verses address the necessity of understanding the other person's point of view. One of the best ways to understand someone is to ask questions. Polite interrogation is one of the surest safeguards against defensiveness. Someone has said that questions are to communication as food is to eating.

The ability to ask questions is a skill that effective conflict resolvers artfully and skillfully perfect. In this chapter I will provide you with a few basic interrogatives to get you started on your quest to understand those with whom you find yourself in conflict. But first let me make a few suggestions about the kinds of questions that I have found to be most effective in conflict resolution.

Since a big part of resolving conflict involves trying to understand the other person's point of view, as a general rule open-ended questions are best. I normally avoid asking "yes" or "no" type questions unless they implicitly encourage an expanded answer. Also, in order to avoid unnecessarily tempting people to become defensive, I avoid asking "why" questions when seeking information. (Jesus saved "why" questions for those occasions when he was attempting to convict people of their sins.) On the pages that follow, I will suggest some better alternatives to the "Why did you do that?" question for getting people to talk about the thoughts and motives of their hearts.

In my book *The Complete Husband* I suggest several questions for a man to ask his wife as he attempts to live with her in an understanding way (1 Peter 3:7). Some of these questions can be adapted to other kinds of close relationship conflicts (such as relationships between family members and close friends). Let's start by looking at a few of these questions that are useful for resolving conflicts of a more intimate nature. Then we will move on to some more generic questions. Keep in mind that the wording of these suggested questions is not suited to everyone's personality (nor are the questions applicable to every circumstance). They are intended only to be used as templates—you will need to personalize and adapt them according to the context in which they are used ("according to the need of the moment"—Eph. 4:29[1]).

A CRACK IN THE DOOR

Before we look at our first question, I would like to say another word about the importance of humility. There is something that humble people do—something that is so disarming and winsome—that it makes almost any conflict enjoyable. They somehow leave a very definite crack in the door that says, "I realize that you may be right and I may be wrong. If you are right, I *really* want to be convinced. So please be patient with me as we discuss these matters. I may press you to prove your points or may ask for examples and applications. I may interact rather passionately

1. "Let no unwholesome word proceed from your mouth, but only such *a word* as is good for edification *according to the need of the moment,* so that it will give grace to those who hear."

with you. But all of this is not done out of arrogance, but rather out of a sincere desire to be persuaded, because I know that I may very well be mistaken." This attitude is antithetical to (and the greatest antidote for) being defensive. It also disarms the defensiveness of others.

As you read through these questions, see if you can spot that unpretentious spirit. To the degree that you become proficient at communicating this "crack in the door" kind of humility in all of your dealings with others—not just in your questioning techniques, but also in your commendations, reproofs, testimonials, and so on—you will be amazed at how much more smoothly your conflicts with others in particular and your relationships in general will go.

1. Exactly what is it that I am I doing or not doing (that I have done or failed to do) that is upsetting (displeasing) to you?[2]

A humble person is always mindful that he is a sinner and that he therefore may very well have done something provocative (even unknowingly so) that contributed to the conflict. By offering to focus first on your own contribution to the argument (by offering to take the beam out of your own eye—see Matt. 7:1–5), you will not only demonstrate humility but also make it easier for your "opponent" to "take the hit" for his contribution to the problem later on.

2. How does (did) it make you feel when I __________? (Identify in biblical terms, if possible, what you know has been a point of contention for the person with whom you are in conflict.)

Having discovered exactly what it is that you have done (or are doing) to hinder the resolution of the conflict, you can begin encouraging the other person to reveal himself to you. In close relationships it can be quite helpful to ask about the other person's feelings. Feelings can give us insight into how an individual thinks and what he values, longs for, and delights in.[3] Knowing these things will enable us to bet-

2. Be careful that your motives for asking these questions are sincere. A sarcastic inflection in your voice will communicate not only insincerity but also an arrogance that will likely inflame rather than quell the conflict.

3. Of course, as Christians, we ought not to live life (or to make our decisions) based primarily

ter understand him and, consequently, to more effectively minister to him in the process of resolving the conflict.[4]

Another reason that it is so important for you to understand the other person's feelings is that his pain may be, in part, the result of your sin. Sometimes all that the person whom you are in conflict with really wants is the acknowledgment that you have, indeed, hurt him and the assurance that you will try hard not do the same hurtful thing again. He concludes that, if you understand how much your action (or lack of action) has hurt him, you will try that much more to keep from doing it again. If you truly understand the extent to which your sinful behavior has hurt the other person, it may very well motivate you to be more considerate of him in the future. Of course (and more importantly), in order for your repentance to be genuine you must also understand that your sin has offended God.

3. What goes (went) through your mind when I ____________? (Identify in biblical terms, if possible, what you know has been a point of contention for the person with whom you are in conflict.)

Having first asked your counterpart to reveal his emotions to you, you are now ready to inquire about his thoughts. By sincerely asking this question, you will be humbly demonstrating to him that you are really trying to see things from his point of view. This will also communicate to him your willingness to repent. "Wow!" he may reason, "since he wants to know the impact that his actions have had on my thoughts and feelings, he must really be serious about not doing this again." Encourage him to be totally candid and frank with you. If appropriate, ask him to give you a verbatim account of his thoughts. ("May I ask what you said to yourself when I did that?") This will help you to see the issue from his perspective (right or wrong). Try to comprehend the full effect that your behavior had on him.

---

on our feelings but rather on the biblical principles that apply to each situation. To do otherwise is dangerous because it leads to a feeling-oriented ("sensual") kind of lifestyle rather than an obedience-oriented lifestyle. Our feelings can lead us astray and tempt us to respond unbiblically to the problems and pressures of life.

4. This may be a novel thought to you, but as Christians we are to love (meet the needs of) even our enemies. Conflicts often reveal to us the greatest needs of our opponents.

YOU ARE WHAT YOU THINK

The problem with most of us is that we listen rather than talk to ourselves. That's right—rather than "speaking the truth in [our] heart[s]" (Ps. 15:2), being "transformed by the renewing of [our] mind[s]" (Rom. 12:2), and "taking every thought captive to the obedience of Christ" (2 Cor. 10:5), many of us preach to ourselves, at hundreds of words per minute, all kinds of fibs, falsehoods, and fabrications manufactured in our deceitful hearts. Rather than passively *listening* to ourselves say something like, "There is no use trying to argue with him," we ought rather to actively *exhort* ourselves by saying something in our hearts like, "By God's grace I am going to do everything within my power to bring about a biblical resolution to this conflict. I *can* do all things through Christ who strengthens me!"

Since what we say to ourselves during a disagreement can make or break the argument, let's look at a few more common examples of unbiblical self-talk to which people often resort when in conflict. After each one I have suggested one biblical alternative (there are any number of possible ones).

- "She's not hearing a word I'm saying! Her mind is made up. I'm done with this conversation. It's over. How can I get out of this mess as quickly as possible?"
- "Perhaps I should ask her to tell me what she thinks I am saying. I may need to clarify my arguments. Then, if it still seems that she is being obstinate, perhaps I can politely ask her how open she is to considering other ways to approach a resolution."

- "He is never going to admit that he is wrong. Why should I bother? I'm getting out of this conflict as fast as I can."
- "The Bible says not to 'answer a fool according to his folly, or you will also be like him,' but rather to 'answer a fool as

his folly *deserves,* that he not be wise in his own eyes.'† I'm not going to leave this conflict until I have at least tried to politely place the ball in his court."

"I'll never be able to match his verbal prowess. I hate it, but unless I want to be outsmarted, I will have to resort to fighting dirty."

"The Bible says, 'The heart of the righteous ponders how to answer.'†† By God's grace, and for the sake of my opponent, I am going to learn how to persuasively argue my case with this person."

"She is starting to win the argument. I had better do something to stop her, or I am going to be embarrassed."

"May the best man win. I am going to be reasonable, like the Bible says that a wise person ought to be, and will seriously consider the validity of her arguments. She may ultimately convince me to see things the way she does. Being embarrassed is not a sin. 'Fighting dirty' is!"

"I've explained this to him a dozen times. I don't have time to do it again right now. I've got to end this NOW!"

"I am to 'be ready in season and out of season; [to] reprove, rebuke, exhort, with great patience and instruction.'"†††

"He's judging (or interrupting, or ignoring, or harassing, or lying to) me again. Who does he think he's talking to? I'm not going to let him get away with this any longer. I've got to stop him! I'm going to scold (or yell at or manipulate or curse or embarrass) him. Maybe then he will learn that he can't do that to me!"

† Proverbs 26:4–5.
†† Proverbs 15:18.
††† 2 Timothy 4:2.

👍 "The Lord's bond-servant must not be quarrelsome, but be kind to all, able to teach, patient when wronged, with gentleness correcting those who are in opposition, if perhaps God may grant them repentance leading to the knowledge of the truth."†

👎 "If she doesn't take a breath and let me speak, I'm going to forget how to defend myself against all of her false accusations, so I have no choice but to forcefully interrupt her."

👍 "I will grab something to write on so that I will not forget. At the first opportunity, I will politely ask to have the floor for equal time."

👎 "He is out to make me look bad (to embarrass me, to intimidate me, to manipulate me, or to otherwise do me harm)."

👍 "I cannot lawfully judge his motives without hard evidence. So I will try to focus on his words and actions, try to believe the best, and, when given the opportunity, politely ask him to tell me what motivated him to say (or do) that."

👎 "I've asked her three times what's wrong, and three times she says 'Nothing!' Really? Does she think I'm that stupid? I'm just going to ignore her until she comes to me and tells me what it is that she's so upset about. I think I'll go for a drive. She can call me when she's ready to talk!"

👍 "She's obviously upset at me. I don't know why. I'm going to politely place the ball in her court and go into 'overcoming evil with good' mode. I am going to kill her with kindness until she opens up. But, whatever I do, I'm not going to retaliate in kind. Now what can I do to begin blessing her?"

† 2 Timothy 2:24–25

4. Is there something that you want (wanted) from me that I'm not (that I wasn't) giving you at the moment?

This question goes beyond feelings and thoughts and helps you to obtain information about the desires and motives of the other person. We have seen that the Bible has much to say about such things. The Word of God is necessary for accurately diagnosing not only our thoughts, but also our motives. "For the word of God is living and active and sharper than any two-edged sword, and piercing as far as the division of soul and spirit, of both joints and marrow, and able to judge the thoughts and *intentions* of the heart" (Heb. 4:12). Fully understanding your opponent involves understanding those desires that generate his thoughts, words, and actions. His desires may be righteous or unrighteous, but if we understand what they are, we will be better able to respond to the underlying issue than if we remain in the dark.

5. Is there something that you would like to see me do to change?

Be especially careful not to ask this question unless you are really committed to making every effort to implement any reasonable suggestion made by your opponent (or to come up with your own biblically based alternative to it).

In many cases, your counterpart will have already thought through some specific changes that he'd like to see you put into practice. In fact, it is possible that he has already intimated (if not clearly articulated) these suggestions to you in the moments preceding your asking this question. So, unless you want to reveal the fact that you have not been listening, don't ask this one unless you are certain that the matter has not been previously mentioned (without first apologizing for not being as attentive as you should have been). I will sometimes ask the question this way (if something has been already mentioned): "In addition to ____________, is there anything else that you would like to see me do differently?" Do you see how questions like these communicate a disarming kind of humility that communicates to others a genuine willingness to make peace?

Sometimes people answer this question in the abstract ("You need to be more considerate of me") rather than in specific and concrete terms ("Please don't throw your clothes on the floor and expect me to pick them up for you"). In such cases you may want to ask the other person to be more specific. "Being inconsiderate" is abstract. "Throwing clothes on the floor instead of in the hamper" is concrete. One requires you to guess what would please the counterpart. The other gives you the exact information that you are looking for. One may not hit the target. The other hits the bull's-eye.

6. How could I have said that differently? (There must have been something about what I said that didn't sit well with you—how could I have said it better?)

This question is especially helpful when it becomes apparent that some kind of "offense" was taken to your previous remark. (Certainly, if you realize that what you said was, in fact, offensive—i.e., sinful—then rather than asking this question you should, after acknowledging what you did wrong, ask, "Will you forgive me?") It may be that your comment was not sinful but could have been said with more grace or compassion. It may be that you misspoke without realizing it. It may be that the other person misunderstood what you said, but asking this kind of question should help the other person over the bump in the road to a biblical resolution.

7. Have I done anything that has made it difficult for us to resolve this issue sooner?

We are sometimes more culpable for causing or exacerbating conflicts than we realize. Perhaps what our offender did to us was in direct response to something that we first did (knowingly or otherwise) to him. Perhaps we waited too long to discuss the matter with the other person out of fear or our own sinful anger (which we should have gotten under control much sooner). Sometimes we sincerely try to overlook an offense or to cover it in love but end up not being able to do so, and then, rather than addressing the matter with the offender, we keep silent and grow increasingly bitter. Perhaps, after we were offended, we did something retaliatory to our offender, which in his eyes was just as obnoxious (if not more so) than what he did to offend us.

8. Is there anything (else) for which I need to ask your forgiveness?

Be it out of fear, ignorance, or a misguided desire for "peace at any price," people in conflict are sometimes hesitant to convict their counterparts of sinful behavior even when it is biblically necessary to do so. Asking this question makes it easier for them to put those things on the table that they might otherwise have been unwilling to disclose. More importantly, it gives you the opportunity to secure from them those three promises of forgiveness that we looked at in chapter 2, and it helps to remove any root of bitterness that may have grown in their hearts. Of course, you may not agree that what "offended" them was something that you are required to ask forgiveness for, but at least the issue will be out in the open and hopefully resolved biblically.

9. What can I do in the future to keep this kind of conflict from happening again?

In cases where the conflict was not the result of someone's sin (in which case the answer to this question should be apparent), it may be especially helpful to discuss what words, actions, and attitudes may be pursued to preemptively smooth out any similar potential rocky roads that the two of you may encounter down the line. "The heart of the righteous ponders how to answer" (Prov. 15:28).

10. I'm sorry, but I do not yet clearly understand what you are saying (or I really want to clearly understand things from your perspective). Would you mind restating that for me?

Disputes sometimes occur simply because one of the parties is misspeaking, misunderstanding, or misinterpreting. If there is any doubt as to what you think you heard, ask politely for clarification. This question often helps an opponent to realize that he did not express himself as clearly as he could have.

11. Am I hearing you correctly? Is this what you are saying?

I am not sure where this question originated, but it is a good one. Although it may smack of Rogerian psychology,[5] repeating back to the other person your perception of what he said accomplishes at least two very important goals. First, it communicates that aforementioned disarming, humble spirit that assuages suspicion and encourages a reciprocal humility. Second, it prevents many common misunderstandings that occur when people use terminology that can have more than one meaning or can conjure up radically different mental images.[6]

12. Perhaps you're right. May I have some more time to think about what you have said?

There may be times when you are simply not sure whether what your opponent has said about your contribution to the conflict is valid. In such cases, it may be appropriate to ask for a postponement of the conflict (or at least a postponement in discussing the specific point of contention) in order to prayerfully "ponder how to answer." In such cases it is important to offer a "rain check" (a specific time to reconvene in order to conclude the matter biblically). Such rain-out games should be replayed as soon after the storm as possible. When Martin Luther was asked to recant his doctrines at the Diet of Worms, he replied that it "would be rash and dangerous for me to reply to such a question, until I had meditated thereupon in silence and retreat, least I incur the anger of our Lord."[7]

5. Carl Rogers was the father of client-centered (person-centered) *non-directive counseling.* (That is an oxymoron if ever there was one.) Because he believed that man was basically good, and had all of the answers to all of his problems within himself, he would never give advice (which up to that point in history was what the word *counsel* universally meant). Rather he would ask questions such as this one to help the client discover the "truth" that resided in his heart. Rogers didn't much appreciate the fact that man was dependent upon God's counsel even in the Garden of Eden (before sin entered the picture).

6. When I say the word *tree,* what comes to your mind? Some of your fellow readers will visualize an oak tree, some a pine, a spruce, a redwood, or one of the maple varieties. The truth is, I was thinking of a weeping willow tree.

7. Martin Luther, *The Life of Luther,* ed. M. Michelet, trans. William Hazlitt (London: David Bogue, 1846), 83.

13. I really want to improve in this area, but I'm afraid that I don't yet see what I'm doing that is troubling to you. Would you be able to give me an example or two of what you are talking about?

Another common problem that occurs during conflict is that patterns of behavior are alleged in general terms with little evidence to support them. These are often initially interpreted as false accusations. A humble person knows that he is capable of just about anything, so rather than responding with defensive incredulity he leaves a crack in the door by asking for more data.

14. I know that this issue is complicated, but could we please focus our attention on trying to resolve the central issues first?

When our adrenaline levels are up and our emotions are high, our minds can more easily wander away from core issues to tangential ones. When this happens, it can be helpful for us to be politely called back to focus on the bull's-eye.

15. May I ask what motivated you to say/do that? (Could it be that the reason you said/did that was _______________?)

When we are in conflict, it is *sometimes* helpful to discuss our motives. As we have seen, it is unbiblical to judge the motives of another, but we may in some cases ask that person to judge his own motives. These two questions can be quite effective. At the beginning of this chapter I said that, in order to preempt getting a defensive response, I generally eschew the word *why* when trying to determine what is going on in the heart of another. But on occasion, not knowing how else to phrase the questions, I have simply stated, "I'm wondering why you said (or did) that. Can you help me to understand?" This wording greatly reduces the accusatory nuance of the word *why*.

16. Is there any way that you could meet me halfway on this issue? (Can you suggest a compromise we could make so that we will both walk away pleased with how this matter was settled?)

It seems rather simple, but by humbly asking your opponent to come up with his own fair solution to the conflict you esteem him more highly than yourself, and you put him in a position to be magnanimous. If you don't believe that the middle-ground he has offered is near enough to the middle, you may respond with something along these lines: "Thank you for offering that. Is there any way you would consider this?"

A MATTER OF CONVICTION

Sometimes the questions we ask while attempting to resolve conflicts are intended to put godly pressure on the other person to make peace—to bring the conflict to a biblical resolution. These questions are asked not just to gain information but also to bring conviction of sin.

17. May I tell you how I perceive what you just said?

Sometimes it helps to ask permission before bringing up a difficult topic. In this case you are about to help the other person to see that what he has communicated may have come across differently than he realized.

18. You seem to be angry at me. May I ask how I have sinned against you?

This question should help the biblically literate person with whom you are in conflict to quickly realize whether his anger is righteous or sinful. If it is the former, he ought to be able to tell you in biblical terms what you have done to provoke his response. If not, it should alert him to the fact that he is struggling with unholy passion, because what he is upset with you about is not upsetting to the Lord. In the first case, *you* may need to repent and seek his forgiveness; in the second, *your opponent* will need to repent (change his thinking about the matter). Or you may find out that he is not angry at you at all, but is angry at someone else or feeling some other emotion.

19. Can you think of a more gracious [or some other appropriate biblical term] way to say (or respond to) that?[8]

This question is rooted in Ephesians 4:29: "Let no unwholesome word proceed from your mouth, but only such a word as is good for

8. Obviously, this question should be asked only when there is a close level of intimacy between the parties. It should probably not be used by subordinates to their superiors unless prior approval to use such familiar language has been given.

edification according to the need of the moment, so that it will give grace to those who hear" (cf. Col. 4:6). As we will see in the next chapter, sometimes simply asking for a redo of a flubbed line is all that is necessary to avoid going down the wrong path.

This little catalog of questions, while not exhaustive, should serve as a basic foundation upon which you can build your own repertoire of troubleshooting questions. Let me again encourage you to modify them in accordance with your own communication style and the personality of the person with whom you are in conflict.

You are now ready to use a resource called the Conflict Journal. I have used it quite beneficially for years in my counseling office. I will typically assign it for homework, instructing my counselees to complete a worksheet for each conflict that took more than fifteen minutes to resolve (or a shorter conflict that ended very badly). When they return to counseling the following week, we unpack their conflicts blow by blow and then reconstruct each one biblically, teaching them how they could have handled each round in the conflict (each verbal exchange) more biblically. If you would like to use this helpful tool, you can find it (along with instructions) in Appendix A.

12

YOU PUT THE WORDS RIGHT INTO MY MOUTH

I LIKE TO FISH. But I love to fly-fish. Do you know what makes fly-fishing different from ordinary fishing? It is how the lure is propelled. When terminal tackle is used in fishing, the tackle itself is weighted and hurled rather forcefully across the water. However, flies are usually constructed of such things as foam, fabric, and feathers. They do not weigh very much and therefore cannot be cast very far (if at all) with an ordinary fishing pole. So, to get those little bugs across the water, weight must be infused into the line. In fly-fishing, the line, not the bait, is hurled across the water. To do this properly takes considerable skill and practice.

If you were to watch an experienced fly-fisher, you would likely be impressed not only with the deftness with which he casts the line, but also with his accuracy. A good caster can repeatedly toss his fly into an eighteen-inch-diameter circle on the surface of the water. How can he do that? It's simple. Practice, practice, and more practice! In my case, I couldn't even describe how I do it. I simply look at the spot where I want the fly to land, my brain makes the appropriate calculations and communicates to my casting arm rather unconsciously—and, most of the time, the fly lands very close to where I want it. Because of practice, it's a point and shoot, second-nature kind of thing. It's easy, automatic, comfortable, and unconscious. I wouldn't know where to begin teaching someone how to do what I can do with a fly-rod, other than to say, "You just have to practice."

But it wasn't always that way. When I began fly-fishing, casting was not so easy, but difficult. It was not automatic, but deliberate.[1] It was not comfortable, but awkward. It was not unconscious, but required much concentration. And so it is with any skill, whether it is learning to putt a golf ball, type eighty words per minute, drive a car, or put on makeup.

PRACTICE AND THE DEVELOPMENT OF HABIT

Developing good conflict-resolution skills takes practice. That's because developing a skill is like developing a habit.

Can you imagine what it would be like if you had to read a driver's manual every time you wanted to go somewhere? After getting into the car you would open up the glove box, pull out the instructions, and read, "First you put the key in the ignition . . ." After checking the diagram to see where the ignition is, you would continue: "Be sure the vehicle is in park . . ." But perhaps you wouldn't be sure exactly what this means, so you would have to turn a few pages to see. By the time you had adjusted your seat and mirrors, figured out how to operate the seatbelt, and decided what radio station you wanted to listen to (after reading the section on how to operate it), you would have used up half your morning before leaving the garage!

But, through training, experience, and habit, you can put the key in the ignition without even looking at either, quickly check the rearview mirror, adjust your seat, buckle your seatbelt, and back out of the garage (after casually opening the garage door with the electronic opener). You can then proceed to the store, executing dozens of operations involving your hands, feet, eyes, and ears in the process. You perform this series of very complex activities all while being mindful of dozens of laws, as well as of the traffic before, behind, and around you, *and* while talking on Bluetooth, listening to the radio, giving instructions to the children

1. Most notably, I would have to sharply turn my neck to look over my shoulder on my back cast to make sure that the line was almost completely uncurled before I started my forward cast.

in the backseat, remembering the last-minute suggestions from your spouse, or (like too many women I've known) applying makeup (which, by the way, is illegal in many states).

What comes to mind when you think of your habits? You may immediately think of some bad habit that you are trying to overcome. For many, this term has negative connotations. Though habits can be good or can be just the standard operations of daily life, our flesh naturally predisposes us to a kind of *training* (or practice) that is corrupt. Interestingly, the word for *training* (*gumnazo*[2]) is used in the Bible not only for training in godliness but also for training in ungodliness. Paul uses it in one of his letters to Timothy, saying, "Discipline yourself for the purpose of godliness" (1 Tim. 4:7).

What does that mean? It means to exercise or to train oneself. If you want to build strength and mass, you don't go to the gym, find the easiest weight you can lift, lift it five times, and then put it back to wait for the next week. It takes repetition, perseverance, and a gradual increase in the level of difficulty (if not exertion) to build your body or to build any other habit worth cultivating. Five minutes a month isn't enough to care for a garden, and it isn't enough to care for your soul, either. In Hebrews 5:14, *gumnazo* is used to speak of training one's conscience to be discerning. "But solid food is for the mature, who because of practice have their senses trained to discern good and evil."

But there is also an improper form of training. Peter, speaking of certain ungodly individuals who had somehow planted themselves alongside the true believers to whom he was writing, uses the same *gumnazo* term to describe the development of a particular wrong habit.

> They [false prophets and teachers] are stains and blemishes, reveling in their deceptions, as they carouse with you, having eyes full of adultery that never cease from sin, enticing unstable souls, having a heart *trained* [*gumnazo*] in greed, accursed children; forsaking the right way, they have gone astray, having followed the way of Balaam, the son of Beor, who loved the wages of unrighteousness. (2 Peter 2:13–15)

2. Notice the similarity between this word and our English words *gymnasium* and *gymnastics*.

> Can an Ethiopian change his skin
> or a leopard its spots?
> Neither can you do good
> who are *accustomed* to doing evil. (Jer. 13:23 NIV)

Apart from Christ, we all have a bent toward developing sinful habits. Apart from Christ and His Word, we will habituate ourselves to speak, act, think, and be motivated in ways that displease God. Left to our own devices, we would be filled with our own ways (see Prov. 1:30–31; 14:14). But with the help of the Spirit and the Scriptures we can train ourselves to think, speak, act, and be motivated biblically.

EXERCISING GODLY COMMUNICATION SKILLS

On the pages that follow, you will learn an exercise that will help you and the people you converse with to improve your ability to effectively resolve conflicts. Before we proceed, let me explain the biblical basis of the exercise.

In Proverbs 15:28 we read, "The heart of the righteous ponders how to answer." Sometimes, in conflict, Christians don't know what to say. So they must study (think through) a good way to answer. Proverbs 16:23 says, "The heart of the wise instructs his mouth, and adds persuasiveness to his lips." A wise person thinks carefully about what he is going to say so that his words will have the greatest possible impact.

I often encourage couples to face and address each other as I am counseling them. There are several reasons why I do this. First, it gets them talking about vital issues (which they have either avoided discussing previously or have been unsuccessful in resolving). The second reason I encourage this practice is to learn what I can about their communication and conflict-resolution techniques. But there is a third and most important reason: I want to train them to communicate and resolve conflicts as effectively as possible.

When I observe patterns of inappropriate speech or overtly sinful forms of communication, I will politely interrupt and ask the offending party to redo what he or she was trying to say. In other words, I have him practice an alternative, more biblical way of communicating.

The *gumnazo* principle can be illustrated with the example of a master and a disciple, or even an intern who is in training to be an expert himself one day. In Jesus' day, a master and his disciples would live together, eat all meals together, and generally go about all their life tasks together.

Think of a blacksmith who is training his apprentice. Imagine the master craftsman explaining and demonstrating the equipment. See him as he tells his apprentice to pay careful attention as he slowly goes through the entire process of making a horseshoe, from lighting the bellows to shoeing the horse's hoof with the finished product, explaining each procedure in great detail. At some point the master craftsman allows the apprentice to help with some of the procedure.

After the Master is convinced that the apprentice understands the entire procedure, he turns the anvil, forge, and hammers over to his disciple. But, rather than standing in front of him to observe his work from afar, the master stands right behind him so that he can correct him on the spot should he make a mistake. Picture this skilled teacher behind his apprentice, placing his hands firmly over the hands of the apprentice as they hold the iron in the fire until the iron has just the right glow of red. Then see the master craftsman (with his hands wrapped around the hands of his young protégé) quickly bringing the iron to the anvil, demonstrating to the apprentice just where to hammer the iron and just how hard to strike it. Then after a few exercises of this hands-on training the master is ready to allow the apprentice to try the procedure by himself. That's "the gumnazo principle" in action!

Like a director of a play, I help my counselees to improve their communication skills by having them rehearse, on the spot, an alternative (biblically acceptable) line in place of the one they have just flubbed. I want them to get it right, even if I have to put the words in their mouths myself. And it's not just their words that are subject to my corrections, but the tone of their voices and their body language as well.

During the early years of my marriage, I made various attempts to use this principle with my wife, Kim. On occasion, when she said something that I deemed to be less than gracious (see Eph. 4:29 and Col. 4:6), I would take the essence of what she had said, repackage it with a more gracious wrapping, and encourage her to repeat it back to me—again, not just with different words, but also with a different tone and possibly a different facial expression.

> Kim (angrily): "Would you take this garbage outside? It's been spilling out onto the floor for two days now!"
>
> Lou (calmly): "Sweetheart, it would really mean a lot to me if you would take the garbage outside."

At this point she would (usually) give it back to me the way I suggested—typically through gritted teeth that would give way to a smile before she finished getting it out. Then I would respond appropriately.

> Kim: "Sweetheart, it would really mean a lot to me if you would take out the garbage."
>
> Lou: "Certainly, dear. It would be my pleasure to take the garbage out for such a lovely and gracious woman as you."

I probably initiated this exercise unilaterally for well over a year. Then one day it happened.

> Lou (in crescendo): "You spent how much for that? I can't believe you bought that without checking with me first! What were you thinking? I thought we agreed that we wouldn't spend more than twenty-five dollars for unbudgeted items without consulting the other person first!"
>
> Kim: "Sweetheart, didn't we agree not to spend more than twenty-five dollars for unbudgeted items without consulting the other person first?"

Lou (through gritted teeth): "Sweetheart, didn't we agree not to spend more than twenty-five dollars for unbudgeted items without consulting the other person first?"

Kim: "We sure did, honey. But, if you remember, we also agreed that if one of us saw something we needed that was on sale (even if it was more than twenty-five dollars and was outside the budget), we could go ahead and purchase it—subject to the other person's approval. And, if the other person didn't like it, we agreed that we would return it for a refund."

Now the point of this exercise is not to show off how cleverly we can think on our feet, but rather to help those whom we love (and ourselves) to learn how to practice biblical communication and to recover from conflicts that would otherwise have gone south in a hurry and ended without resolution.

So this is essentially the exercise I would like to propose: when either you, or people with whom you regularly converse, believe that the other is violating any number of biblical communication principles, the pre-agreed-upon response will be to prompt the other person to redo the offending line. Depending on the person you are talking with, and what that person prefers, the prompt may be made in several different ways.[3]

It may be communicated in the form of a question.

- "Would you please try that again by asking me a question rather than something that comes across as an accusation?"
- "Would you like to try that again, as per our agreement, without the sarcasm?"
- "Would you mind asking me what my motives for doing that were instead of uncharitably judging them?"

3. These are only suggested prompts. There are certainly many other (and even better) ways to select and syntactically arrange words that will encourage the rewording of an inappropriate response.

- "Honey, do you think you could please repeat those instructions so as to make it clear that you are talking to your 'co-heir,' 'weaker vessel' wife rather than one of your subordinates at work?"

Or the prompt can take on the tenor of a coach who is demonstrating to one of his players how to improve his game.

- "Let's try that again with a little more grace and a lot less salt."
- "Honey, that was kind of harsh. I think that can be said with more gentleness."
- "Son, that really came across disrespectfully. Please see if you can make that point more politely."
- "Please say that again without rolling your eyes."

Or you can simply suggest a better (more biblical) way to make the point.

- "May I suggest a more gracious way to say that?"
- "I think it would be more appropriate if you were to say it this way . . ."
- "Please try it this way . . ."
- "It would really make it much easier for me to do what you are asking if you made your request like this . . ."

With certain family members, it might even be acceptable to skip the polite suggestion and simply prompt them with the correction (the revised version) itself. (Use your imagination to figure out what may have prompted each reworded line.)

- "Sweetheart, would you mind helping me locate my keys? I seem to have misplaced them again."
- "I'm going to need your undivided attention for a few minutes. When would be a good time for us to talk?"

- "Dad, I was wrong for being so disrespectful to you. Will you forgive me?"
- "Honey, would you mind very much stopping at the next gas station to ask for directions?"

Of course, certain things ought not to be said at all, and there is really no good way to redo these types of remarks. In such cases, probably the best responses would be to either overlook the comment or point out that the comment was rude or disrespectful and request the other person to ask for your forgiveness for making it.

The directives found in Luke 17:3 may be applicable to certain forms of sinful communication. "If your brother sins, rebuke him; and if he repents, forgive him." We don't often seriously consider the idea of pressuring people to ask for our forgiveness (especially for something as "minor" as an inappropriate comment), but as we have seen, if it is something that cannot be overlooked, this is the biblical thing to do. Of course, if the other person is willing to show repentance for what he said by cooperating with this rewording exercise, his cooperation could be taken as the equivalent of saying "I repent." ("And if he sins against you seven times a day, and returns to you seven times, saying, 'I repent,' forgive him"—Luke 17:4.)

Now admittedly, this exercise seems a bit childish. But that is probably more a function of our pride (which resists the idea of relearning how to communicate at the hands of a peer or family member) than anything else. The concept is certainly a biblical one—not only on the face of it (see Prov. 15:28) but also in the spirit. (I'm referring to that spirit of humility that we looked at in the previous chapter that, generally speaking, communicates from the posture of a learner and a servant and leaves a crack in the door for the possibility that it may be wrong.)

The time that you invest up front doing this exercise should save you much time (and aggravation) in the long run. This is so for at least two reasons. In the short term, by immediately replacing unbiblical patterns of speech with biblical ones, you will train yourself to communicate more biblically. (Your heart will teach your lips how.) The more you (and your opponent) do this, the less time it will take you to solve conflicts. Second, you will learn over time how to stop stepping on those unique land mines that seemingly explode only in the mind of your foil and will instead learn how to speak his language (in a way that most effectively gets through to him).

13

HAVE WE GONE TOO FAR?

HOW FAR IS TOO FAR? I mean, how far into a conflict (in terms of minutes) are most people willing to go before they conclude that they have reached the point of no return—the point at which the conflict cannot be salvaged? Would you say about sixty minutes? Forty? Twenty? Ten? Five?

You say, "I guess that depends on the reasonableness of both participants in the conflict."

Okay. Suppose that they are both reasonably reasonable. How far is too far?

I have not been able to find the national average, but for the purpose of our discussion, let's say that most people are willing to give it about twenty minutes.

The real question I want to address in this chapter is, "At what point in a conflict that is headed in the wrong direction can one party turn things around and get the conflict back on track?"

In the course of any conflict, each participant is usually attempting to persuade the other over to "his way of thinking." Of course, each person ought also to be trying to fully understand the other person's point of view. As the conversation unfolds, back and forth they go, each fervently trying to persuade (and understand) the other. It may take five minutes or it may take fifty minutes. But by the time the conflict is over, hopefully either one will persuade the other, they will both persuade each other and will come up with some form of hybrid resolution (agreement), or they will come to the realization that it is perfectly acceptable for them to disagree about the matter. The bottom line is that at the end of the day they will both have the same "bottom line"—they will be speaking the same thing. They will be in agreement with each other.

Let's consider the following conflict.

Wife: "Honey, are we lost?"
Husband: "No, we're not. I know exactly where we are."
Wife: "But we've passed this gas station six times already."
Husband: "It was three. I know it's around here somewhere."
Wife: "Well, maybe we should ask for directions."
Husband: "That's not necessary. It's got to be around here somewhere."
Wife: "Okay, but we're already ten minutes late."
Husband: "I think it's just around the corner."
Wife: "I think we're lost."
Husband: "We're not lost!"
Wife: "I thought you said you knew how to get there."
Husband: "I do know how to get there . . . from work."
Wife: "There's that gas station again. Would you please . . ."
Husband: "I think I'll go in and ask for directions."

Notice that this couple ultimately made it to the same "bottom line." The husband conceded that they were lost (at least by inference) and that he should therefore ask for directions. They ultimately spoke the same thing—they agreed.[1]

But what do you suppose would happen if one of them prematurely terminated the conflict by blowing up (out of anger) or clamming up (let's say, out of fear)? The dispute would come to a screeching halt, the remainder of the conflict would not take place, and there would be no resolution. What a pity that would be!

1. By the way, this is an example of where one might choose to overlook an offense or talk about it later, as the husband chooses to overlook his wife's passionate persistence as he accepts her point that he does indeed need to ask for directions.

HELPING THE OTHER PERSON TO COMMUNICATE

As we saw in chapter 2, blowing up and clamming up are not biblical responses to conflict. Both reactions break the communication circuit, which causes the lights to go out immediately. When one person trips the circuit breaker, the other ought to make every effort to switch it back on immediately by gently calling the other person back to the conflict—and, if necessary, by calling him to repentance.

This can be done in a variety of ways.[2] Essentially, the person who has not blown the circuit may urge the person who has to redo his sinful response, ask forgiveness for it (in certain cases),[3] and come back to the table recommitted to resolving the conflict according to biblical principles. Of course, it may be necessary to take a short break (for a few minutes) for the person who is upset to collect his composure before the conflict resumes. And there may be occasions when the conflict will have to be postponed, but preferably not before the person who broke the circuit (who prematurely halted the conversation by either blowing up or clamming up) has sought forgiveness and committed to finish the conflict in accordance with biblical principles later on—until, in other words, he offers a rain check to the party who came to the conflict expecting a fair fight.

Communicating with the One Who Blows Up

Here are a few examples of what "calling the other back to the table" might[4] sound like. Let's begin with what can be said by the one who is trying to help the "blower-upper."

- "I think I know why you are upset. I shouldn't have said that. It was ________________ [identifying in biblical terms the exact nature of your own sin]. Will you please forgive me and allow me to try making my point a different way?"

2. Some of the methodologies discussed in the last chapter are also applicable here.

3. It may be wise in some cases to overlook the offense or to cover it for love's sake.

4. These are just suggestions. They are not the only or even the best options available. If you can come up with better "lines" or can improve on the ones I have suggested, by all means do so.

- "You seem quite upset. If I have sinned somehow, please tell me and I will ask your forgiveness. But please, let's not end our conversation this way."
- "Please come back to the table. May I pray for us? And then can we try to get this conflict resolved in a God-honoring way?"
- "The Bible tells us to try to get our differences resolved quickly. Can we please try a little longer to get on the same page?"
- "We may not be able to get this conflict resolved today, but can we at least try to get our relationship resolved before the sun goes down?"
- "The Bible says, 'Be angry and do not sin.' I realize that you're upset, but the way you are trying to solve this conflict is sinful. I think the best thing you can do right now is to seek my forgiveness for ________________ [identifying in biblical terms the exact nature of your opponent's sin] and to continue having this discussion with me according to biblical principles."
- "Could you repeat that in a different way?" (or "Would you repeat that please?")

Communicating with the One Who Clams Up

Now, let's look at a few "call back" options for one who is trying to assist the "clammer-upper."

- "I think I know why you are troubled [or whatever other descriptive term is appropriate]. I shouldn't have said that. It was [identifying in biblical terms the exact nature of your own sin]. Will you please forgive me and allow me to try making my point a different way?"
- "You seem to be rather frustrated with me. If I have sinned somehow, please tell me and I will be happy to ask your forgiveness. But please, let's not stop trying to resolve this issue."
- "Please don't stop now. Can we pray and ask the Lord to help us to get through this in a way that pleases Him?"
- "May we please keep trying to resolve this issue? If you would like to take a little break, perhaps we can do that. But we must

make every effort to maintain the unity of the Spirit in the bond of peace. So I would like to keep trying to resolve this."

- "Please tell me, exactly, what is it you see that I'm doing or saying that is tempting you to withdraw from this conversation, so that we may continue."
- "This issue is very important to me. I am willing to do whatever is biblically necessary to get things between us resolved quickly, effectively, and with a minimum amount of sin. What can I do to make it easier for you to continue?"
- "How about we simply take a fifteen-minute break, spend a little time in private prayer, and then come back to the table for one more round of talks. I think we will both do better if we have some time to compose our thoughts."

Let me give you a word of caution at this point: There may be circumstances when there is good reason to postpone initiating (or participating in) a conflict. If the other person is enraged or is under the influence of a substance, for example, it may be best to hold off having the discussion until the person is in full control of his faculties. If he has serious character issues—if he is what the Bible calls "an angry man," or a fool, or a "scorner"—it may be wise to seek counsel before you proceed with the conflict (if you proceed at all).[5]

RECOVERING A CONFLICT THAT STARTS BADLY

Now the thing that most people don't realize (and the most important point I want to make in this little chapter) is that most conflicts

5. There are certain kinds of people who the book of Proverbs warns us not to confront. For if we do, there will be consequences. It is my belief that these warnings apply generally to unbelievers. The Proverbs contain truisms—i.e., *principles* (things that are generally true but not necessarily true in all cases). On the other hand, Matthew 18:15, Luke 17:3, and Galatians 6:1 are *imperatives* that instruct us about how to deal with believers. I am persuaded that the New Testament imperatives "trump" the Old Testament principles, and therefore professing Christians (who are members in good standing in Bible-believing churches), as a rule, ought to be confronted even if they possess these ungodly characteristics.

that go south are quite recoverable—even if the participants have been battling it out in the most unbiblical fashion for thirty minutes or longer. Let me say it again: humility begets humility. Even after twenty minutes (or more) of knock-down, drag-out quarreling, either party, by recognizing his own sinful contributions to the problem, confessing them, seeking forgiveness for them, and recommitting to proceed according to biblical principles, can often turn the entire conflict 180 degrees around—and can do it pretty much "on a dime." So often when one person does what Jesus said to—looking at and removing the beam in his own eye *first*—the other person will usually follow suit. Why? Because there is something quite disarming about humility! Allow me to illustrate how this can work.

Soon after the argument begins, Barney and Betty passionately embark on shifting the blame for the problem (an unresolved conflict from the night before) to each other. As the conversation rages on for well over twenty minutes, they begin interrupting each other. Barney raises his voice, makes several bitterly sarcastic comments to Betty, and calls her a very unflattering name. She retaliates by judging his motives quite uncharitably, talking to him in the most demeaning way, and exaggerating something that he has done far beyond almost all recognition. They are both very hurt and so angry that they have little interest in the validity of the other person's perspective. At this point, all they really want to do is retaliate.

Then, at twenty-six minutes and twelve seconds into the conflict, Barney remembers that all is not necessarily lost. "It will be hard," he tells himself, "but by God's grace I'm going to be the first one to put his neck on the chopping block."

So, after a silent prayer of repentance to God and a plea for the grace to clothe himself with humility, he says to Betty, "Hold on! You think I'm to blame, and I think you're to blame. Let me go first. I need to ask your forgiveness for the terrible way I have been talking to you for the last few minutes. I have been sinfully angry, and in the process have been very harsh with you. I have unjustly shifted the blame to you, and I shouldn't have called you that terrible name. I shouldn't have even allowed it to go through my mind. I have been way too sarcastic and vindictive with you. I'm sure that I have hurt you very much, and I am sorry for that. I know I don't deserve it, but do you think you could find it in your heart to forgive me?"

"Sure I'll forgive you. But you really are sorry!"

"I know. Is there anything else I need to ask your forgiveness for?"

"I suppose that covers it."

At this point Barney is trying to figure out how to talk to Betty about the things she has done to offend him, in the hopes of getting her to ask for forgiveness. Betty knows what is coming next, so she preempts him by saying, "Barney, before you go any further, let me ask your forgiveness for what I know I have done wrong. To begin with, I am also guilty of blame shifting and of judging your motives. And I was way too angry and disrespectful to you. Will you forgive me for these things?"

"Sure, but I think you forgot something."

"I probably did. What else do I need to make right with you?"

"I think that you falsely accused me by your hyperbolic account of our discussion last night."

"You're right. I didn't mean to falsely accuse you. I just thought that if I exaggerated what you said a little (. . . all right, maybe more than 'a little'), you would realize how much your words hurt me."

"Honey, I can appreciate the fact that you want me to understand the impact of your words, but do *you* understand the impact of *your* words on me? When you exaggerated what I said (especially with the tone in your voice and the contorted expression that you put on your face), I became so angry at what I perceived was a blatantly false accusation that, at that moment, I really couldn't have cared less about how much my words might have hurt you."

"I understand. You're right. I shouldn't have done it. Will you please forgive me?"

"I will. And thank you."

"Thank you for going first—for showing more humility than I did."

"You're welcome. So where do we go from here? Shall we continue with our discussion, or shall we take a little break?"

"I would like to take a little break. But I promise, when we get back together, I will have a much better attitude."

"Me too! Thank the Lord for giving us the grace to turn around this disastrous conversation."

Now, of course, things will probably not go this smoothly the first time you try to stick out your neck. But, even if it takes a little longer (or a lot longer) to turn your next conflict around than it took Barney and Betty, it will almost certainly take less time to resolve things with humility than with pride. "Through insolence comes nothing but strife" (Prov. 13:10; cf. 28:25).

"But what if I humble myself by sticking my neck on the chopping block first, and instead of responding in kind, my opponent tries to chop off my head?"

Then perhaps you should let him. Continue to respond in humility until you have secured his forgiveness. If, after a reasonable amount of time, he will not reciprocate by voluntarily acknowledging his sin, you may rightly pressure him to assume responsibility for it—that is, you may then use the Scriptures to convict him. If he will not hear you, it may[6] then be necessary to get another believer involved.

TURNING AWAY WRATH

Even in the midst of a heated conflict, a humble spirit can often disarm a proud and angry opponent. "A gentle answer turns away wrath, but a harsh word stirs up anger" (Prov. 15:1).

There was no love lost between Esau and his brother, Jacob. "So Esau *bore a grudge against* Jacob because of the blessing with which his father had blessed him; and Esau said to himself, 'The days of mourning for my father are near; then I will kill my brother Jacob'" (Gen. 27:41). It was so bad that when Jacob left his father-in-law, Laban, to return home, he was afraid for his life, believing that Esau still had it in for him. He pleaded with God, saying, "Deliver me, I pray, from the hand of my brother, from the hand of Esau; for I fear him, that he will come and attack me and the mothers with the children" (Gen. 32:11). But besides

6. I say "may" because, as a Christian, you always have the option of "overlooking," "covering," or "taking it on the chin"—in other words, putting up with wrong (see 1 Cor. 6:7) for a few rounds before you move on to the next phase of the Matthew 18:15–17 procedure.

praying, Jacob humbled himself before his offended brother, sending him presents, bowing down seven times, and repeatedly referring to himself (indirectly through his family members) as "your servant" and to Esau directly (face to face) as "my lord." What he didn't know was that Yahweh had been working in his brother's heart. What was the result? In the midst of this contrition, the Bible says, "Then Esau ran to meet him and embraced him, and fell on his neck and kissed him, and they wept" (Gen. 33:4).

David, by humbling himself before King Saul, evoked a humble response from his insanely jealous and suspicious persecutor on more than one occasion.

> Now afterward David arose and went out of the cave and called after Saul, saying, "*My lord the king!*" And when Saul looked behind him, *David bowed with his face to the ground and prostrated himself.* David said to Saul, "Why do you listen to the words of men, saying, 'Behold, David seeks to harm you'? Behold, this day your eyes have seen that the Lord had given you today into my hand in the cave, and some said to kill you, *but my eye had pity on you*; and I said, '*I will not stretch out my hand against my lord, for he is the Lord's anointed.*' Now, *my father*, see! Indeed, see the edge of your robe in my hand! For in that I cut off the edge of your robe and did not kill you, know and perceive that there is no evil or rebellion in my hands, and I have not sinned against you, though you are lying in wait for my life to take it. May the Lord judge between you and me, and may the Lord avenge me on you; *but my hand shall not be against you.*" . . . When David had finished speaking these words to Saul, Saul said, "Is this your voice, my son David?" Then Saul lifted up his voice and wept. He said to David, "*You are more righteous than I; for you have dealt well with me, while I have dealt wickedly with you.* You have declared today that you have done good to me, that the Lord delivered me into your hand and yet you did not kill me. For if a man finds his enemy, will he let him go away safely? *May the Lord therefore reward you with good in return for what you have done to me this day.* Now, behold, I know that you will surely be king, and that the kingdom of Israel will be established in your hand." (1 Sam. 24:8–12, 16–20)

> Then Saul recognized David's voice and said, "Is this your voice, my son David?" And David said, "It is my voice, *my lord the king.*" He also said, "Why then is my lord pursuing *his servant*? For what have I done? Or what evil is in my hand?" . . . Then Saul said, "*I have sinned.* Return, my son David, for I will not harm you again because my life was precious in your sight this day. *Behold, I have played the fool and have committed a serious error.*" . . . So David went on his way, and Saul returned to his place. (1 Sam. 26:17–18, 21, 25)

And let's not forget Abigail's response to David when her husband, Nabal, was incredibly rude to David and his men.

> But Nabal answered David's servants and said, "Who is David? And who is the son of Jesse? There are many servants today who are each breaking away from his master. Shall I then take my bread and my water and my meat that I have slaughtered for my shearers, and give it to men whose origin I do not know?" (1 Sam. 25:10–11)

Notice how Abigail's grace and humility not only disarm David but also prevent him from carrying out his vindictive plan to kill Nabal and his household.

> Then Abigail hurried and took two hundred loaves of bread and two jugs of wine and five sheep already prepared and five measures of roasted grain and a hundred clusters of raisins and two hundred cakes of figs, and loaded them on donkeys. She said to her young men, "Go on before me; behold, I am coming after you." But she did not tell her husband Nabal. It came about as she was riding on her donkey and coming down by the hidden part of the mountain, that behold, David and his men were coming down toward her; so she met them. Now David had said, "Surely in vain I have guarded all that this man has in the wilderness, so that nothing was missed of all that belonged to him; and he has returned me evil for good. May God do so to the enemies of David, and more also, if by morning I leave as much as one male of any who belong to him." When Abigail saw David, she hurried and

> dismounted from her donkey, and fell on her face before David and *bowed herself to the ground.* She fell at his feet and said, "On me alone, *my lord,* be the blame. And please let *your maidservant* speak to you, and listen to the words of your maidservant. Please do not let my lord pay attention to this worthless man, Nabal, for as his name is, so is he. Nabal is his name and folly is with him; but I your maidservant did not see the young men of *my lord* whom you sent. Now therefore, *my lord,* as the Lord lives, and as your soul lives, since the Lord has restrained you from shedding blood, and from avenging yourself by your own hand, now then let your enemies and those who seek evil against my lord, be as Nabal. Now let this gift which your maidservant has brought to my lord be given to the young men who accompany *my lord. Please forgive the transgression of your maidservant;* for the Lord will certainly make for my lord an enduring house, because *my lord* is fighting the battles of the Lord, and evil will not be found in you all your days. Should anyone rise up to pursue you and to seek your life, then the life of *my lord* shall be bound in the bundle of the living with the Lord your God; but the lives of your enemies He will sling out as from the hollow of a sling. And when the Lord does for my lord according to all the good that He has spoken concerning you, and appoints you ruler over Israel, this will not cause grief or a troubled heart to my lord, both *by having shed blood without cause and by my lord having avenged himself.* When the Lord deals well with my lord, then remember *your maidservant.*" Then David said to Abigail, "Blessed be the Lord God of Israel, who sent you this day to meet me, and blessed be your discernment, and blessed be you, who have *kept me this day from bloodshed and from avenging myself by my own hand.* Nevertheless, as the Lord God of Israel lives, who has restrained me from harming you, *unless you had come quickly to meet me, surely there would not have been left to Nabal until the morning light as much as one male.*" So David received from her hand what she had brought him and said to her, "Go up to your house in peace. See, I have listened to you and granted your request." (1 Sam. 25:18–35)

Of course, there is no guarantee that humility will always beget humility in conflict—especially when God has hardened someone's heart (like Pharaoh's) for his own purposes. But we are to "clothe ourselves with humility" because it is what we have been commanded to do (not because we believe that it will get us what we want). Nevertheless, humility is far more effective in bringing about a successful resolution to conflicts than arrogance is.

Here is a worksheet to help you to get started planning how you might leave that crack in the door the next time you are in conflict. In the column on the left, record the name (or initials) of the persons with whom you are most likely to be in conflict (probably the ones with whom you have had the most conflict in the past). In the right column, record some of the ways you can demonstrate humility to that person during your next conflict.

Person with whom I might have a conflict	What I can say/do to clothe myself with humility

14

THE HIDDEN PREREQUISITE

I WAITED TO TELL YOU THAT, technically, there is another prerequisite to solving conflicts God's way hidden[1] in the Ephesians 4 passage. It's diligence: "*being diligent* to preserve the unity of the Spirit in the bond of peace" (v. 3). I say that this present active participle is a prerequisite because if you lack diligence you will find it difficult to consistently implement the instructions of this verse.

The Greek word for *diligent* is *spoudazontes*.[2] It means to make a zealous effort, to do one's best. It characterizes the total conduct of the Christian as he grows in his Christian life.[3] In other words, it has to do with exerting the energy necessary to bring about in the daily reality of one's life on earth (progressive sanctification) what has been accomplished in books of heaven (positional sanctification). In early church literature it was used to denote striving after true Christian conduct.[4]

1. I say that it is hidden because, in our modern versions, this injunction is separated from the character traits in verse 2 by the verse number (3), which breaks the flow of the sentence a bit. Also, the present active participle in the original is not passive (as the last prerequisite, forbearance, is in verse 2). This gives it more of a "don't stop doing this" flavor than the previous four characteristics have (the first three of which are simply nouns).

2. It is a present active participle in the Greek. Hence it is essentially a verb.

3. *Theological Dictionary of the New Testament*, trans. and ed. Geoffrey W. Bromiley, vol. 7, Σ, ed. Gerhard Friedrich (Grand Rapids: Eerdmans, 1971), 565.

4. Ibid.

But it involves more than just action. An assumed motivation associated with this word might well be rendered, "Make this your highest priority," or "Pour yourself into this task."[5] So to be diligent is not to have a casual or laid-back attitude. Being a peacemaker is hard work. It requires determination.

Today, as throughout church history, there are those who would have us "look to Christ" for our spiritual growth in a manner that is passive (and reflective) more than it is active. In his booklet *Temptation*, Jay Adams explains that balance is necessary to grow by grace.

> The teaching in Christian circles today tends to offer one of two basic options: (1) inaction on your part in lieu of contemplation and prayer; or (2) obedience to biblical commands that leads to growth. . . .
>
> While the two options are often set in opposition to each other, it is incorrect to view matters that way. Aspects of both must be combined in order to take in the full scope of biblical teaching. It is surely not impossible to consider one's ways, pray about them, and then do what God's Word directs.[6]

The balance between the two can be clearly seen in at least three passages in the New Testament. The first is 1 Corinthians 15:10. "But by the grace of God I am what I am, and His grace toward me did not prove vain; but *I labored* even more than all of them, *yet not I, but the grace of God with me.*" Paul labored (often to the point of exhaustion, as the Greek indicates), but he realized that it was God who was doing it through him. In Colossians 1:29 we see the same dynamic.

> We proclaim Him, admonishing every man and teaching every man with all wisdom, so that we may present every man complete in Christ. For this purpose also *I labor, striving* according to *His power, which mightily works within me.* (Col. 1:28–29)

5. Daniel B. Wallace, "Crisis of the Word: A Message to Pastors and Would-Be Pastors (2 Timothy 2:15)," *Conservative Theological Journal* 1, no. 2 (1997): 109.

6. Jay E. Adams, *Temptation: Applying Radical Amputation to Life's Sinful Patterns* (Phillipsburg, NJ: P&R Publishing, 2012), 6–7.

The same energy[7] (see Col. 2:12) that raised Christ from the dead worked in Paul as he labored. The present active tense of this verb (the same word for *labor* as in 1 Cor. 15:10) is continuous. Like the Energizer Bunny, it keeps going and going and going. The word *striving* is *agonizomai*. It assumes the exertion of energies.

In Philippians 2:12–13 we again find this "He works / I work" principle. "*Work out your salvation* with fear and trembling; for *it is God* [the Holy Spirit] *who is at work in you*, both to will and to work for His good pleasure." The salvation that we are commanded in this passage to work out is obviously not the destination of our soul after death. God has already worked that out for us through Christ's work on the cross. The directive to work out our salvation (or to bring it to completion) addresses our responsibility to actively participate in the work of progressive sanctification. So to cooperate with the Spirit (and to let Him lead you) you must, by faith and in dependence upon Him, do what the Bible says is necessary to grow as a Christian.

This book is filled with contemplative material intended to get you to look deep into your heart through the lens of Scripture and to prayerfully reflect on your thoughts and motives. But it also contains much in the way of actions to be taken—exercises to practice, words to say, and things to do in order to help you learn how to solve conflicts God's way. But the bottom line is that they will do you little good unless you put forth effort, as the Scriptures command. You must pursue peace. And you must develop the mind-set of a peacemaker.

In Romans 14:19, Paul says, "So then let us pursue what makes for peace and for mutual upbuilding" (ESV). The word that is rendered *pursue* in this passage means "to seek after" (see 1 Thess. 5:15). But it can also mean to persecute, as it does in Romans 12:14: "Bless those that persecute you." If we render the Romans 12 passage with that meaning, it sounds something like this: "So then let us persecute one another in the process of making peace."

Have you ever considered Hebrews 12:14? "Pursue peace with all men, and the sanctification without which no one will see the Lord."

7. The word *power* here is *energeia* in the original.

The Greek imperative for *pursue* is used here. So this passage commands us to *pursue* not only peace with all men (believers and unbelievers) but also sanctification, or holiness. That's right; we are to pursue peace with unbelievers as well as with believers. "All *types of* men" is the idea. Of course, it is not always possible for Christians to be at peace with unbelievers—even in marriage (see 1 Cor. 7:15). But we must *try*, according to Romans 12:18: "If possible, so far as it depends on you, live at peace with all men." Although we may not always be able to resolve conflicts with unbelievers, there is no good reason why two *believers* cannot learn how to be at peace with each other.

Romans 12:18 has two clauses—one is conditional, the other unconditional. The first stipulation is the *conditional* one: "*If possible* . . . live at peace with all men." The second clause is *unconditional*: "*So far as it depends on you*, be at peace with all men." You and I must "pursue peace with all men" (Heb. 12:14) *regardless* of their response to us. Our obedience to God does not depend on the response of others. Our love for our neighbors (or enemies) should not be conditional—not predicated on their love for us. Regardless of our offenders' willingness to be at peace with us, *we* should be willing to be at peace with them (initiating and pursuing them if necessary)—especially when they are fellow believers.

If the person with whom you are having a conflict is not at peace with you, don't jump to the conclusion that it is because he is not at peace with God. It's possible that the reason you are not at peace with each other is because of some things that "depend on you." Let me suggest some reasons that your offender may not be at peace with you.[8] Here are three self-evaluation questions to consider if an opponent has sinned against you.

1. Have I *provoked* my opponent to sin? Your opponent's contention with you may, in part, be a sinful response to an offense that you first committed against him. While he is not thereby exonerated, you are required to seek his forgiveness for any sin you may have committed that provoked him to sin in the first place.

8. Adapted from my booklet *Bitterness: The Root That Pollutes* (Phillipsburg, NJ: P&R Publishing, 2008). I am indebted again to Jay Adams and his little booklet *How to Overcome Evil: A Practical Exposition of Romans 12:14–21* (1977; repr., Phillipsburg, NJ: P&R Publishing, 2010) for these self-evaluation questions.

2. Have I *protracted* (aggravated) his sin by a sinful response in return? Is it possible that, rather than responding with good to your opponent's sin, you responded in kind (perhaps with even more evil than he inflicted against you) and that such a sinful response on your part has contributed greatly to the lack of peace between you?

3. Have I *prolonged* the problem by not dealing with it quickly? Conflicts between believers are to be resolved expeditiously. "If therefore you are presenting your offering at the altar, and there remember that your brother has something against you, leave your offering there before the altar and go; first be reconciled to your brother, and then come and present your offering" (Matt. 5:23–24). The longer you wait to resolve conflicts, the more bitterness and suspicion can take root and fester.

Other passages in the New Testament speak to our responsibility to pursue peace. In 1 Peter 3 we are exhorted,[9]

> To sum up, all of you be harmonious, sympathetic, brotherly, kind-hearted, and humble in spirit; not returning evil for evil or insult for insult, but giving a blessing instead; for you were called for the very purpose that you might inherit a blessing. For,
>
> > "The one who desires life, to love and see good days,
> > Must keep his tongue from evil and his lips from speaking deceit.
> > He must turn away from evil and do good;
> > He must seek peace and pursue it.
> > For the eyes of the Lord are toward the righteous,
> > And His ears attend to their prayer,
> > But the face of the Lord is against those who do evil." (1 Peter 3:8–12)

The word for *harmonious* (v. 8)[10] denotes being like-minded. It is a compound term combining the ideas of "one and the same" and "mind." It might be better to think of it in terms of "having the same attitudes" or

9. These words are an extension of the injunction that precedes them. Although there is no imperative in the initial part of this verse, it is implied.

10. This is the only place in the New Testament where this exact word is used.

"having thoughts that follow the same path."[11] Peter goes on to quote a few verses from Psalm 34. Psalm 34:14 (verse 11b in 1 Peter 3) is the one that I want to unpack a bit for you. It has to do with our topic of diligently pursuing peace. This little line contains two imperatives: "The one who desires life, to love and see good days," it says, "*must seek* peace and *pursue* it."

The word for *seek* is the same term (and in the same active voice) that Jesus uses in Matthew 6:33: "But seek first His kingdom and His righteousness, and all these things will be added to you." It is used quite often in the Greek New Testament. A few of the basic meanings include "to inquire or ask about something," "to look for something in the hope of finding it," and "to desire and attempt to acquire something." Peace between believers is something that we as followers of Christ should want, hope for, and actively attempt to obtain.

The term for *pursue* is the same "follow after" and "persecute" word (*diṓkō*) that we see in Romans 12:14; 14:19; and Hebrews 12:14. It also is in the active voice, indicating that we are to do the pursuing.

We looked earlier at Colossians 3:15. It deserves a closer look here. "Let the peace of Christ rule in your hearts, to which indeed you were called in one body; and be thankful." This has become one of the most misapplied passages in the New Testament. Many people wrongly teach that the *peace* Paul is referring to is that internal, somewhat subjective peace that passes all understanding, which God gives to those who trust in Him. Believing that this text may be used to determine God's will in decision making (guidance), proponents of this view maintain that we ought not to make any decision if we don't have such peace.[12] But the context of this verse is not about guidance, but rather about how we are to relate to one another in Christ, putting on "heart[s] of compassion, kindness, humility, gentleness and patience; bearing with one another, and forgiving each other" (Col. 3:12–13).

The present, active imperative of the verb is rendered, "Let it [the peace of Christ] rule." *Rule* denotes acting as an arbiter or an umpire

11. Johannes P. Louw and Eugene A. Nida, *Greek-English Lexicon of the New Testament: Based on Semantic Domains*, 2nd ed. (New York: United Bible Societies, 1989), Logos Bible Software e-book.

12. There may be a bit of sound wisdom in that guiding principle, but it is derived from such texts as Romans 14:13 and 1 Corinthians 8:7, not from this one.

or a referee. In other words, the peace that flows out of our union with Christ is what is to "call the shots" in our dealings with others. Again, this is an imperative—it is a command for us to obey.

I would like for us to consider yet another interesting passage once more. Do you remember the two women who couldn't get along with each other, whom I briefly mentioned in chapter 5?

> I urge Euodia and I urge Syntyche to live in harmony in the Lord. Indeed, true companion, I ask you also to help these women who have shared my struggle in the cause of the gospel, together with Clement also and the rest of my fellow workers, whose names are in the book of life. (Phil. 4:2–3)

Something is rather odd in the way that Paul approaches these hard-working women. He *doesn't* say to them, "I urge Euodia *and* Syntyche to live in harmony in the Lord." He says, "I *urge* Euodia *and I urge* Syntyche to live in harmony in the Lord." Did you catch that? Paul doesn't address them both with the one verb *urge*, but rather repeats the same verb twice. He says, "I urge Euodia *and I urge* Syntyche." Why does he do that? He does it to stress the point that they both have a biblical responsibility to get along with each other in the Lord. Allow me to say it one more time: God doesn't want loose ends between Christians to be forever flapping in the breeze. He wants them tied up, and He puts the responsibility on both parties (the offended, as in Luke 17:3, and the offender, as in Matt. 5:24).

Euodia *and* Syntyche were also advised to accept the assistance of their "true companion" in the process. This leads to another element of making every effort to maintain unity: we must sometimes involve others in the process. If you are unsuccessful at resolving matters between you and another believer, remember this: you have not made every effort to maintain the unity of the Spirit in the bond of peace until you have enlisted the help of another mature Christian. I would again urge you to consult Ken Sande's book *Peacemaker* to learn how to do this in great detail.[13]

13. Another *very* helpful resource for this process is Jay E. Adams's book *Handbook of Church Discipline: A Right and Privilege of Every Church Member* (Grand Rapids: Zondervan, 1986).

As a counselor on staff at and an elder in my local church, I have frequently been called upon to help two members to resolve their differences when their attempts to do so between themselves has failed. You might be surprised to know that it is not always because someone has sinned. In other words, I'm not called upon only to be the second witness of a Matthew 18 type dispute. Sometimes it is a conflict of differentness, or one of righteousness, that prompts one or both parties to seek my help. John Calvin says that peacemakers are "those who not only seek peace and avoid quarrels, as far as lies in their power, but who also labor to settle differences among others, who advise all men to live at peace, and take away every occasion of hatred and strife."[14]

Of course, much more can be said about this matter than I have said in these few pages. Much more will doubtless be forthcoming from other Christian authors who are committed to the biblical peacemaking process. I pray that what I have written herein will be a helpful addition to the body of work currently in print and that it will strengthen the church of Jesus Christ around the world. From cultivating proper motives and attitudes to learning and sharpening your communication skills, by God's grace you can become a person who is proficient at promoting peace.

14. John Calvin, "Matthew 5:9," *Commentary on a Harmony of the Evangelists: Matthew, Mark, and Luke*, trans. William Pringle (Edinburgh, 1845), 1:264.

Appendix A

HOW TO USE A CONFLICT JOURNAL

HERE IS A TOOL that you can use to help you (and those to whom you minister) to implement the various conflict-resolution principles in this book. A conflict journal is composed of worksheets on which individuals can record, word for word, an account of the disputes in which they are involved so that they may both analyze their own conflict-resolution abilities and sharpen their conflict-resolution skills.

On the first several lines of the journal, record the context in which the conflict took place (time of day, location, and general activities of the participants). On the lines that follow, record the actual verbatim account of the conflict.

After completing the journal, set aside some time to review it, taking note of the extent to which you responded biblically to the conflict. Then go over it again, this time trying to determine at every point (exchange) how you may have more effectively used the things you have learned in this book. Consider finding a spiritually mature accountability partner to help you to review your journal entries.[1]

Several versions of the journal are provided on the pages that follow for use in a variety of contexts and depending on who initiates the conversation. These may be photocopied and used in accordance with the aforementioned instructions.

1. Be sure that the person who is holding you accountable cannot identify the persons with whom you are in conflict (unless you have permission to disclose their identities).

CONFLICT JOURNAL

Circumstances surrounding the conflict: ______________________________

____

____

____

Husband: ____

____

Wife: ____

____

Husband: ____

____

Wife: ____

____

Husband: ____

____

Wife: ____

____

Husband: ____

____

Wife: ____

____

Husband: ____

____

Wife: ____

____

Husband: ____

____

Wife: ____

____

Husband: ____

____

Wife: ____

____

Husband: ____

____

Wife: ____

____

Husband: ____

____

Wife: ____

____

Husband: ____

____

Wife: ____

____

Husband: ____

____

Wife: ____

____

CONFLICT JOURNAL

Circumstances surrounding the conflict: ______________________

____

____

____

Wife: ______________________

____

Husband: ______________________

____

Wife: ______________________

____

Husband: ______________________

____

Wife: ______________________

____

Husband: ______________________

____

Wife: ______________________

____

Husband: ______________________

____

Wife: ______________________

____

Husband: ______________________

____

Wife: ____

____

Husband: ____

____

Wife: ____

____

Husband: ____

____

Wife: ____

____

Husband: ____

____

Wife: ____

____

Husband: ____

____

Wife: ____

____

Husband: ____

____

Wife: ____

____

Husband: ____

____

CONFLICT JOURNAL

Circumstances surrounding the conflict: ______________________

____

____

____

Parent: ______________________________________

____

Child: ______________________________________

____

Parent: ______________________________________

____

Child: ______________________________________

____

Parent: ______________________________________

____

Child: ______________________________________

____

Parent: ______________________________________

____

Child: ______________________________________

____

Parent: ______________________________________

____

Child: ______________________________________

____

Parent: ______________________________

____

Child: ______________________________

____

Parent: ______________________________

____

Child: ______________________________

____

Parent: ______________________________

____

Child: ______________________________

____

Parent: ______________________________

____

Child: ______________________________

____

Parent: ______________________________

____

Child: ______________________________

____

Parent: ______________________________

____

Child: ______________________________

____

CONFLICT JOURNAL

Circumstances surrounding the conflict: ______________________

____

____

____

Child: ____

____

Parent: ____

____

Child: ____

____

Parent: ____

____

Child: ____

____

Parent: ____

____

Child: ____

____

Parent: ____

____

Child: ____

____

Parent: ____

____

Child: ____

____

Parent: ____

____

Child: ____

____

Parent: ____

____

Child: ____

____

Parent: ____

____

Child: ____

____

Parent: ____

____

Child: ____

____

Parent: ____

____

Child: ____

____

Parent: ____

____

CONFLICT JOURNAL

Circumstances surrounding the conflict: ____________________

____

____

____

Me: ____________________

____

Him/Her: ____________________

____

Me: ____________________

____

Him/Her: ____________________

____

Me: ____________________

____

Him/Her: ____________________

____

Me: ____________________

____

Him/Her: ____________________

____

Me: ____________________

____

Him/Her: ____________________

____

Me: ____

____

Him/Her: ____

____

Me: ____

____

Him/Her: ____

____

Me: ____

____

Him/Her: ____

____

Me: ____

____

Him/Her: ____

____

Me: ____

____

Him/Her: ____

____

Me: ____

____

Him/Her: ____

____

Appendix B

CONFLICTS WITH UNBELIEVERS

AS FOLLOWERS OF JESUS CHRIST, we are commanded to pursue peace with believer and unbeliever alike.

> If possible, so far as it depends on you, be at peace with *all men.* (Rom. 12:18)

> Pursue peace with *all men,* and the sanctification without which no one will see the Lord. (Heb. 12:14)

But the way that we approach conflicts with the believer in most cases is going to be different from the way we approach them with the unbeliever.

First of all, we know from the beginning that a conflict with a believer has a much greater likelihood of ending peacefully than a conflict with an unbeliever does. This is so primarily because, as we have seen, Jesus doesn't want there to be loose ends between His followers that haven't been properly tied up. He tells both the offended party as well as the offending party to initiate the peacemaking process. So, while it is not always possible for believers to get along with unbelievers (see 1 Cor. 7:15), it is possible for two believers to live (or to learn to live) at peace with each other.

Second, Christians have access to more biblical peacemaking resources than do unbelievers. We have the Scriptures, which, as we have seen, provide quite a few insights into conflict resolution. We have the Holy Spirit, who supernaturally enables us to obey these conflict-solving directives and principles, and we have the local church, which is a repository of teachers, counselors, and mediators.[1]

Third, we stand a better chance of seeing "eye to eye" with believers, with whom we have so much in common, than we do with unbelievers, whose worldview is very often quite different from (if not antagonistic to) ours.

So what are the differences between the way we resolve conflicts with believers and the way we attempt to do so with unbelievers? An entire book would need to be written in order to address this question adequately. For now, I can suggest only a few basic principles for your consideration.

1. We may use the Scriptures more readily with believers than with unbelievers.

Whether it is bringing conviction, exhorting, persuading, defending, instructing, or anything else we might use the Scriptures for in conflict with a fellow believer, we must take care not to give that which is holy to the dogs (unbelievers) or to throw our pearls before swine (unbelievers), lest they trample them under their feet and turn and tear us to pieces (see Matt. 7:6). Concerning unbelievers, the Bible also says, "But a natural man does not accept the things of the Spirit of God, for they are foolishness to him; and he cannot understand them, because they are spiritually appraised" (1 Cor. 2:14).

So, while we may be able to use biblical truth and principles,[2] we may not often be able to quote chapter and verse to them.

But, on the other hand, the Word of God is swift and powerful; it can be effectively used to convict unbelievers of their sin. I had a professor

1. In fact, we are told to avoid entering into the civil court system to settle disputes with each other (1 Cor. 6:1–8), where we would be less likely to have the dispute settled biblically.

2. Jay E. Adams, *The Christian Counselor's New Testament* (Stanley NC: Timeless Texts, 1977), 165.

who would use an analogy to demonstrate how powerful Scripture can be even with someone who doesn't believe that it is what it is.

Two men were dueling over the affection of a woman. The swords they were using were sharp. The first took a swipe at the other's neck in the hopes of severing his opponent's head from its body. The second took a step back in order to avoid getting beheaded and, after the swipe, proudly said to the first, "You missed me." The first smiled and said, "Oh, no I didn't! Just try to wiggle your head!"

The point is that just because someone doesn't believe in the sharpness of the Sword (or doesn't feel its penetrating edge), that does not mean it can't slice. So we must use discernment to know how, to what degree, and when to use the Scriptures when confronting unbelievers. Certainly the use of the Word is essential when we are presenting the gospel. And there are times when the Scriptures may be effectively used (although prudently so) in relational conflicts with those who do not profess Christ. "The reason I cannot do what you would like is because, as a Christian, I am instructed to ____________." I have known several unbelieving spouses who were quite open to discussing the Bible with their believing husbands and wives.

This is not to say that when we have differences with unbelievers we shouldn't use the conflict-resolving principles set forth in the Bible. Indeed, sometimes they will still be quite effective. It's a matter of knowing that an unbelieving opponent may not want to resolve conflicts with us and that he may not be playing by the same rules, or fighting according to them. On the other hand, sometimes unbelievers are more adept at conflict resolution than believers are.

2. We must wisely make the most of the opportunities we have to speak with unbelievers.

Scripture gives us another set of specific instructions on communicating with unbelievers.

> Conduct yourselves with wisdom *toward outsiders*, making the most of the opportunity. Let your speech always be with grace, as though

> seasoned with salt, so that you will know how you should respond to *each person.* (Col. 4:5–6)

We are to walk in wisdom toward outsiders (unbelievers). To walk has to do with the way we conduct ourselves. It is often our behavior that first attracts unbelievers to the gospel message that we proclaim to them (how we handle the stresses and pressures of life; how we handle conflicts—especially with them). This wise walking before them has to do with things that they observe about us—not just our actions, but also our words. What does this wisdom look like? What does it taste like? When you bite into it, it tastes like peace.

> But the wisdom from above is first pure, then peaceable, gentle, reasonable, full of mercy and good fruits, unwavering, without hypocrisy. And the seed whose fruit is righteousness is sown in peace by those who make peace. (James 3:17–18)

So we must make the most of the opportunities that we have when around unbelievers—especially those challenging opportunities like differences of opinion (or worldview), disagreements, confrontations (in both directions), hostilities, and even persecutions. How are we to do this? Again, it is with our speech! "Let your speech always be with grace, as though seasoned with salt."

We are at all times to speak graciously to all people. The idea here is that "practice makes perfect." That is, if we always follow this advice in all circumstances (as well as the advice of Ephesians 4:29: "Let no unwholesome word proceed from your mouth, but only such *a word* as is good for edification according to the need *of the moment,* so that it will give grace to those who hear"), we will know how to answer all sorts of people—even unbelievers. We will learn it through practice and experience.

Not only is our speech to be gracious, it is to be seasoned with salt. It is to be full of taste, appetizing, and appealing. Whether your food is savory or sweet, a little bit of salt brings out more of the flavor—it makes things more palatable.

3. We may use likeminded mediators more readily with believers than with unbelievers.

As followers of Jesus Christ, we have our own divinely inspired conflict-resolution manual. In the Bible we find principles and directives (rules of engagement, if you please) to guide our attempts to resolve our conflicts. There are things we are allowed to do, and things we are forbidden to do, in the process of reconciliation. Principles of justice help us to decide how to make equitable decisions. We have rules about involving others and not involving others. And people in the church are (or at least should be) equipped to help handle disputes between members who need such assistance.

> So if you have such cases, why do you lay them before those who have no standing in the church? I say this to your shame. Can it be that there is no one among you wise enough to settle a dispute between the brothers? (1 Cor. 6:4–5 ESV)

However, finding a Christian mediator who an unbeliever would be willing to go to (let alone to trust) may be difficult. And it could be dangerous (if not disastrous) for a Christian to go to a mediator who doesn't understand biblical principles of justice and conflict resolution.

4. We may use ecclesiastical authorities more readily in our conflicts with believers than with unbelievers.

More specifically, the Lord has placed over each member of His church overseers (pastors and elders) whose job it is to assist those under their care to resolve conflicts biblically. These ecclesiastical shepherds, though they are not infallible, have been given the responsibility and authority to adjudicate differences between the sheep, according to the aforementioned biblical principles and directives. Individual members of the flock are to submit to the leadership and authority of the overseers.[3]

3. I believe that, since the ruling bodies of churches are capable of making erroneous judgments, it is vital to have in place some form of adjudicating body outside the local church to which members may appeal should they believe that the decision handed down by the local church leadership was biblically flawed. This is the big idea behind the Presbyterian form of church government. But

5. We may have more serious conflicts with unbelievers than with believers.

Christians don't often persecute Christians the way that non-Christians sometimes do.[4] We are given clear instruction about how to respond to evil individuals in Romans 12:17–21. Verse 21 is the summary statement of the paragraph. "Do not be overcome by evil, but overcome evil with good."

> Never pay back evil for evil to anyone. Respect what is right in the sight of all men. If possible, so far as it depends on you, be at peace with all men. Never take your own revenge, beloved, but leave room for the wrath of God, for it is written, "Vengeance is Mine, I will repay," says the Lord. "But if your enemy is hungry, feed him, and if he is thirsty, give him a drink; for in so doing you will heap burning coals on his head." Do not be overcome by evil, but overcome evil with good.

I have previously expounded this passage and will not fully repeat here what I have said elsewhere.[5] But I would like to make a few applications of this passage to conflicts with unbelievers.

First, you may not retaliate in kind. You may fight back against evil, but you may not fight back with any weapons that are not biblically certified as "good" or "righteous" weapons.

Second, you must prepare a battle plan. The word translated as "respect" in the NASB is actually a participle that literally means to think of beforehand. God is saying that Christians must plan their next response to evil before the next battle. We must anticipate beforehand (see Prov. 15:28) how we are going to respond to the conflict so that, when we find ourselves in the heat of the battle, we will not respond to evil in kind but rather will respond to it with good. This is how soldiers

---

independent churches can also create a voluntary structured agreement with other likeminded churches so that the members of all the churches will have the security of knowing that an appeal can be made to an objective collection of overseers outside of (and above) its own leadership.

4. Of course, there are notable exceptions (see Ps. 55:12–15).

5. For a more complete understanding of these directions, see my booklet *Bitterness: The Root That Pollutes* (Phillipsburg, NJ: P&R Publishing, 2008) and Jay E. Adams, *How to Overcome Evil: A Practical Exposition of Romans 12:14–21* (1977; repr., Phillipsburg, NJ: P&R Publishing, 2010).

are prepared for battle in basic training. They are drilled on how to fight before the battle so that, in the heat of combat, they will respond automatically in the right way.

Third, you must, as much as it depends on you, be at peace with the unbeliever, *regardless* of that person's response to you. "Pursue peace with all men" (Heb. 12:14). Your obedience to God does not depend on the response of others. Your love for your neighbor (or enemy) should not be conditional, in that it is not predicated on his love for you. Regardless of your offender's willingness to be at peace with you, *you* should be willing to be at peace with him, or initiating and pursuing attempts at such.

Fourth, do not take your own revenge! Vengeance is not for you to take personally (individually). It is a judicial issue, not a personal one. Ultimately, God is the one who will (directly or indirectly) right all wrongs. Vengeance does not belong to you; it belongs to God.

Fifth, look for ways to meet the needs of your unbelieving opponent. The ultimate weapon to use against those who habitually offend us is *love*. We love them by meeting their needs. If they are hungry, feed them. If they are thirsty, give them a drink. Study your opponent. Learn what his needs are. Then take a look at your resources to see if you can somehow provide for them.

There is much more that can be said about this than I am able to do here. (For example, there are times when we may have to *flee* conflicts with unbelievers—see 2 Sam. 15:14; Matt. 10:23—or *appeal to a secular authority*—Acts 25:11). But I trust that these few guiding principles will be helpful to you as you consider how to conduct yourself when you are in conflict with someone who does not profess Christ.

Appendix C

BIBLICAL ALTERNATIVES TO COMMONLY USED TERMS FOR SIN

FOR MANY YEARS, attempts have been made to reclassify what God has called "sin" in terms that are more socially acceptable. This is being done by political organizations, by the media, as well as by the scientific community. Things that once were classified by society as sin are now being reclassified with more politically correct terms and scientific nomenclature.[1] Those who dislike orthodox Christianity (and are eager to suppress the truth in unrighteousness) are often eager to neutralize or intimidate those of us who are followers of Christ. But this book is for Christians, and as Christians we ought to use the most precise biblical language we know in our attempts to resolve conflicts with other Christians—especially conflicts that involve sin.

Below are some terms commonly used in conflict that are often

1. For example, the *Diagnostic and Statistical Manual* of the American Psychiatric Association typically refers to mental illness classifications as "disorders" (see American Psychiatric Association, *Diagnostic and Statistical Manual of Mental Disorders*, 5th ed. [Arlington: American Psychiatric Publishing, 2013]). What many people fail to realize is that in order for something to be classified as a disorder there must be some kind of universal standard of order. But there is not! Indeed, it has been well established that among the so-called mental health professionals worldwide there is absolutely no consensus on pretty much anything. Freudians disagree with Rogerians, Youngians disagree with Maslowians, Skinnerians often disagree with fellow Skinnerians.

less than accurate and/or that tend to minimize the sinfulness of the problems they attempt to signify, listed along with possibilities for alternate, biblical ways to word them.

Commonly Used Terms	Possible Sin Involved	Related Scripture
Addicted to	In bondage to Overtaken by Enslaved to	John 8:34 Romans 6:15–23 Galatians 6:1
Annoyed (Irritated)	Impatient Intolerant	Proverbs 12:16 1 Corinthians 13:4, 7 Ephesians 4:2
Bipolar	Double-minded Unstable Given to change Intemperate (feeling-oriented)	2 Peter 1:5–9; 3:16 James 1:8; 4:8 Proverbs 24:21
Closure (e.g., bringing or getting)	Resolving the conflict (or problem) Being at peace	Psalm 34:14 Ephesians 4:3 Hebrews 12:14 Romans 14:19
Codependency	Idolatrous relationship Inordinate relationship Being a people pleaser	John 12:42–43 Galatians 1:10 Ephesians 6:5–9 Colossians 3:22 1 John 5:21
Control freak	Oppressive Overbearing Having an idolatrous desire to control	Matthew 23:1–4 3 John 9–10
Defense mechanism	Unbiblical response	2 Corinthians 10:4–5 Ephesians 4:17–18
Defensive	Proud Unreasonable	1 Samuel 15:13–21 James 3:17

Dismissive†	Despising (thinking lightly of) Thinking around Thinking down toward	1 Timothy 4:12 Titus 2:15
Dysfunctional	Disorderly Disharmonious Unbiblical Out of sync with Scripture	Matthew 12:25; 22:29 1 Corinthians 14:33, 40
Feeling frustrated	Feeling angry	Esther 3:5–6 Job 32: 1–5
Hurt	Bitter (resentful) Unforgiving	Ephesians 4:31–32 Hebrews 12:15
"I feel"	"I think" "I believe" "I am convicted about" "I am persuaded"	Romans 8:38 Romans 14: 5, 14 Philippians 1:25 2 Timothy 1:12
In denial	Self-deceived	Jeremiah 17:9 Obadiah 3 John 8:43–44 James 1:22 Revelation 3:17
Low self-esteem / Poor self-image	Inferiority judgment Inaccurate self-image Fear of man	Romans 12:3 Philippians 4:8††
Make a mistake	Sin Do wrong	1 Samuel 15:13–34 Colossians 3:25 James 5:16 1 John 1:8–10; 5:17

† This term is actually more biblically accurate than most people realize. The word for *despise or disregard in Titus 2:15 literally means "to think around" and by implication means "to be dismissive of."*

†† Whatever is true (accurate or conforms to reality) . . . dwell on these things.

Narcissistic	Selfish Self-centered Self-willed	Philippians 2:3 2 Timothy 3:2 Titus 1:7 James 3:14–16
Oversensitive	Proud Weak (brother)	Ecclesiastes 7:21–22 Romans 14:1 1 Corinthians 8:11 Galatians 4:16
Paranoid	Suspicious Not believing "all things"	1 Samuel 18:6–9 1 Chronicles 19:3–5 Proverbs 9:8 1 Corinthians 13:7 1 Timothy 6:4
Passive-aggressive	Vindictive	Romans 12:19–21
Play that card	Manipulate	Matthew 22:15–22
Pushed my buttons	Provoked me to anger	Numbers 20:10–12 Proverbs 14:17 1 Corinthians 13:5 James 1:19
Share	Gossip about Slander	Psalm 50:20; 105:5 Proverbs 17:19 2 Corinthians 12:20 James 4:11
Ugly	Rude Harsh Unkind	1 Corinthians 13:5 1 Samuel 25 Proverbs 12:18 Ephesians 4:31–32
Upset	Angry Offended (sinned against) Distressed	Ecclesiastes 7:9 Proverbs 29:11 Daniel 6:14 Matthew 17:27 Ephesians 4:31

Venting	Intemperance Foolishness	Proverbs 25:28; 29:11 Galatians 5:16–24
"You're lying"[†]	"I don't remember it that way" "I'm not sure that's accurate"	Jeremiah 37:11–15 1 Corinthians 13:7

Use the space below to record additional terms that you use or hear other people use, which are too wide-ranging or imprecise to resolve conflicts effectively. Then search the Scriptures for possible alternatives. Record your findings in the space provided.

Commonly Used Terms	Possible Sin Involved	Related Scripture

† While *lying* itself is a biblically accurate term already, it is equally biblical to allow an opponent a chance to rephrase or clarify what he is saying, instead of uncharitably accusing him of a sin without understanding his full point of view.

Was this book helpful to you?
Consider writing a review online.
The author appreciates your feedback!

Or write to P&R at editorial@prpbooks.com
with your comments. We'd love to hear from you.

Also from P&R Publishing

"Far and away the best material on anger I have read, thoroughly biblical and immensely practical. Jones does a masterful job of helping us identify anger in our lives, then gives us biblical steps for uprooting it. Every Christian ought to prayerfully read this book and apply its teaching."
—**Jerry Bridges**, author, *The Pursuit of Holiness*

"Most of us find it all too easy to use words like *hurt*, *frustrated*, and *troubled* to conceal the fact that we are often controlled by sinful anger. This book cuts through this disguise, exposes our bondage to anger, and marks a clear path to peace and freedom."
—**Ken Sande**, President, Peacemaker Ministries

Also from P&R Publishing

Commonplace, familiar sins are dangerous—they sneak in and become habits! Rush Witt defines these subtle sins that seem so unkillable, then shows how change is possible through Christ.

"Rush Witt's *Diehard Sins* is a clarion call for holiness that also provides us with meaningful and theologically rich resources to fight indwelling sin. This book is a careful and refreshing resource that every Christian should read."
—**R. Albert Mohler Jr.**, President, The Southern Baptist Theological Seminary